Cognitive Intelligence and Robotics

Series Editors

Amit Konar, Department of Electronics and Telecommunication Engineering, Jadavpur University, Kolkata, India

Witold Pedrycz, Department of Electrical and Computer Engineering, University of Alberta, Edmonton, AB, Canada

Cognitive Intelligence refers to the natural intelligence of humans and animals, it is considered that the brain performs intelligent activities. While establishing a hard boundary that distinguishes intelligent activities from others remains controversial, most common behaviors and activities of living organisms that cannot be fully synthesized using artificial means are regarded as intelligent. Thus the acts of sensing and perception, understanding the environment, and voluntary control of muscles, which can be performed by lower-level mammals, are indeed intelligent. Besides the above, advanced mammals can perform more sophisticated cognitive tasks, including logical reasoning, learning, recognition, and complex planning and coordination, none of which can yet be realized artificially to the level of a baby, and thus are regarded as cognitively intelligent.

This book series covers two important aspects of brain science. First, it attempts to uncover the mystery behind the biological basis of cognition, with a special emphasis on the decoding of stimulated brain signals or images. Topics in this area include the neural basis of sensory perception, motor control, sensory-motor coordination, and understanding the biological basis of higher-level cognition, including memory, learning, reasoning, and complex planning. The second objective of the series is to publish consolidated research on brain-inspired models of learning, perception, memory, and coordination, including results that can be realized on robots, enabling them to mimic the cognitive activities performed by living creatures. These brain-inspired models of machine intelligence complement the behavioral counterparts studied in traditional artificial intelligence.

The series publishes textbooks, monographs, and contributed volumes.

More information about this series at http://www.springer.com/series/15488

Paramartha Dutta · Asit Barman

Human Emotion Recognition from Face Images

 Springer

Paramartha Dutta
Department of Computer
and Systems Sciences
Visva-Bharati University
Santiniketan, West Bengal, India

Asit Barman
Department of Computer Science
and Engineering and Information
Technology
Siliguri Institute of Technology
Siliguri, West Bengal, India

ISSN 2520-1956   ISSN 2520-1964   (electronic)
Cognitive Intelligence and Robotics
ISBN 978-981-15-3885-8   ISBN 978-981-15-3883-4   (eBook)
https://doi.org/10.1007/978-981-15-3883-4

This Springer imprint is published by the registered company Springer Nature Singapore Pte Ltd.
The registered company address is: 152 Beach Road, #21-01/04 Gateway East, Singapore 189721, Singapore

I dedicate this book to my parents Harimohan Barman and Maya Barman and my wife Karmukta Adhikari Barman. They all kept me going and this book would not have been possible without them.

Asit Barman

Preface

This book provides a Human emotion recognition from face images using different modalities. Key topics of discussion include facial expression recognition. Special emphasis is given on grid formation, distance signature, shape signature, texture signature feature selection, classifier design, and combination of signatures to improve performance of emotion recognition. There is an increasing demand for emotion recognition in diverse fields, including psychotherapy, biomedicine, and security in government, public, and private agencies. Now we describe the proposed book chapter-wise.

In Chap. 1, we describe emotion and types of emotion. There are various types of emotions but we consider only six basic emotions for this book. In this chapter, we also mention the importance of emotions. Nowadays artificial intelligence is a vast research exploration in almost all areas. A human being can easily understand the emotions by looking at another person. Now we want to build a system so that our system has the ability to recognize the emotions from different human face images. The comprehensive survey work will also be considered to explain the different methodologies of human emotion recognition.

In Chap. 2, we consider a distance signature from human faces to recognize emotion. Distance feature has great significance in recognizing facial expressions. Identifying accurate landmarks is vital as well as a challenging issue in the field of affective computing. Appearance model is used to detect the salient landmarks on human faces. These salient landmarks are used to form a grid on the human face. Distances are determined from one landmark point to another landmark point in a grid and are normalized. A novel concept of corresponding stability index is introduced which eventually is found to play an important role to recognize the facial expressions. Statistical analysis such as range, moment, skewness, kurtosis, and entropy are calculated from normalized distance signature to supplement the feature set. This enhanced feature set is supplied into a Multilayer Perceptron (MLP) to arrive at different expression categories encompassing anger, sadness, fear, disgust, surprise, and happiness. We experimented our proposed system on Cohn-Kanade (CK+), JAFFE, MMI, and MUG benchmark databases for training and testing our experiment and establish its superior performance over the other existing competitors.

In Chap. 3, we consider a shape signature from human faces to recognize the emotion. In this chapter, we propose a novel framework for expression recognition by using salient landmark-induced shape signature. Detection of effective landmarks is achieved by appearance-based models. A grid is formed using the landmark points and accordingly several triangles within the grid on the basis of a nose landmark reference point are formed. Normalized shape signature is derived from the grid. Stability index is calculated from shape signature which is also exploited as a significant feature to recognize the facial expressions. Statistical measures such as range, moment, skewness, kurtosis, and entropy are used to supplement the feature set. This enhanced feature set is fed into Multilayer Perceptron (MLP) and Nonlinear Auto Regressive with eXogenous (NARX) to differentiate the expressions into different categories. We shall investigate our proposed system on Cohn-Kanade (CK+), JAFFE, MMI, and MUG benchmark databases to conduct and validate our experiment and shall be able to establish its performance superiority over other existing arts.

In Chap. 4, we consider a texture signature from human faces to recognize the emotion. Texture characteristics among the landmark points reflected in human faces are important features in the recognition of facial expression. Here, we propose a salient feature-based facial expression on texture characteristics. Detection of effective landmarks is performed by appearance-based models and corresponding texture regions are extracted from face images. Local Binary Pattern (LBP) is used to compute the texture feature. Texture feature is used for normalizing texture signatures. In addition, we introduce stability indices corresponding to texture features which are exploited as features in the present scope. Moreover, statistical features such as moment, skewness, kurtosis, and entropy are also supplemented to the feature set. These salient features together are used as an input to Nonlinear Auto Regressive with eXogenous (NARX) for recognition of the human facial expression. The Cohn-Kanade (CK+), Japanese Female Facial Expression (JAFFE), MMI, and MUG benchmark databases are used to conduct the experiments and the results justify the effectiveness of the proposed procedure.

In Chap. 5, we consider individual signature (distance and shape) to form a joined Distance-Shape (D-S) signature for recognizing the emotion. Individual signature feature plays a crucial role in recognizing facial expressions. Identification of proper landmark point is a challenging issue in emotion recognition as well as face identification. Appearance model shall be put into use to identify the landmarks from expressed images. These identified landmark points generate a grid on a expressed face and also are used to form probable triangles within the grid. The stability indices are determined from both individual signature features (distance and shape) which play a significant role in recognizing emotion. Statistical parameters, viz. moment, range, skewness, entropy, and kurtosis are computed from both normalized signature for the formation of indispensable feature set. This feature set is used as input to Multilayer Perceptron (MLP) to categorize the emotion into six categories, viz. sadness, anger, disgust, fear, surprise, and happiness. We examine the suggested method on benchmark datasets (Cohn-Kanade (CK+), MMI, JAFFE, & MUG) to validate the system performance of emotion detection.

In Chap. 6, we consider a combination of distance and texture signature from human faces to recognize the emotion. Distance characteristics among the landmark points as well as texture characteristics are formidable features in emotion recognition from an expressed image. This chapter provides a novel framework of emotion recognition by considering salient features-based approach of distance and texture characteristics. Accurate landmark detection of a facial image is imperative to achieve improved accuracy of the individual signature (distance and texture). Detection of effective landmarks is performed by appearance-based models. A grid is formed using the landmark detection points and inter-landmark distances are considered in specific order to obtain the distance signature. Texture signature based on the textures appearing on a face is considered. Both these signatures are taken in a normalized form in the present scope. Distance and texture signatures are used for normalizing the distances and texture signatures. In addition, we introduce stability indices corresponding to distance and texture feature pair which are exploited as features in the present scope. Moreover, statistical features such as moment, skewness, kurtosis, and entropy are also supplemented in the feature set. These salient features together are used as input to Multilayer Perceptron (MLP), Radial Basis Function Network (RBFN), and Nonlinear Auto Regressive with eXogenous input (NARX) for recognition of the human facial expression. The benchmark CK+, MMI, JAFFE, and MUG datasets are examined on the suggested methods to measure the performance of emotion recognition. The joined Distance-Texture (D-T) signature also plays a significant recognition rate of emotion than the individual signature.

In Chap. 7, we consider a combination of shape and texture signature from expressed images to recognize the emotions. Shape and texture features proposed individually and combined form a novel framework of emotion identification through considering salient landmarks-based triangle formation and texture characteristics. Accurate landmarks detection on a facial image improves the accuracy of emotion identification by use of shape and texture signature features. Detection of effective landmarks is achieved by a well-known appearance-based model. A grid is formed using the landmark points and accordingly, several triangles are formed within the grid on the basis of a nose landmark reference point to compute the normalized shape signature. Subsequently, texture regions are extracted from the salient landmark points to find normalized texture signature. Stability indices are measured from both individual signature (shape and texture) for exploiting a valuable feature to identify the emotion. Statistical analyzes such as moment, range, skewness, entropy, and kurtosis are considered to form an enhanced feature set. Individual and joined signature features are provided to Multilayer Perceptron (MLP) and Deep Belief Neural (DBN) network to detect the emotion into six categories. We investigate our suggested method on CK+, MMI, JAFFE, and MUG datasets to conduct and validate the experiment and establish its performance superiority over other existing competitors.

In Chap. 8, we propose a joined distance, shape, and texture (D-S-T) signature feature from human faces to recognize the expressions. Distance, shape, and texture signatures have great significance in recognizing emotions. Extracting the accurate landmark points on the face image is a challenging task in the field of human emotion detection. Appearance model is used to identify the proper landmarks on the faces. These proper landmark points are used for the formation of a grid on the human face. Now triangles are identified among the grid and texture regions are marked from salient landmark points. Distance, shape, and texture signatures are determined from the grid. Now we merge distance, shape, and texture signatures to get Distance-Shape-Texture (D-S-T) signature trio feature for facial expression recognition.

Santiniketan, India
Siliguri, India

Paramartha Dutta
Asit Barman

Acknowledgements

We would like to thank Prof. Maja Pantic for providing access to the MMI database.

We also would like to thank Prof. Dr. A. Delopoulos for providing access to the MUG database.

We would like to say sincere thanks to our colleague Prof. Sathi Ball for her constant encouragement.

We express our special thanks to Dr. Sumana Kundu for her genuine support throughout this work.

Contents

Contents   xvii

About the Authors

Paramartha Dutta is currently a Professor at the Dept. of Computer and System Sciences at Visva-Bharati University, West Bengal. He completed his Bachelor's and Master's in Statistics at the Indian Statistical Institute, Kolkata, in 1988 and 1990, respectively. He received his Master's in Computer Science from the Indian Statistical Institute, Kolkata, in 1993, and his Ph.D. from the Bengal Engineering and Science University, Shibpur, in 2005.

He is the co-author of 6 books, co-editor of 10 books, and he has published over 230 research papers in peer-reviewed journals and conference proceedings. He is a Fellow of IETE, OSI, IE India, a senior member of ACM, IEEE, CSI, and IACSIT, and a member of ACCS, IAPR, ISCA, ISTE, and SSI.

Asit Barman Asit Barman is an Assistant Professor at the Dept. of Computer Science & Engineering and Information Technology of Siliguri Institute Technology. He served as a Lecturer at the Dept. of Information Technology at the Calcutta Institute of Technology, West Bengal from 2008 to 2009.

He received his B.Tech. in Information Technology from the West Bengal University of Technology in 2006 and his M.Tech. in Information Technology from the University of Calcutta, Kolkata, in 2008. Currently, he is pursuing a Ph.D. at the University of Calcutta under the guidance of Prof. Paramartha Dutta. He is a member of the IEEE society.

Chapter 1
Introduction

The definition of the emotions [1] is the changes in psychological states that comprise thoughts, physiological changes, feelings, and expressive behaviors to act. The accurate combination of the psychological changes fluctuates from emotion to emotion and it is not necessarily accompanied by behaviors. This complex of states and behaviors is triggered by an event that is either experienced or recalled. You are insulted by anyone. Depending on the perception of the insult, you may act angry or annoyed. If you feel angry, your face may redden or your heartbeat may become faster than the normal mental state, etc. Apart from this, you may take action against the person who was insulting. A similar kind of action of emotion can be given for fear, happiness, disgust, sadness, surprise, and many others. There are also some emotions that are less clear, in that they do not always occur changes in physiological states and do not always express in behavioral change; for example, regret. Having made a decision or taken a course of action that turns out badly, one may well feel strong regret, but this subjective experience will typically not be accompanied by changes in physiology or behavior.

When we consider the borderline cases of emotion such as physical pain, anxiety, sexual arousal, boredom, depression, irritability, all of which can be seen as examples of affective states, there are also many complications that arise to define the psychological states. In [1], the psychologists try to differentiate the emotion and borderline-emotion among affective states that have a clear object. Those that do not, considering that emotion is a term that should be reserved for psychological states that have an object. For example, chronic pain, general states of boredom, depression, or irritability are not considered as emotions.

The human mind can analyze the emotions with associated mood, temperament, and personality. The computer system seeks to evaluate human emotions by analyzing digital images as input. The fact that the world is three-dimensional while computer vision is two-dimensional is basically one of the main problems that

© Springer Nature Singapore Pte Ltd. 2020
P. Dutta and A. Barman, *Human Emotion Recognition from Face Images*,
Cognitive Intelligence and Robotics,
https://doi.org/10.1007/978-981-15-3883-4_1

complicate computer system for computation. Human faces are nonrigid objects with a high degree of variability in size, shape, color, and texture. The face databases are hugely considered for experimentation of different algorithms proposed in facial expression recognition systems. Any automated system for face and facial gesture recognition has immense potential in the identification of criminals, surveillance, and retrieval of missing children, office security, credit card verification, video document retrieval, telecommunication, high-definition television, medicine, human-computer interfaces.

Everyday most of the people can interact with each other either directly or indirectly in the world. In direct interaction, they can communicate with each other face-to-face and in an indirect way they can communicate with each other through a phone call, text message, etc. In some professions, interaction with people is the main task to perform duties like call centers, sales executives, etc. Nowadays people can easily access the emotion label of different people when he/she is interacting with each other directly or indirectly with the great advancement of technology. With the advancement of 4G technology in the mobile communication field, one may interact face-to-face with others while talking. At that moment he/she can easily access the mood of the third party so that interaction will certainly result in social as well as professional benefits. There are two reasons to consider the mood of the human. Firstly, what are the emotions? A mental state that arises spontaneously rather than through conscious effort and is often accompanied by physiological changes and these physiological changes are recognized from the outer world. Depending on the changes in mood, he/she can easily understand the mood. Secondly, major human emotions have changes in day-to-day life: Happiness, Sadness, Anger, Surprise, Fear, Surprise, and many more.

Expression and Emotion
The emotions [2] can be analyzed from the expressed face and other parts of the body. If someone feels intensely angry, sad, fear, surprise, we observe the changes of expressions on a particular face image and try to differentiate among the emotions. The fluctuation of the different facial images on emotions helps to understand how someone is feeling without nonverbal communication. It is sometimes argued that the nonverbal communication of emotion is more important and effective than verbal communication. This is true of interpersonal communication whereby one or both persons are unable to communicate verbally because they are prelingual as in the case of infants or deaf or simply unable to speak to each other.

Ekman [3] showed that there is a close relationship between emotion and facial behavior. They proposed a system that has the capability of facial expression recognition. They showed two kinds of research methods. The first method is based on Darwin's idea that the expressed emotions are universal and they are also independent of culture. Ekman et al. took face images that were identified by Westerners as explicitly expressing a few emotions and they also evaluated these to persons in a variety of other cultures. The most telling studies are those conducted in preliterate cultures such as the highlands of Papua New Guinea. Ekman and Frisen [4] recalled, "Isolated from Western culture, the New Guinea Fore was able to match the photographs with the appropriate stories". The subtle creases of a grimace tell the same story around the world, to preliterate New Guinea tribesmen, Japanese and American college students alike. "The implication?" If you meet a native in New Guinea or your old boss in a Manhattan bar, you will be able to interpret their facial expressions easily, knowing how they feel or how they want you to think they feel.

The second line of research pursued by Ekman and colleagues [3] evaluated different emotions that are accompanied by measurable differences in facial behavior. In this method, researchers used the Facial Action Coding System (FACS) which is a measurement system for coding all visible movement in the human face. In this research, for example, that happiness and disgust, as induced by film clips, are associated with different facial actions. This seemingly uncontroversial finding has been the subject of some debate in the literature. Various researchers proposed different types of stimuli to induce emotional states. The surprise is an example and has failed to find that these states are accompanied by distinct facial actions (brow-raising, eye-widening, jaw-dropping) that would be expected if the notion of a facial affect program were correct. Other researchers have questioned the assumption that there is a close relationship between emotion and facial action, arguing instead that facial actions evolved to communicate intentions or motives, not emotions, to conspecifics. This line of argument leads one to predict that facial behavior should vary as a function of how social a situation is, rather than how emotional it is.

1.1 About Emotion

The most notable research into the topic came from psychologist Ekman [3], who pioneered research into emotion recognition in the 1960s. His team of researchers provided their test subjects with photos of faces showing different emotional expressions. The test subjects define the emotional states from each photo, based on a predetermined list of possible emotions. Through these studies, Ekman found a high agreement across members of Western and Eastern cultures when it came to selecting emotional labels that corresponded with facial expressions. They defined the universal emotions those indicating happiness, disgust, anger, sadness, surprise, and fear. Working with Friesen, Ekman established that the findings of the study correlated with Fore tribesmen in Papua New Guinea, whose members could not have learned the meaning of expressions from exposure to media. Instead, they inherently displayed the expressions without ever having been primed for them, leading Ekman and Friesen [3] to determine that they were universal.

1.1.1 Types of Emotions

There are different types of emotion. The emotions are identified as happiness, sadness, disgust, fear, surprise, and anger. A brief description of each emotion is given below:

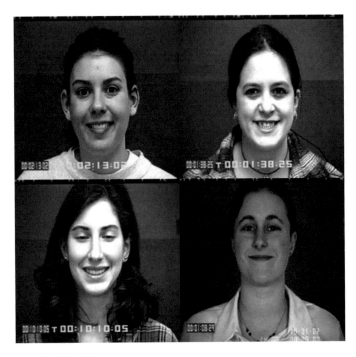

Fig. 1.1 Examples of happiness

Happiness: Happiness is incorporated with a state of mind that reflects satisfaction, pleasure, or joy. Happiness is one of the most common emotions and we consider it throughout different philosophical, religious, and biological approaches. All of these observations try to define the source of happiness. Philosophers define happiness as stemming from the living of a good life or the flourishing of one's soul, rather than it just being an emotion. Today we often associate happiness with pleasure. Happiness is characterized by a facial expression that causes someone to raise the corners of their mouth upwards. An example of happiness is shown in Fig. 1.1.

Disgust: Disgust is incorporated with things that are offending, inedible, and infectious. For example, someone might be offended by some hurtful things you have said, or they might be disgusted by your behavior. To sum it up, disgust is relative to something revolting and is experienced primarily in retaliation to the sense of taste and secondarily in retaliation to anything which elicits a similar feeling through senses of smell and touch. Disgust is characterized by a facial expression that causes someone to raise their upper lip, wrinkle their nose bridge, and raise their cheeks. Surprisingly, however, disgust is one of the six emotions that decreases heart rate. Here we consider an example to show the disgust emotion which is available in Fig. 1.2.

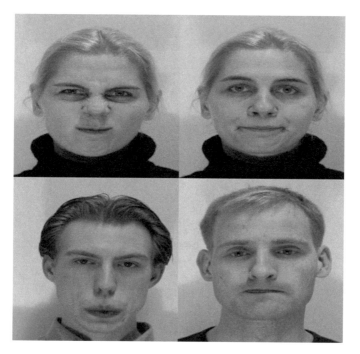

Fig. 1.2 Examples of disgust

Fear: Fear is incorporated with stimuli of danger or threatening. It is a basic survival mechanism that occurs in response to a traumatic presence, such as pain or the impending threat of pain. Fear is the same as the behaviors of escape, and avoidance, but it is not the same with anxiety which deals with the direct physical reaction to threats that are perceived to be unavoidable and uncontrollable. When discussing fear, it is said to cause a person to raise their brows, open their mouth slightly, and open their eyes in a manner that is wider than normal. The example of fear is shown in Fig. 1.3.

Anger: Anger is incorporated within the range of minor irritation to intense rage. Physically, anger causes someone to experience an increased heart rate, heightened blood pressure, and abnormal levels of adrenaline and noradrenaline. You may often hear as anger being associated with the fight or flight brain response when a person is introduced to an experience that causes them to feel threatened or in pain. When someone chooses to take action against whatever threat is causing them trauma or pain, anger is thought to be the dominant response and emotion that is expressed in a cognitive and physiological way. Anger is characterized by a facial expression that causes someone to lower their brows, press their lips together firmly, and bulge their eyes. The example of anger is shown in Fig. 1.4.

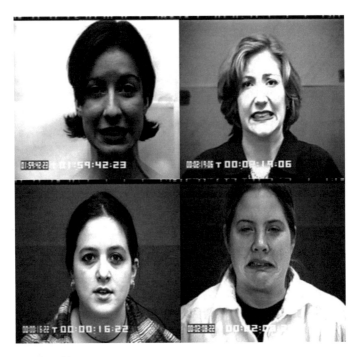

Fig. 1.3 Examples of fear

Surprise: Surprise is incorporated with a brief state of being. This brief state of being is invoked by an unexpected relevant event. However, the surprise is not always a traumatic emotional experience. The surprise has also been categorized into being valent, which means that it spans the spectrum of being neutral, pleasant, and unpleasant. Surprise is characterized by a facial expression that causes someone to arch their brows, open their eyes widely, and drop their jaw. Here we consider an example to show the surprise emotion which is available in Fig. 1.5.

Sadness: Sadness is incorporated with the feelings of disadvantage, loss, and helplessness. Often, humans react to being sad by becoming quiet and they experience a lack of energy and a need to be withdrawn. Sadness is defined as the direct opposite of happiness and can also be characterized as sorrow, grief, misery, and melancholy. Sadness exists in two main ways: the temporary lowering of one's mood or the chronic, persistent lowering of one's mood often associated with depression. Sadness is characterized by a facial expression that causes someone to lower the corners of their mouth, and raise the inner portion of their brows. Here an example is indicated in Fig. 1.6 to show the disgust emotion.

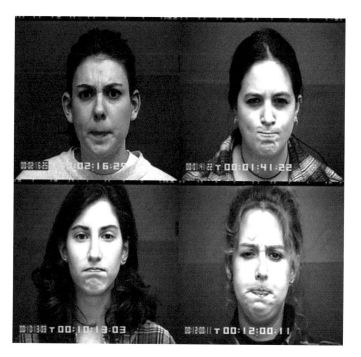

Fig. 1.4 Examples of anger

1.2 Database of Facial Expression

Images used for facial expression recognition are static images or image sequences. An image sequence potentially contains more information than a still image, because the former also depicts the temporal information. The usage of these databases is restricted for research purposes only. Most commonly used databases include Cohn-Kanade facial expression database [5], Japanese Female Facial Expression (JAFFE) database [6], MMI [7], and MUG [8] database. Currently, 3D databases are used to a larger extent. The description mainly emphasizes the techniques used during the development of the database. This is followed by a few of the face images from the database. Finally, the salient features of the database are listed. Each of the explained databases is briefly described below.

Cohn-Kanade facial expression database

Subjects in the available portion of the database [5] were 97 university students enrolled in introductory psychology classes. They ranged in age from 18 to 30 years. Sixty-five percent were female, fifteen percent were African-American, and three percent were Asian or Latino. The observation room was equipped with a chair for the subject and two Panasonic WV3230 cameras, each connected to a Panasonic S-VHS AG-7500 video recorder with a Horita synchronized time-code generator. One of the cameras was located directly in front of the subject and the other was

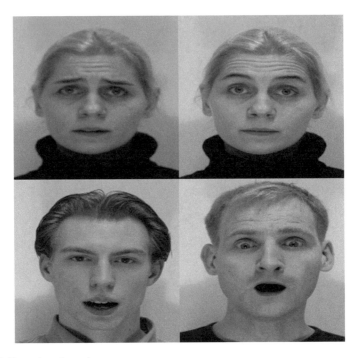

Fig. 1.5 Examples of surprise

positioned 30° to the right of the subject. Only image data from the frontal camera are available at this time. Subjects were instructed by an experimenter to perform a series of 23 facial displays that included single action units (e.g., AU 12, or lip corners pulled obliquely) and combinations of action units (e.g., AU 1 + 2, or inner and outer brows raised). Each emotion began from a neutral face and it ended in expressed face. Before performing each display, an experimenter described and modeled the desired display. Six of the displays were based on descriptions of prototypic basic emotions (i.e. joy, surprise, anger, fear, disgust, and sadness). Image sequences from neutral to target display were digitized into 640 by 480 or 490-pixel arrays with 8-bit precision for grayscale values. The images are available in png and jpg. Images are labeled using their corresponding VITC. The final frame of each image sequence was coded using Facial Action Coding System (FACS) which describes the subject's expression in terms of action units (AUs). FACS codes were conducted by a certified FACS coder.

Salient features:

1. Usage of two types of illumination (fluorescent and incandescent lights);
2. Blinking, a non-prototypic gesture, considered in the database (Fig. 1.7).

JAFFE database
Ten female subjects posed for the six basic expressions: happiness, sadness, anger, disgust, fear, and surprise and one for the neutral face. Each of the subjects posed

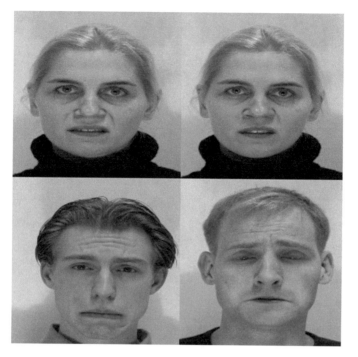

Fig. 1.6 Examples of sadness

with three to four examples per expression to make a total of 219 images [6]. The still images were captured in a controlled environment (pose and illumination). The semantic ratings of the expressions were performed from psychological experiments averaged over 60 Japanese female subjects as ground truth. According to Michael J Lyons, any expression is never a pure expression but a mixture of different emotions. So, a 5-level scale was used for each of the expression images (5 for high and 1 for low). Considerably low-resolution images used 256×256 with the number of subjects just equal to 10 (smallest in comparison with other databases) (Fig. 1.8).

Salient features:

1. First ever facial expression database to consider occlusions in face images.
2. Inclusion of scream, a non-prototypic gesture, in the database.
3. To enable testing and modeling using this database, 22 facial feature points are manually labeled on each face.

MMI database

The developers of MMI [7] **MMI** facial expression database are from the Man-Machine Interaction group of Delft University of Technology, Netherlands. This was the first web-based facial expression database. The basic criteria defined for this database include easy accessibility, extensibility, manageability, user-friendliness,

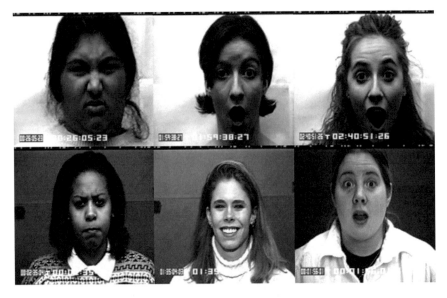

Fig. 1.7 Dataset of CK+

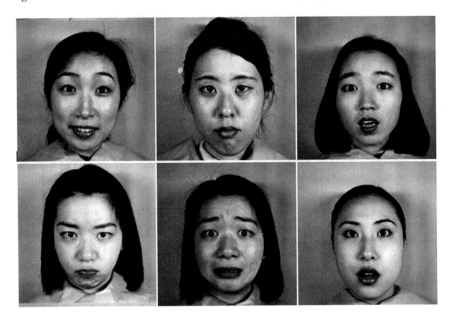

Fig. 1.8 Dataset of JAFFE

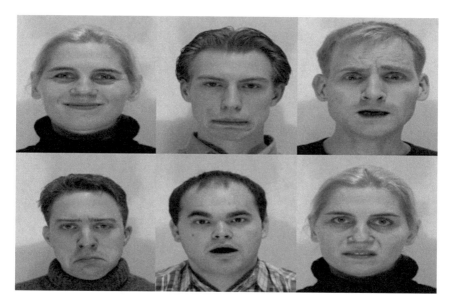

Fig. 1.9 Dataset of MMI

online help files, and various search criteria. The database contains both still as well as video streams depicting the six basic expressions: happiness, anger, sadness, disgust, fear, and surprise. The activation of the individual facial action muscles is taken care of. The database was built using JavaScript, Macromedia Flash, MySQL, PHP, and Apache HTTP server. JavaScript was used for the creation of dynamic pages, Macromedia Flash was used to build rich Internet applications (animation features), MySQL was chosen for the database server, PHP due to its compatibility with MySQL and is an open-source platform, Apache HTTP server for its open-source application, security, extendibility, and efficiency. This database provides users with a very good repository, which is easily searchable. Over 200 images and 800 video sequences can be accessed by the user. There are a good 308 number of active users of this database currently.

Salient features:

1. First web-based facial expression database.
2. Includes both still images and image sequences (Fig. 1.9).

MUG Database

The MUG [8] facial expression database was created by the MUG group. It contains several image sequences of an adequate number of subjects for the development and the evaluation of facial expression recognition systems that use posed and induced expressions. The image sequences were captured in a laboratory environment with high resolution and no occlusions. In the first part of the database 86 subjects performed the six basic expressions according to the emotion prototypes as defined in the Investigators Guide in the FACS manual. The image sequences start and stop

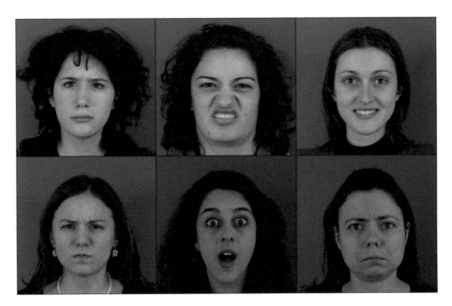

Fig. 1.10 Dataset of MUG

at the neutral state and follow the onset, apex, offset temporal pattern. The publicly available sequences count up to 1462. Landmark point annotation of 1222 images is available as well. In the second part of the database 82 of the subjects were recorded while they were watching an emotion-inducing video. This way several authentic expressions are recorded (Fig. 1.10).

1.3 Survey Work

The affective [9] computing is a human-computer interaction in which a system has the capability to recognize and appropriately find its users' emotions. A computing system with this capacity could gather information to user emotion from a different source. When we consider emotional states, they have significant changes in facial expressions, posture, gestures, and speech. These emotions are recognized and interpreted by a computer. A built-in camera takes images of the user and proposed systems are considered to process the extracted information to produce an output. Identifying emotional states requires the extraction of meaningful features from the gathered data. A machine learning system is used to detect the different modalities, such as speech recognition and facial expression detection.

A vast area in affective computing [9] is the building of a proposed system to exhibit either innate emotional capabilities or that are capable of convincingly simulating emotions. Due to the changes in current technological capabilities, a more practical approach is the simulation of emotions in conversational agents in order to enrich and facilitate interactivity between humans and machines. Two major categories are considered in emotions of machines such as Emotional Speech and Facial affect detection. Emotional speech includes algorithms, databases, and speech descriptors. Facial affect detection includes body gesture and physiological monitoring.

Affective computing tries to address one of the major drawbacks of online learning versus in-classroom learning by the teachers. In classroom learning, a teacher can easily identify the understanding behavior of the students and then take action. To overcome this type of problem, an e-learning-based affective computing is used to adjust the presentation style of a computerized tutor when a learner is bored, interested, frustrated, or pleased. In psychological health services, i.e. counseling, affective computing is used when determining a client's emotional state. Robotic systems have the capability of processing of affective information that exhibits higher flexibility while one works in uncertain or complex environments.

There are many applications around Social Monitoring. In this context, a car can observe the emotional state of all occupants and engage in additional safety measures, such as alerting other vehicles if it identifies the anger of the driver. Affective computing has the capability in human-computer interaction, such as affective states measure the user's performance. For example, an emotion monitoring agents sending a warning before one sends an angry email so that companies would be able to use affecting computing to infer whether their products will or will not be well used by the respective market.

Facial expression recognition is an active research area in the field of affective computing. There are many approaches to recognize facial expressions, i.e. holistic approach and geometric approach. In this paper, we discuss the various approaches of facial expression recognition. There are different methods of feature extraction such as appearance-based method, geometric-based method, texture-based method, etc. and in the current research, mostly used methods are geometric-based method and appearance-based method. Geometric-based feature extraction method extracts feature information using shape, distance, and position of facial components, and appearance-based feature extraction method uses appearance information such as pixel intensity of face image. After getting the features, classification methods are applied to recognize facial expression. Among the frequently used classifiers, Artificial Neural Networks (ANN), Support Vector Machine (SVM), and Deep Learning achieve good performance in facial expression recognition.

Ekman and Frisen [4] recognized six basic emotions, viz. happiness, sadness, surprise, fear, anger, and disgust. In [10], the authors identified action units of the facial action coding system. This FACS is an anatomically based approach allowing movement of different parts of the face to be described. It consists of 44 unique and visually distinguishable movements called AUs.

In [11], the authors proposed an optical flow approach that detects facial muscle actions which can be identified as facial expressions. Facial expressions are the result of facial muscle actions that are triggered by the nerve impulses generated by emotions. The muscle actions have the movement and deformation of facial skin and facial features such as eyes, mouth, and nose. Facial skin has a texture region, which helps to extract the optical flow. They also extracted muscle actions from external appearance. The authors proposed the recognition method in two ways. First, the optical flow fields of skin movement were extracted in muscle windows, each of which defines one primary direction of muscle contraction to correctly extract muscle movement. Second, a 15-dimensional feature vector was used to identify the most active points in terms of the flow variance. The expression recognition system used the feature vector to classify the image sequences into several classes of facial expression. Preliminary experiments indicated an accuracy of approximately 80% when recognizing four types of expressions: happiness, anger, disgust, and surprise.

In [12], the authors proposed a method for analysis and representation of facial dynamics for facial expression recognition from image sequences. They developed an optical flow computation to identify the direction of rigid and nonrigid motions that were caused by human facial expressions. Recognizing six facial expressions, as well as eye blinking, were explained from image sequences.

In [13], the authors proposed a radial basis function network architecture that learns the correlation of facial feature motion patterns and human expressions. They proposed a hierarchical approach which at the highest level identifies expressions, at the mid-level determines the motion of facial features, and at the low level recovers motion directions. Individual expression networks were trained to recognize the smile and surprise expressions. Each expression network was trained by viewing a set of sequences of one expression for many subjects. The trained neural network was then tested for retention, extrapolation, and rejection ability. Success rates were 88% for retention, 88% for extrapolation, and 83% for rejection.

In [14], the authors described a parametrized model of facial appearance which takes into account all these sources of variability. The model represents both shape and gray-level appearance and was generated by performing a statistical analysis over a set of training images. A robust multiresolution search algorithm was incorporated to fit the model to new face images. This allows the main facial features to be located, and a set of shape and gray-level appearance parameters to be recovered. A good approximation to a given face can be reconstructed using less than 100 of these parameters. This representation could be used for tasks such as image coding, person identification, 3D pose recovery, gender recognition, and expression recognition. Experimental results were shown for a database of 690 face images obtained under widely varying conditions of a 3D pose, lighting, and facial expression. The system performed well on all the tasks listed above.

In [15], the authors proposed a neural network-based facial expressions with human subjects over a set of experiments using interpolated imagery. The experiments for both the human subjects and neural networks make use of interpolations of facial expressions from the images of facial affect database [4]. The only difference in materials between those used in the human subjects experiments and the interpolated images are constructed image-quality morphs versus pixel averages. The neural network correctly recognizes the categorical nature of the human responses, showing sharp transitions in the labeling of images along the interpolated sequence.

For a demonstration of categorical perception [16], the model indicates the biggest discrimination between transition images at the crossover point. The model also takes the shape of the reaction time curves of the human subjects along with the sequences. Finally, the network matches the human subject's judgments of which expressions are being mixed in the images. The main drawback of this model is that there are intrusions of neutral responses in some transitions, which are not seen in the human subjects. They attribute this difference between the pixel average stimuli and the image quality morph stimuli. These results indicted that a simple neural network classifier, with no access to the biological constraints that are presumably imposed on the human emotion processor, and whose only access to the surrounding culture is the category labels placed by American subjects on the facial expressions, can nevertheless simulate fairly well the human responses to emotional expressions.

In [17], the author proposed feature-based facial expression recognition which was classified by a two-layer perceptron. They proposed two types of features extraction from face images: the geometric positions of a set of fiducial points on a face, and a set of multiscale and multi-orientation Gabor wavelet coefficients at these points. These features used either independently or jointly. The performance of the expressions with different types of features was compared which noticed that Gabor wavelet coefficients were much more powerful than geometric positions. First layer of the perceptron actually acted on a nonlinear dimensionality reduction of the feature space. They also studied the needed number of hidden units. They showed that five to seven hidden units were more sufficient to represent the space of facial expressions. The authors also experimented the importance of each individual fiducial point to facial expression recognition. Sensitivity analysis proved that cheeks and forehead points carry little useful information. They studied the importance of image scales. This experiment indicated that facial expression recognition was a low-frequency process, and a spatial resolution of 64 pixels $\times$ 64 pixels was probably enough.

Anderson et al. [18] developed a six basic facial expression system. Their system was built upon three components. The first one is a face tracker (derivative of ratio template) to detect the location of the face. The optical flow algorithm used to track the motion within the face as the second component. Expression recognition engine used as the last component. Support Vector Machines and Multilayer Perceptrons were used to recognize the expressions. They achieved recognition accuracy of 81.8%.

Kotsia and Pitas [19] identified expressions by mapping a Candide grid, a face mask with a low number of polygons, onto a face image. The grid was initially placed randomly on the image, then it was placed manually on the human face. Kanade-Lucas-Tomasi tracker was used to track the grid. The geometric displacement information provided by the grid was used as an input feature for multiclass SVMs. The expressions were anger, disgust, fear, happiness, sadness, and surprise. They evaluated the model on the Cohn-Kanade dataset and an accuracy of 99.7% has been achieved.

Zhang and Ji [20] and Tian et al. [21] combined the geometric features and the transient features (local texture information) to enhance recognition accuracy of facial expressions. Thus, transient features were extracted by the Canny edge detection operator in [20] and [21] which were neither variable nor robust to luminance and albedo variations. Manual interactions were considered in [21] for template-based geometric feature extraction, which was inconvenient to users.

The geometric feature is another important visual cue for facial expression recognition than the local texture. This is because a facial expression automatically produced a corresponding geometric deformation. In [22], the effect of landmarks associated with their geometric feature was demonstrated in face recognition and facial expression recognition. The geometric coordinates of the landmark cannot be used to directly train the classifier, because various researchers may have different face configurations. Therefore, the relative distances [23] are computed to measure the geometric distance. Some methods, such as [24], carry out facial expression recognition based on the geometric feature extracted by the Active Appearance Model in one step. In [23], the authors presented a two-step approach in which both the geometric feature extraction and the action unit recognition precede the expression prediction.

Facial expression recognition is a type of visual learning process. Existing facial expression recognition algorithms can be separated into two groups, i.e. feature-based and appearance-based. The feature-based approach finds features (feature points and the motion of feature points) and tracks them along with the images, and then, classification is done based on these extracted features. According to [25], the appearance-based approach usually uses as a part of or the whole face image as a high-dimensional vector. After that, some dimensionality reduction learning methods, e.g., principle component analysis, linear discriminant analysis, locality preserving projection [26], and graph embedding [27], are considered to obtain the subspace representation of the original input. Finally, classification is performed in the learned subspace. Feature-based approach provides good intuitive explanations for expression recognition. These methods require little time and space costs for computation. Appearance-based methods are useful in discovering both the discriminative information and the manifold structure using a subspace learning method, but their time and space costs are huge. Moreover, all the face images have to carefully be aligned and cropped.

Zhang and Ji [20] and Tian et al. [21] used a Canny operator to identify the high gradient components. Martinez [28] proposed that the local texture information introduced by the face motion was important for facial expression deduction. These approaches have validated the advantages of local texture information in facial expression recognition. However, neither the threshold-based nor the Canny-based method is robust and flexible in extracting the transient features with albedo and lighting variations. Guo and Dyer [29] considered the Gabor wavelet coefficient to extract local texture information. Gabor features are sensitive to scale and rotation variations in local regions of interest points [30]. Another drawback is that Gabor features are sensitive to skin albedo. For example, if one person's skin is much smoother than that of another person, the Gabor filter responses will be quite different between these two people, even if they have the same expression. Ma and Khorasani [31] carried out facial expression recognition using 2D discrete cosine transform over the entire face image. A constructive one-hidden-layer feedforward neural network has been used to classify the expressions.

In [32], authors presented an appearance feature-based facial expression recognition system using Kohonen Self-Organizing Map. Appearance features were extracted using uniform Local Binary Patterns from equally subdivided blocks applied over face image. The dimensionality of the LBP feature vector was reduced using Principal Component Analysis (PCA) to avoid redundant data that leads to unnecessary computation cost.

Jizheng et al. [33] proposed a facial expression recognition by exploiting the structural characteristics and the texture information hiding in the image space. Firstly, the feature points were marked by an Active Appearance Model. Secondly, three facial features, which are feature point distance ratio coefficient, connection angle ratio coefficient and skin deformation energy parameter, were proposed to eliminate the differences among the individuals. Finally, a radial basis function neural network was used as a classifier for facial expression recognition.

Happy and Routray [34] proposed a novel framework for expression recognition by using salient facial patches. A few prominent facial patches, depending on the position of facial landmarks, were extracted which are active during emotion elicitation. These active patches are further processed to obtain the salient patches which contain discriminative features for classification of each pair of expressions, thereby selecting different facial patches as salient for different pair of expression classes. One against one classification method is adopted using these features. The salient features from these patches are used as an input of a multiclass classifier to classify expressions into six basic categories.

In [35], the authors proposed a method that uses a combination of two methods, convolutional neural networks to detect faces and a rule-based algorithm to recognize the expression. The rule-based algorithm was used to enhance the subject of independent facial expression recognition. This procedure used rules like the distance between eyes and mouth, length of a horizontal line segment in mouth, and length of a horizontal line segment in eyebrows. The experiments were carried out with 10 persons only and the authors report the results of detecting smiling faces only (i.e. happiness), which was 97.6%.

In [36], MLP-based training algorithm tried to find synthesis parameters as the number of patterns corresponding for subsets of each class to be presented initially in the training step, the initial number of hidden neurons, the number of iterations during the training step as well as the MSE predefined value. The suggested algorithm was developed in order to classify a facial expression.

Shan et al. [37] have created an emotion recognition system based on Local Binary Patterns (LBP). The LBPs are calculated over the facial region. These extracted LBP features are used as a feature vector. The features depend on the position and size of the sub-regions over which the LBP is calculated. AdaBoost is used to find the sub-regions of the images which contain the most discriminative information. Different classification algorithms have been evaluated of which an SVM with Boosted-LBP features performs the best with a recognition accuracy of 95.1% on the Cohn-Kanade (CK+) database.

Lucey et al. [5] created the Extended Cohn-Kanade (CK+) dataset. This dataset contains emotion annotations as well as action unit annotations. In regards to classification, they also have evaluated the datasets using Active Appearance Models (AAMs) in combination with SVMs. To find the position and track the face over different images, they have employed AAM which generates a mesh out of the face. From this mesh, they have extracted two feature vectors. First, the normalized vertices with respect to rotation, translation, and scale, second, a grayscale image from the mesh data and the input images have been extracted. They have chosen a cross-validation strategy, where one subject is left out in the training process, achieving an accuracy of over 80%.

Let us now look at the main parts of the face and the role they play in the recognition of expressions. As we can imagine, the nose, the eyebrows, and mouth are the parts of the face that carry the maximum amount of information related to the facial expression that is being observed. This is shown to be true by Pardas and Bonafonte [38]. Their work shows that surprise, joy, and disgust have very high recognition rates (of 100%, 93.4% and 97.3%, respectively) because they involve clear motion of the mouth and the eyebrows. Another interesting result from their work shows that the mouth conveys more information than the eyebrows. The tests they evaluated with only the mouth being visible gave a recognition accuracy of 78% whereas tests evaluated with only the eyebrows visible gave a recognition accuracy of only 50%. Another occlusion related study by Bourel et al. has shown that sadness is mainly conveyed by the mouth [39]. Occlusion related studies are important because in real-world scenarios, partial occlusion is not uncommon. Everyday items like sunglasses, shadows, scarves, facial hair, etc can lead to occlusions and the recognition system must be able to recognize expressions despite these occlusions. Kotsia et al. [40]'s study on the effect of occlusions on face expression recognizers shows that the occlusion of the mouth reduces the results by more than 50%. This number perfectly matches with the results of Pardas and Bonafonte (that we have seen above). Thus we can say that, for expression recognition, the eyebrows and mouth are the most important parts of the face with the mouth being much more important than the eyebrows. Kotsia et al. also showed that occlusions on the left half or the right half of the face do not affect the performance [40]. This is because of the fact that the facial expressions are symmetric along the vertical plane that divides the face into left and right.

Affective computing collects the cues of emotional state from a variety of sources, including facial expressions, muscle tension, speech patterns, heart rate, pupil dilation, and body temperature. The equipment such as sensors, cameras are used for measuring the emotion and big data, deep learning, and analytic engines are used for analyzing the emotion. Till now many companies have launched facial expression recognition analyzers. For example, IBM Watson APIs include Tone Analyzer and Emotion Analysis.

1.4 Sum-up Discussion

In this chapter, we give a description of the emotion detection system from face images. There are many parts of this chapter. First, a definition of the emotion is provided and also how it is interrelated with affective computing. The term emotion and facial expression are considered to show the relationship between them and also defines the type of emotions. The detailed survey work is presented here to obtain an idea of the emotion recognition system. The rest of this book consists of the following chapters. In the second chapter, a distance signature is proposed to categorize the emotions into six basic categories.

References

1. S.E. Kitayama, H.R.E. Markus, *Emotion and Culture: Empirical Studies of Mutual Influence* (American Psychological Association, 1994)
2. B. Parkinson, A.H. Fischer, A.S.R. Manstead, *Emotion in Social Relations: Cultural, Group, and Interpersonal Processes* (Psychology Press, 2005)
3. R. Ekman, *What the Face Reveals: Basic and Applied Studies of Spontaneous Expression Using the Facial Action Coding System (FACS)* (Oxford University Press, USA, 1997)
4. P. Ekman, W.V. Frisen, *Emotion in the Human Face* (Prentice Hall, Eagle Woods Cliffs, NJ, 1975)
5. P. Lucey, J.F. Cohn, T. Kanade, J. Saragih, Z. Ambadar, I. Matthews, The extended cohn-kanade dataset (ck+): a complete dataset for action unit and emotion-specified expression, in *Computer Society Conference on Computer Vision and Pattern Recognition-Workshops* (IEEE, 2010)
6. M. Lyons, S. Akamatsu, M. Kamachi, J. Gyoba, Coding facial expressions with gabor wavelets, in *Third IEEE International Conference on Automatic Face and Gesture Recognition, 1998. Proceedings* (IEEE, 1998), pp. 200–205
7. M.F. Valstar, M. Pantic, Induced disgust, happiness and surprise: an addition to the mmi facial expression database, in *Proceedings of International Conference on Language Resources and Evaluation, Workshop on EMOTION* (Malta, 2010), pp. 65–70
8. N. Aifanti, C. Papachristou, A. Delopoulos. The mug facial expression database, in *11th International Workshop on Image Analysis for Facial Expression Database* (Desenzano, Italy, 2010), pp. 12–14
9. R.W. Picard, R. Picard, *Affective Computing*, vol. 252 (MIT press Cambridge, 1997)
10. P. Ekman, W.V. Friesen, *Facial Action Coding System* (1977)
11. K. Mase, Recognition of facial expression from optical flow. IEICE Trans. (E) **74**, 3474–3483 (1991)
12. Y. Yaccob, L. Davis, Recognizing facial expressions by spatio-temporal analysis, in *Proceedings of the 12th IAPR International Conference on Pattern Recognition, Conference A: Computer Vision & Image Processing*, vol. 1 (IEEE, 1994), pp. 747–749
13. M. Rosenblum, Y. Yacoob, L.S. Davis, Human expression recognition from motion using a radial basis function network architecture. IEEE Trans. Neural Netw. **7**(5), 1121–1138 (1996)
14. A. Lanitis, C.J. Taylor, T.F. Cootes, Automatic interpretation and coding of face images using flexible models. IEEE Trans. Pattern Anal. Mach. Intell. **19**(7), 743–756 (1997)
15. Curtis Padgett and Garrison W Cottrell. A simple neural network models categorical perception of facial expressions, in *Proceedings of the Twentieth Annual Cognitive Science Conference* (1998), pp. 806–807
16. S. Harnad, Psychophysical and cognitive aspects of categorical perception: a critical overview, in *Categorical Perception: The Groundwork of Cognition* (Cambridge University Press, 1987), pp. 1–52
17. Z. Zhang, Feature-based facial expression recognition: sensitivity analysis and experiments with a multilayer perceptron. Int. J. Pattern Recogn. Artif. Intell. **13**(06), 893–911 (1999)
18. K. Anderson, P.W. McOwan, A real-time automated system for the recognition of human facial expressions. *IEEE Trans. Syst. Man Cybern. Part B (Cybern.)* **36**(1), 96–105 (2006)

19. I. Kotsia, I. Pitas, Facial expression recognition in image sequences using geometric deformation features and support vector machines. IEEE Trans. Image Process. **16**(1), 172–187 (2007)
20. Y. Zhang, Q. Ji, Active and dynamic information fusion for facial expression understanding from image sequences. IEEE Trans. Pattern Anal. Mach. Intell. **27**(5), 699–714 (2005)
21. Y.I. Tian, T. Kanade, J.F. Cohn, Recognizing action units for facial expression analysis. IEEE Trans. Pattern Anal. Mach. Intell. **23**(2), 97–115 (2001)
22. J. Shi, A. Samal, D. Marx, How effective are landmarks and their geometry for face recognition? Comput. Vis. Image Underst. **102**(2), 117–133 (2006)
23. M.F. Valstar, M. Pantic, Biologically versus logic inspired encoding of facial actions and emotions in video, in *2006 IEEE International Conference on Multimedia and Expo* (IEEE, 2006), pp. 325–328
24. S. Park, J. Shin, D. Kim, Facial expression analysis with facial expression deformation. In *19th International Conference on Pattern Recognition, 2008. ICPR 2008* (IEEE, 2008), pp. 1–4
25. D. Cai, X. He, Y. Hu, J. Han, T. Huang, Learning a spatially smooth subspace for face recognition, in *IEEE Conference on Computer Vision and Pattern Recognition, 2007. CVPR'07* (IEEE, 2007), pp. 1–7
26. W. Li, S. Prasad, J.E. Fowler, Hyperspectral image classification using gaussian mixture models and markov random fields. IEEE Geosci. Remote Sens. Lett. **11**(1), 153–157 (2014)
27. X. He, M. Ji, H. Bao, Graph embedding with constraints, in *IJCAI9*, 1065–1070 (2009)
28. A.M. Martínez, Recognizing imprecisely localized, partially occluded, and expression variant faces from a single sample per class. IEEE Trans. Pattern Anal. Mach. Intell. **24**(6), 748–763 (2002)
29. G. Guo, C.R. Dyer, Learning from examples in the small sample case: face expression recognition. IEEE Trans. Syst. Man Cybern. Part B (Cybern.) **35**(3), 477–488 (2005)
30. J. Han, K.-K. Ma, Rotation-invariant and scale-invariant gabor features for texture image retrieval. Image Vis. Comput. **25**(9), 1474–1481 (2007)
31. L. Ma, K. Khorasani, Facial expression recognition using constructive feedforward neural networks. IEEE Trans. Syst. Man Cybern. Part B (Cybern.) **34**(3), 1588–1595 (2004)
32. A. Majumder, L. Behera, V.K. Subramanian, Local binary pattern based facial expression recognition using self-organizing map, in *2014 International Joint Conference on Neural Networks (IJCNN)* (IEEE, 2014), pp. 2375–2382
33. J. Yi, X. Mao, L. Chen, Y. Xue, A. Compare, Facial expression recognition considering individual differences in facial structure and texture. IET Comput. Vis. **8**(5), 429–440 (2014)
34. SL Happy and Aurobinda Routray, Automatic facial expression recognition using features of salient facial patches. IEEE Trans. Affect. Comput. **6**(1), 1–12 (2015)
35. M. Matsugu, K. Mori, Y. Mitari, Y. Kaneda, Subject independent facial expression recognition with robust face detection using a convolutional neural network. Neural Netw. **16**(5), 555–559 (2003)
36. H. Boughrara, M. Chtourou, C.B. Amar, L. Chen, Facial expression recognition based on a MLP neural network using constructive training algorithm. Multimedia Tools Appl. **75**(2), 709–731 (2016)
37. C. Shan, S. Gong, P.W. McOwan, Facial expression recognition based on local binary patterns: a comprehensive study. Image Vis. Comput. **27**(6), 803–816 (2009)
38. M. Pardàs, A. Bonafonte, Facial animation parameters extraction and expression recognition using hidden markov models. Signal Process. Image Commun. **17**(9), 675–688 (2002)
39. F. Bourel, C.C. Chibelushi, A.A. Low, Recognition of facial expressions in the presence of occlusion, in *BMVC*, pp. 1–10 (2001)
40. I. Kotsia, I. Buciu, I. Pitas, An analysis of facial expression recognition under partial facial image occlusion. Image Vis. Comput. **26**(7), 1052–1067 (2008)

Chapter 2
Distance Signature for Recognizing Human Emotions

2.1 Introduction

The previous chapter did get hold of a comprehensive survey of the relevant literature. As a result, the shortcomings of the existing art could be identified and as such we could come out with motivation in favor of overcoming these drawbacks. The question of a new approach devoid of such drawbacks was felt strongly. Human emotion recognition plays a significant role in the field of affective computing when a system in classifying the emotions. In this chapter, we introduce a distance signature-based emotion recognition from human face images. Human face regions such as mouth, jaw, eyes, eyebrows, etc. have a crucial role in differentiating the emotions from one face to another. Active Appearance Model is used on an expressed face images to detect the landmarks. Salient landmarks are identified in and around the regions of eyebrows, eyes, mouth, and nose of a typical human face image. Among these landmark points, we only consider three points on each eyebrow, four points on each eye, three points on the nose, and four points on mouth region. These salient identified landmarks are used to form a grid on the face image. Now we measure the useful Euclidean distances within the grid. These distances are normalized called distance signature. Subsequently, the stability index is calculated from the normalized distance signature which also is found to play an important role to distinguish the emotions from one to another. Statistical measures encompassing range, moment, skewness, kurtosis, and entropy are computed from the normalized distance signature. These features are further supplemented with the features stated already to recognize the expressed emotions into different categories. These features are used as input to the multilayer perceptron for training and the subsequent are used for classification of six basic expressions.

© Springer Nature Singapore Pte Ltd. 2020
P. Dutta and A. Barman, *Human Emotion Recognition from Face Images*,
Cognitive Intelligence and Robotics,
https://doi.org/10.1007/978-981-15-3883-4_2

Organization of This Chapter

This chapter is organized into seven parts. In the first part, consisting of Sect. 2.1, we introduce distance signature useful for human emotion recognition.

The second part of the chapter explores the proposed framework of emotion recognition of distance signature and landmark detection using the AAM model. This part also elaborates grid formation using salient landmark points and distances.

The third part of this chapter, consisting of Sect. 2.3, shows the discussion on feature extraction mechanism. In this part we also discuss distance signature apart from formation and functioning of stability index. Statistical measures such as range, moment, skewness, kurtosis, and entropy are considered to supplement the realization of complete feature set.

The next part, comprising Sects. 2.4 and 2.5 show the training of MLP. This part also makes a detailed discussion about the classification of emotions into different categories.

The penultimate part of the chapter discusses the experiment and result analysis on four benchmark databases.

The chapter sums up with a conclusion in Sect. 2.7.

2.2 Block Diagram of Proposed Emotion Recognition System

The proposed procedure of distance signature-based facial expression recognition is indicated in Fig. 2.1. Active Appearance Model (AAM) [1] is used to detect the landmark points from face images. The few salient landmarks are extracted from the eyebrows, eyes, mouth, and nose region for the formation of a grid. A grid is constituted with extracted landmarks on the face image. These 21 landmark points

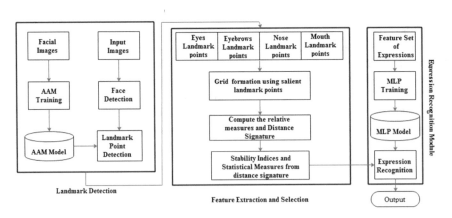

Fig. 2.1 Block diagram of proposed methodology

are linked to each other and labeled in an array of a specific order for the formation of a grid. The Euclidean distances are computed from each pair of landmarks within the grid. These distances are normalized and it measures in a particular order called distance signature. We shall see as to how effectively we apply this property in the facial expression recognition being considered. This normalized distance signature is also used to derive the stability index. The normalized distance signature is also used to find the statistical features such as range, moment, kurtosis, skewness, and entropy to enrich the significance of a feature set. These features are fed as input to a multilayer perceptron to recognize the emotions.

2.2.1 Landmark Detection Using AAM

Effective feature extraction is vital in recognizing emotions. For this reason, proper landmark identification on the face images is a challenging task to get the prominent features. The study of the landmark identification of different facial expressions is available in [2]. According to [3], the landmark points are sensitive to extract the prominent feature set for the deformations and displacement of the facial components during the variation of the emotions. The extensive study of the landmark identification from the different facial expressions is available in [2, 4]. It is noticed that the few facial landmarks hold common properties in changing expressions and some have an important characteristic to categorize the emotions from one face to another (Fig. 2.2).

There are many approaches in landmark detection but in this chapter, an appearance model is used to exact landmark points. The various types of landmark detection are studied in [2, 4] on the face image during different facial expressions. It is observed that some facial regions hold common properties in changing expressions

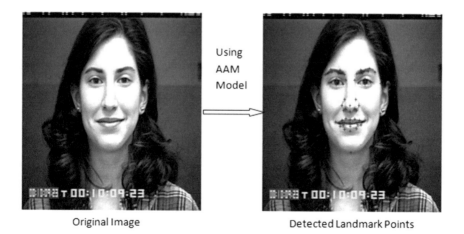

Original Image   Detected Landmark Points

Fig. 2.2 AAM fitting landmark points of happiness

and some are very prominent characteristics to differentiate the expressions from one face images to another. For that reason landmark points on the face images are actively considered in differentiating expressions from one face to another face of the same person. To get hold of the landmark points, at first a shape model on a face image is considered. After that Active Appearance Model (AAM) is used on that face image to get the exact landmark points to that face image. The shape model consists of a set of annotating u landmarks $[x_1, y_1, \ldots x_u, y_u]$ among D training images $1 \le i \le D$. These landmark points specify the shape model of each face image. Next, the similarity transformations from the original shapes are removed by Procrustes analysis and get D similarity-free shapes. Finally, Principal Component Analysis (PCA) is used on these shapes to get a shape model that represents the mean shape and n eigen shape vectors $[s_0, S]$. The model basically holds shape variation due to pose and expression. Assume that we are given a new similarity-free shape s. Then, the model can be used to represent s as

$$s = s_0 + Sp, p = S^T(s - s_0) \tag{2.1}$$

Finally, the similarity transforms of the shape matrix S is appended with 4 similarity eigenvectors. Now all eigenvectors are re-orthonormalized, and then Eq. 2.1 is applied.

Learning the appearance model requires removing shape variation from the texture. This can be achieved by first warping each I_i to the reference frame defined by the mean shape s_0 using a motion model W. Finally, PCA is applied to the shape-free textures, to obtain the appearance model defined by the mean appearance and m appearance eigenvectors $[A_0, A]$. The model captures appearance variation, for example, due to identity and illumination. The model can be used to represent a shape-free test texture I as

$$I = A_0 + Ac, c = A^T(I - A_0) \tag{2.2}$$

We used piecewise affine warps $W(x, p)$ as the motion model in this work. Briefly, to define a piecewise affine warp, one first needs to triangulate the set of vertices of the given shapes. Then, each triangle in s and the corresponding triangle in s_0 can define an affine warp. The collection of all affine warps defines a piecewise affine warp which is parameterized with respect to p. Finally, a model instance is synthesized to represent a test object by warping I from the mean shape s_0 to s using the piecewise affine warp define by s_0 and s.

2.2.2   Formation of Grid

We use AAM [1] to obtain the landmarks from the expressed image. First, we consider a shape model to identify the landmark points using AAM. As we consider the shape model, the landmark points are known to the system. These known landmark points

Fig. 2.3 Salient landmark
points detection of happiness
using AAM model

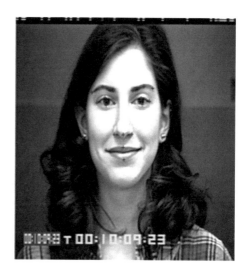

are used to identify the salient landmark points on the mouth, nose, eyebrows, and
eyes region due to their sensation of various expressions. The extraction of landmark
detection for different facial expressions is shown in Fig. 2.3. These salient landmarks
are marked on the eyebrows (one in mid-position of two corner points and another
two are corner points), eyes (two points are in mid-position of upper eyelid and
lower eyelid, two corner points), mouth (two points are in mid-position of the upper
lip and lower lip, two corner points of lips), and nose (two corner points of nostril
and remaining one in upper-position of nose). Now identified landmark points are
connected with each other, forming a grid as depicted in Fig. 2.4.

We have identified 21 landmark points, while $\frac{21(21-1)}{2}$, i.e. 210 distances possible
among the grid. These 21 landmarks are joined to each other to form an array. The
connection points are stored in an array in a particular way to form a grid in Fig. 2.5.
The dimension of this array is 21×11. The first row is joined with the second row,
then the first row is joined with the third and so forth until the first row is joined
with the last row. Next, the second row is joined with the first row, the second row is
joined with the third. and so on and so forth until the second row is connected with
the last row. Remaining rows maintain the same mechanism until last row landmarks
are joined to each other. A grid is formed through the identified points as depicted
in Fig. 2.5.

The process of grid formation implies the following sequence of events:

1. Identification of the landmark points using AAM.
2. Few prominent landmarks are marked on eyebrows, eyes, mouth, and nose
   regions.
3. These landmark points are connected to each other to form a grid as shown in
   Fig. 2.4.

Fig. 2.4 Formation of grid
using salient landmark points
of happiness

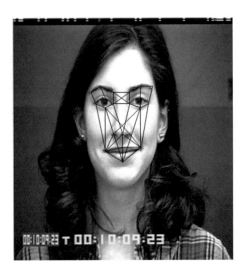

Fig. 2.5 Grid formation
using AAM

```
Grid=
[18 20 22 23 25 27 37 38 40 42 43;
 20 22 23 25 27 37 38 40 42 43 45;
 22 23 25 27 37 38 40 42 43 45 46;
 23 25 27 37 38 40 42 43 45 46 48;
 25 27 37 38 40 42 43 45 46 48 32;
 27 37 38 40 42 43 45 46 48 32 34;
 32 18 20 22 23 25 27 37 38 34 36;
 34 18 20 22 23 25 27 36 37 38 40;
 36 18 20 22 23 25 27 37 38 40 42;
 37 38 40 42 43 45 46 48 49 52 55;
 38 40 42 43 45 46 48 49 52 55 58;
 40 42 43 45 46 48 49 52 55 58 32;
 42 43 45 46 48 49 52 55 58 32 36;
 43 45 46 48 49 52 55 58 32 34 36;
 45 46 48 49 52 55 58 32 34 36 18;
 46 48 49 52 55 58 32 34 36 18 20;
 48 49 52 55 58 32 34 36 18 20 22;
 49 52 55 58 32 34 36 18 20 22 23;
 52 55 58 32 34 36 18 20 22 23 25;
 55 58 32 34 36 18 20 22 23 25 27;
 58 32 34 36 18 20 22 23 25 27 37]
```

2.3 Feature Extraction

Facial expression recognition to a large extent relies on an appropriate selection of facial features from face images. Feature extraction mechanisms are a challenging task in facial expression recognition. These features have the capability of making fine distinctions of facial expression recognition. We consider various types of features used in our proposed facial expression recognition system.

2.3.1 Distance Signature

We consider eyebrows, eyes, mouth, and nose regions to extract the proper landmark points on face images. These salient landmark points are used to form a grid on the face image. There are 210 distinct distances possible within the grid. Euclidean distances are calculated among pairs of landmark points in the grid using Eq. 2.3

$$d = \sqrt{(x_1 - x_2)^2 + (y_1 - y_2)^2} \qquad (2.3)$$

where Euclidean distance is denoted by d. The first row landmark point is denoted by (x_1, y_1) and the second row landmark point is denoted by (x_2, y_2). Now these distances [5] are normalized as

$$\beta_i^f = \frac{d_i^f}{\sum_{i=1}^{n} d_i^f} \quad f = 1, 2, \ldots, m \text{ and } i = 1, 2, \ldots, n \qquad (2.4)$$

where m is the total number of facial images and n is the total number of distances. A set of β_i^f values in an appropriate sequence constitutes the distance signature and various d_i^f are the distances. These normalized distances are considered as a distance signature.

To understand the distance signature, we consider an example which is shown in Fig. 2.6. In this figure the six basic emotions are considered, viz. surprise, happiness, sadness, fear, disgust, and anger to calculate the distance signatures. The distance signatures are shown in Fig. 2.7. The surprise emotion is shown in Fig. 2.6 (a) and the corresponding distance signature of this emotion is shown in Fig. 2.7 column 1. The happiness is shown in Fig. 2.6 (b) and corresponding distance signature of this emotion is calculated in Fig. 2.6 column 2. The sadness is considered in Fig. 2.6 (c) to show the corresponding distance signature in Fig. 2.7 column 3. The fear is considered in Fig. 2.6 (d) to show the corresponding distance signature in Fig. 2.7 column 4. The disgust is considered in Fig. 2.6 (e) to show the corresponding distance signature in Fig. 2.7 column 5. In the same way, anger is considered in Fig. 2.6 (f) to show the corresponding distance signature in Fig. 2.7 column 6. This way the distance signature is derived.

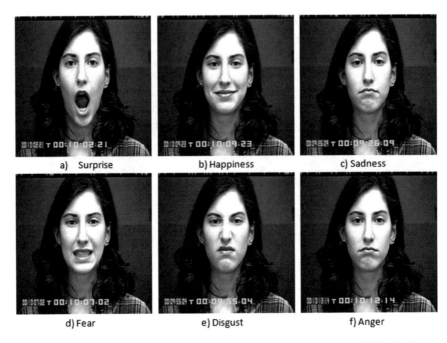

a) Surprise   b) Happiness   c) Sadness

d) Fear   e) Disgust   f) Anger

Fig. 2.6 Six basic emotions are considered to calculate the distance signature of CK+ database

2.3.2 Stability Index

Normalized distance signature is calculated from the grid out of face images using Eq. 2.4. This signature is considered to compute the stability index of face images. Stability index is yet another formidable feature for its sensitivity to expressions to classify the facial expression. The normalized distance signature is deduced using Eq. 2.5

$$(\mu_i^r)^f = \frac{(d_i^r)^f}{(\sum_{i=1}^{n} d_i^r)^f} \tag{2.5}$$

where the rth order distance signature is computed for each face image. In this experiment, we use rth order as $r = 1, 2, \ldots, 8$. We subsequently calculate the rth order differential as

$$\Delta(d_i^r)^f = (\mu_i^r)^f - (\mu_i^{r-1})^f \tag{2.6}$$

where we set a threshold upon the analysis of the differences of higher-order factors. Given a preassigned small positive threshold λ, we identify that order r for which $\Delta(d_i^r)^f \leq \lambda$, for the first time (i.e. the smallest value of r). This order r is considered as a stability index of the distance signature. Our experiment reveals that the value of r may go up to 8 with the images we considered.

	1	2	3	4	5	6
1	0.0015	0.0017	0.0017	0.0017	0.0018	0.0017
2	0.0015	0.0017	0.0017	0.0017	0.0018	0.0017
3	0.0025	0.0028	0.0027	0.0028	0.0027	0.0029
4	0.0015	0.0017	0.0018	0.0017	0.0018	0.0016
5	0.0014	0.0016	0.0017	0.0015	0.0017	0.0015
6	0.0074	0.0082	0.0082	0.0080	0.0083	0.0081
7	0.0055	0.0059	0.0059	0.0056	0.0056	0.0058
8	0.0061	0.0067	0.0067	0.0067	0.0068	0.0067
9	0.0066	0.0072	0.0071	0.0072	0.0074	0.0074
....						....
....						....
....						....
199	0.0077	0.0078	0.0078	0.0077	0.0077	0.0077
200	0.0093	0.0072	0.0067	0.0077	0.0070	0.0068
201	0.0032	0.0034	0.0034	0.0032	0.0031	0.0033
202	0.0045	0.0050	0.0048	0.0049	0.0050	0.0050
203	0.0033	0.0035	0.0035	0.0035	0.0031	0.0035
204	0.0067	0.0074	0.0074	0.0073	0.0076	0.0074
205	0.0063	0.0068	0.0068	0.0067	0.0069	0.0068
206	0.0036	0.0040	0.0039	0.0038	0.0039	0.0039
207	0.0079	0.0076	0.0079	0.0076	0.0075	0.0079
208	0.0067	0.0072	0.0073	0.0071	0.0072	0.0073
209	0.0075	0.0065	0.0070	0.0066	0.0071	0.0070
210	0.0091	0.0071	0.0066	0.0075	0.0069	0.0066

Fig. 2.7 Distance signature of six basic emotions on CK+

The determination of stability index [5] implies the following sequence of events:

1. Normalized distance signatures are calculated from among the grid of face images.
2. Higher-order signatures are computed from distance signatures.
3. A threshold is selected upon the experimentation of the differences of higher-order factors.
4. The higher order attaining below the preset threshold for the first time is treated as a stability index of that particular face image.

Now we consider face images indicated in Fig. 2.6 to derive the corresponding stability indices of six basic emotions, viz. surprise, happiness, sadness, fear, disgust, and anger. The stability index of surprise is calculated as of Fig. 2.6 (a). The stability index of happiness is identified as of Fig. 2.6 (b). The stability index of sadness is calculates as 430 of Fig. 2.6 (c). The stability index of fear is computed as 433 of Fig. 2.6 (d). The stability index of disgust is calculated as 428 of Fig. 2.6 (e). The stability index of anger is calculated as 427 of Fig. 2.6 (f).

2.3.3   Statistical Measures of Distance Signature

Many number of features are yielding promising recognition rate in facial expression. For this reason, we compute statistical measures. The statistical measures such as range, moment, skewness, kurtosis, and entropy are considered to meaningfully augment the feature set.

Range
In statistics, range is defined as the difference between the maximum and minimum of observations. It is intuitively obvious as to why we define range in statistics this way. The range should suggest how diversely spread out the values are, and by computing the difference between the maximum and minimum values, we get an estimate of the spread of the data.

For example, suppose an experiment involves finding out the weight of lab rats and the values in grams being 320, 367, 423, 471, and 480. In this case, the range is simply computed as (480–320) = 160 grams.

Moment
The mathematical concept of moments are found to have been used for many years in many fields, such as pattern recognition and image understanding. The mean is the first statistic moment. The subsequent six statistical features are median, mode, variance, standard deviation, skewness, and kurtosis. The skewness denotes the third-order moment, which characterizes the degree of asymmetry of the distribution of underlying data around its mean, or the degree of deviation from symmetry about the mean. The kurtosis is the fourth-order moment of data distribution and is a measure of the degree of the sharpness inherent in the underlying histogram and is a measure of the flatness or peakedness of a curve.

When moments are used to describe an image, the global properties of respective images are exploited. A significant work considering moments for the specific pattern recognition has been reported by Hu [6]. He derived a set of seven-moment invariants, using nonlinear combinations of geometric moments. These invariants remain the same under image translation, rotation, and scaling. When a set of values has a sufficiently strong central tendency, that is, a tendency to classify around some particular value, then it may be useful to characterize the set by a few numbers that are related to its moments. In statistics, the moment measures something relative to the center of the values. The moment [6] is computed as

$$l_k = \sum_{i=1}^{n} b(i, k) \times v(i) \tag{2.7}$$

where $v = (v_1, v_2, \ldots, v_n)$ represents the normalized distance signature and $b(i, k)$ is i raised to power of k, where $k = 1, 2, 3, 4$.

Skewness
Skewness is a measure of the asymmetry of the data around the mean. On the other hand, skewness refers to the asymmetry or latch of symmetry in the distance of a frequency distribution. If skewness is negative, the data is spread out more to the left of the mean than to the right. If skewness is positive, the data is spread out more to the right. The skewness of the normal distribution (or any perfectly symmetric distribution) is zero. The third central moment is the measure of the asymmetry associated with the distribution. The normalized third central moment is called skewness. A distribution that is skewed to the left (the tail of the distribution is longer on the left) will have negative skewness. A distribution that is skewed to the right (the tail of the distribution is longer on the right) will have positive skewness. Skewness [6] is defined as

$$u = \frac{\sum_{i=1}^{n} b(i, 3)^2 \times v(i)}{\sum_{i=1}^{n} b(i, 2)^3 \times v(i)} \tag{2.8}$$

where u indicates the skewness of distance signature.

Kurtosis
Kurtosis is a measure of how outlier prone a distribution is. Distributions of data and probability distributions may not always be of the same shape. Some are asymmetric and skewed to the left or to the right. Another feature to consider when talking about distribution is the shape of the tails of the distribution on the far left and the far right. Kurtosis is the measure of the thickness or heaviness of the tails of a distribution which is defined as

$$q = \frac{\sum_{i=1}^{n} b(i, 4)}{\sum_{i=1}^{n} b(i, 2)^2 \times v(i)} \tag{2.9}$$

where q indicates the kurtosis of distance signature.

Entropy
Entropy is a measure of unpredictability of the state of its average information content. To get a basic understanding of this term, we consider the example of a political poll. Usually, such polls happen because the outcome of the poll is not known beforehand. In other words, the outcome of the poll is relatively unpredictable, and actually

performing the poll and learning the results gives some new information; these are just different ways of saying that the a priori entropy of the poll results is large. Now, consider the case that the same poll is performed a second time shortly after the first poll. Since the result of the first poll is already known, the outcome of the second poll can be predicted well and the results should not contain much new information; in this case the a priori entropy of the second poll result is small relative to that of the first. Entropy [7] is defined as

$$En = -\sum_{i=1}^{n} p_i \log p_i \qquad (2.10)$$

where p_i contains the histogram count of the distance signature and $\sum_{i=1}^{n} p_i = 1$, $0 \le p_i \le 1$.

2.4 Feature Selection

Distance signature is obtained using Eq. 2.4. The stability index is computed from the distance signature to get prominent features. The huge number of features yields promising facial expression recognition than a fewer number of features. For this reason, statistical measures such as range, moment, skewness, kurtosis, and entropy are computed from both distance and shape signatures. Now the extracted features are combined to get a feature set of a particular emotion. The feature extraction mechanism is available in Algorithm 2.1.

2.5 Training of MLP

A MLP [8] with one layer comprising z hidden units is discussed here. Indicate that it is a supervised mode of learning. Also elaborate as to how data are partitioned into training data and testing data, in general, and then explain in the present scope. The y output unit has v_{ok} as associated bias. It is found that both input and hidden units have biases. The training procedure of MLP involves the following steps:

1. Initialization of the weights.
2. Feedforward flow of signals.
3. Backpropagation of errors reported at the output layer.
4. Updation of the weights and biases along the connecting edges.

Algorithm 2.1 : *Distance Feature Extraction(D)*

1: **begin**
2:    Identify the landmark points l_i using AAM [1].
3:    The eyes, nose, mouth and eyebrows regions are used to extract salient landmark points $l_i (i = 1, 2, \ldots, 21)$.
4:    These salient landmark points l_i are connected with each other to form a grid.
5:    Distances (d_i where $i = 1, 2, \ldots, n1$) are calculated from the grid.
6:    Normalize the distances using Eq. 2.4 to obtain distance signature (β_i).
7:    Find stability index $(\beta_i^r)^f$ from distance signature using Eq. 2.5 and corresponding differences of higher-order signatures are calculated using Eq. 2.6.
8:    Calculate range, moment [l_k (*where* $k = 1, 2, 3, 4$)], skewness (u) and kurtosis (q) using Eqs. 2.7, 2.8 and 2.9.
9:    Also calculate entropy (En) from distance signature using Eq. 2.10.
10:    $D \leftarrow [range, (\beta_i^{r1}), l_k, u, q, En]$.
11:    Return D.
12: **end**

During the first step for the sake of the initialization of the weights, some small values are assigned corresponding to the connecting edges. At the time of feedforward step, each node x_i receives an input signal and sends this signal from the input layer to each hidden unit $z_1, z_2, \ldots, z_p$. Each hidden unit calculates the activation function and sends this signal z_j to each output unit. The output unit calculates the activation function to form the response of the network for the given input unit pattern.

During the backpropagation of errors, each output unit compares its computed activation y_k with its target value t_k to determine the associated error for that pattern with that unit. Based on that error, the factor $\delta_k (k = 1, 2, \ldots, m)$ is computed and is used to distribute the error at output unit y_k back to all units in the previous layer. Similarly, the factor $\delta_j (j = 1, 2, \ldots, p)$ is computed for each hidden unit z_j.

During the last step, the weights and biases are updated using the δ factor and the activation function.

The various parameters considered in the training algorithm are as follows:

- x = input of training pattern;
- $x = (x_1, x_2, \ldots, x_n)$;
- $t = (t_1, t_2, \ldots, t_k)$ = output of target pattern;
- v_{oj} = bias on hidden unit j;
- z_j = hidden unit j;
- w_{ok} = bias on output unit k; and
- y_k = output unit $k = 1, 2, \ldots .6$.

The training algorithm used in the MLP network is as follows clearly indicating various phases:

Algorithm 2.2 MLP training algorithm

1: Initialize the weights to small random values.
2: While stopping condition is false, do step 3–14.
3: For each training pair do step 4–13.

Feedforward
4: Each input unit receives the input signal x_i and transmits this signal to all units in the hidden layers.
5: Each hidden unit $(z_j, j = 1, 2, \ldots, p)$ sums its weighted input signal $z_{in} = v_{oj} + \sum_{i=1}^{n} x_{ij} v_{ij}$. After calculating this signal is used activation function $z_j = f(z_{in})$ and sends this signal to all units of the output layers.
6: Each output unit $(y_k, k = 1, 2, \ldots, m)$ sums its weighted input signals using $y_{in} = w_{ok} + \sum_{j=1}^{p} z_j w_{jk}$ and applies its activation function to calculate the output signals $y_k + f(y_{in})$.

Backpropagation of errors
7: Each output unit $(y_k, k = 1, 2, \ldots, m)$ receives a target pattern corresponding to an input pattern, error is calculated as $\delta_k = (t_k - y_k) F(y_{in})$.
8: Each hidden $(z_j = j = 1, 2, \ldots, n)$ sums its delta input units in the layer $\delta_{in} = \sum_{\delta_j w_{jk}}$. The error term is calculated as $\delta_j = \delta_{in} f(z_{in})$.
   Updation of weights and biases
9: Each output unit $(y_k, k = 1, 2, \ldots, m)$ updates its bias and weights $(j = 0, 1, \ldots, p)$. The weight correction is given by $\Delta w_{jk} = \alpha \delta_k z_j$ and bias is given by $w_{ok} = \alpha \delta_k$.
10: Therefore weights updations are $w_{jk}(new) = w_{jk}(old) + \Delta w_{jk}$ and $w_{ok}(new) = w_{ok}(old) + \Delta w_{ok}$
11: Each hidden unit $(z_j, j = 1, 2, \ldots, p)$ updates its bias and weights $(i = 0, 1, \ldots, n)$.
12: The weight correction is given by $\Delta v_{ij} = \alpha \delta_j x_i$ and bias is given by $v_{oj} = \alpha \delta_j$.
13: Therefore weights updations are $v_{ij}(new) = v_{ij}(old) + \Delta v_{ij}$ and $v_{oj}(new) = v_{oj}(old) + \Delta v_{oj}$.
14: Test the stopping condition. The stopping condition may be minimization of the errors.

2.5.1 Classification

A multilayer perceptron is a feedforward artificial neural network model that maps a set of input data onto a set of appropriate outputs [9]. The extracted features of every face image are represented by a vector of 9 elements. These features are used as Min-Max process to normalize each row feature vector. Extracted features are used as input to MLP network producing output responses as per minimum errors. The network consists of a number of 9 input nodes in the input layer, a hidden layer consisting of the number of 8 intermediate nodes and an output layer containing 6 nodes. The weights usually excite or inhibit the signal that flows through the edge. The perceptron is found capable of classifying a facial expression into six basic expressions, viz. anger, fear, disgust, sadness, happiness, and surprise.

2.6 Experiments and Results

Distance signature-based facial expression recognition is validated on Cohn-Kanade (CK+) [10], JAFFE [11], MMI [12], and MUG [13] benchmark databases to evaluate the performance of the proposed method. Twenty-one landmark points have been obtained via the AAM model to form a grid that is used to calculate the distances. These distances are normalized and subsequently, features are considered to recognize the different emotions. Obtained results are compared with different state-of-art methods to evaluate the effectiveness of the proposed method. The benchmark databases contain six basic facial expressions: anger, disgust, fear, happiness, sadness, and surprise.

2.6.1 Experimental Result on CK+ Dataset

The Cohn-Kanade (CK+) database is a combination of 100 university students aged between 18 and 30 years. CK+ includes both posed and non-posed (spontaneous) expressions and additional types of metadata. For posed expressions, the number of sequences is increased from the initial release by 22% and the number of subjects by 27%. As with the initial release, the target expression for each sequence is fully Facial Action Coding System coded. In addition, validated emotion labels have been added to the metadata. Thus, sequences may be analyzed for both action units and prototypic emotions. Each sequence goes from neutral to target display, with the last frame being action unit coded.

To evaluate the system performance, a total of 849 images were selected (566 for training and 283 for testing) and could achieve an average rate of 98.6% for training. Table 2.1 shows the classification of different expressions. Anger is classified into 49 images properly but 2 images are misclassified with surprise. Disgust classifies 45 images correctly and 2 images are confused with anger and happiness. Fear recognized 23 images properly and 1 image is confused with happiness. Happiness identified 63 images correctly whereas 1 image is misclassified as anger. Sadness

Table 2.1 The Confusion Matrix shows the correct classification of expressions on CK+ database using distance signature

	Anger	Disgust	Fear	Happiness	Sadness	Surprise
Anger	49	0	0	0	0	2
Disgust	1	45	0	1	0	0
Fear	0	0	23	1	0	0
Happiness	1	0	0	63	0	0
Sadness	0	0	0	0	47	2
Surprise	0	1	0	1	0	46

identified 47 images correctly and 2 images are confused as surprise. In the same way, surprise identifies 46 images perfectly and 2 images are misclassified with happiness and disgust.

The average recognition rate of each expression is 96.1% for anger, 95.7% for disgust, 95.8% for fear, 98.4% for happiness, 95.9% for sadness, and 95.8% for a surprise. The average recognition accuracy of 96.3% with the highest recognition accuracy 98.4% in case of happiness and the lowest 95.8% in case of surprise is achieved. The average performance of the distance signature is 96.3% as evident.

False Acceptance Rate (FAR): This is defined as a percentage of impostors accepted by the biometric system. In biometric identification system the users are not making claims about their identity. Hence it is necessary that this percentage is as small as possible so that the person not enrolled in the system must not be accepted by the system. Thus False Acceptance must be minimized in comparison to False Rejections.

Here, we assume as FP: False Positive
FN: False Negative
TN: True Negative
TP: True Positive

$$FAR = \frac{FP}{FP + TN} \tag{2.11}$$

False Rejection Rate (FRR): This is defined as a percentage of genuine users rejected by the biometric system. In the verification biometric system, the user will make claims of their identity and hence the system must not reject an enrolled user and the number of False Rejections must be kept as small as possible. Thus False Rejection must be minimized in comparison to False Acceptance. It is defined as

$$FRR = \frac{FN}{FN + TP} \tag{2.12}$$

Error Rate (ERR) : EER [14] is computed as the incorrect predictions of all items divided by the total number of items in the database. If a system produces 0, it indicates the best error rate. In the same way, the worst is 1. It is also defined as

$$ERR = \frac{FP + FN}{TP + TN + FP + FN} \tag{2.13}$$

Equal Error Rate (EER) : EER [15] computes the performance of a system with another system (lower is better) by measuring the equal (if they are not equal then nearly equal or minimum distance) of FRR and FAR.

In a biometric analysis, the system assigns all appropriate targets a "score" between in the interval [0, 1]. The target 1 indicates a full match and 0 indicates no match at all. If we set a threshold as 0, all the users including the genuine (positive) and the impostors (negative) are authenticated. If we consider a threshold to 1, there is a high risk that no one may be authenticated. Therefore, in real applications, the threshold is considered between 0 and 1.

Table 2.2 The FAR, FRR, and ERR of distance signature on CK+ Database

	FAR	FRR	ERR
Anger	0.008	0.039	0.014
Disgust	0.004	0.042	0.010
Fear	0.000	0.041	0.003
Happiness	0.013	0.015	0.014
Sadness	0.000	0.040	0.007
Surprise	0.017	0.041	0.021

The recognition performance of the proposed system is measured in terms of the FAR, FRR, and ERR. The FRR, FAR, and ERR of distance signature using MLP for CK+ dataset are shown in Table 2.2.

Table 2.2 shows the MLP-based EER of distance signature is 0.014. This EER indicates that the distance signatures produce higher recognition accuracy for MLP.

2.6.2 Experimental Result on JAFFE Dataset

The JAFFE [11] database contains 213 images. Six basic expressions, in addition to the neutral face (seven in total), are available in this database. These expressions are happiness, sadness, surprise, anger, disgust, and fear. The images were taken from 10 Japanese female models, and each emotion was subjectively tested on 60 Japanese volunteers. There are three samples, corresponding to each facial expression of each person. In the JAFFE database, each subject posed 3 or 4 times for each expression.

In our discussion, a total of 213 images were considered (116 for training and 97 for testing) and acquires 96.6% for training. In Table 2.3, the confusion matrix shows the performance of different expressions. From this table, one may observe that anger, disgust, happiness, sadness, and surprise are classified correctly but fear is

Table 2.3 The recognition matrix shows the correct classification of expressions on JAFFE dataset using distance signature

	Anger	Disgust	Fear	Happiness	Sadness	Surprise
Anger	21	0	0	0	0	0
Disgust	0	20	0	0	0	0
Fear	2	1	11	0	0	0
Happiness	0	1	0	13	0	0
Sadness	0	0	0	1	13	0
Surprise	0	0	0	0	1	14

Table 2.4 The FAR, FRR, and ERR of distance signature on JAFFE Database

	FAR	FRR	ERR
Anger	0.026	0.000	0.020
Disgust	0.025	0.000	0.020
Fear	0.000	0.214	0.030
Happiness	0.011	0.071	0.020
Sadness	0.011	0.071	0.020
Surprise	0.000	0.066	0.010

misclassified with anger and disgust. This is because fear and happiness expressions share common distances during the time of feature extraction within the grid.

The average classification rate of individual expressions is 100% for anger, disgust, sadness, and surprise, 78.6% for fear, and 85.7% for happiness. The average recognition accuracy of 94% with correct recognition in case of anger, disgust, sadness, and surprises and the lowest 78.6% in case of fear is achieved. The average recognition rate of the distance signature approach is 94%.

We also consider FAR, FRR, and ERR to compute the system performance. The recognition rate of the proposed system is measured in terms of the false FRR, FAR, and ERR. The FRR, FAR, and ERR of distance signature using MLP for CK+ dataset are shown in Table 2.4.

Table 2.4 indicates the MLP-based EER of distance signature. This EER value indicates that the distance signatures ensure higher recognition accuracy for MLP.

2.6.3   Experimental Result on MMI Dataset

The MMI facial expression database was created by the Man-Machine Interaction Group, Delft University of Technology, Netherlands. This database is initially established for research on machine analysis of facial expressions. The database consists of over 2,900 videos and high-resolution still images of 75 subjects of both genders with age range from 19 to 62 years having either a European, Asian, or South American ethnic background. These samples show both non-occluded and partially occluded faces, with or without facial hair and glasses. In our experiments, 96 image sequences were selected from the MMI database. The only selection criterion is that a sequence can be labeled as one of the six basic emotions. The sequences come from 20 subjects, with 16 emotions per subject. MMI database offers a more challenging issue for facial expression recognition compared to CK+. First, different people give the pose of the same expression in various ways. Secondly, some expressions are found having accessories, such as glasses, headcloth, or mustache.

Table 2.5 The recognition matrix shows the correct classification of expressions on MMI dataset using distance signature

	Anger	Disgust	Fear	Happiness	Sadness	Surprise
Anger	24	3	2	0	0	0
Disgust	0	17	0	0	3	1
Fear	2	1	10	0	0	1
Happiness	0	2	0	14	0	0
Sadness	0	0	0	0	18	0
Surprise	1	1	1	0	2	10

A total of 325 images were selected (212 for training and 113 for testing) to assess the performance of expressions from the MMI database and an average recognition rate of 92.5% could be achieved for training. The proposed procedure uses a total of 113 images to test the performance of expressions. Table 2.5 shows the performance of facial expressions. The anger is classified into 24 images accurately but 5 images are misclassified with fear and disgust. Disgust recognized 17 images correctly and 4 images are misclassified with sadness and surprise. Fear is classified into 10 images properly and 4 images are wrongly classified as anger, disgust, and surprise. Happiness identified 14 images correctly and 2 images are misclassified with disgust. Sadness is classified correctly. Surprise is classified into 10 images properly but 5 images are misclassified with anger, disgust, fear, and sadness. From this, we observe that most expressions share common distances during the time of feature extraction within the grid. The expressions of fear and surprise are challenging expressions to be correctly classified.

The average recognition rate of each expression is 82.8% for anger, 81% for disgust, 71.4% for fear, 87.5% for happiness, 100% for sadness, and 66.7% for a surprise. The average recognition accuracy of 81.5% with the highest recognition accuracy 100% in case of sadness and the lowest 66.7% in case of surprise is achieved. Our experience indicates that the MMI database is more challenging than the CK+ and JAFFE for facial expression recognition. The average performance of the distance signature is reported to the tune of 81.5%. The FAR, FRR, and ERR are measured to show the recognition rate of the proposed system. The recognition rate of the proposed system is measured in terms of the FRR, FAR, and ERR. The FRR, FAR, and ERR of distance signature using MLP for CK+ dataset are shown in Table 2.6.

Table 2.6 indicates the MLP-based EER of distance signature. This EER value indicates that the distance signatures ensure higher recognition accuracy for MLP.

Table 2.6 The FAR, FRR, and ERR of distance signature on MMI Database

	FAR	FRR	ERR
Anger	0.035	0.172	0.070
Disgust	0.076	0.190	0.097
Fear	0.030	0.285	0.061
Happiness	0.000	0.125	0.017
Sadness	0.052	0.000	0.044
Surprise	0.020	0.333	0.061

2.6.4 Experimental Result on MUG Dataset

In the MUG [13] database 35 women and 51 men, all of the Caucasian origin between 20 and 35 years of age participated. Men are with or without beards. The subjects are not wearing glasses except for 7 subjects in the second part of the database. There are no occlusions except for a few hairs falling on the face. The images of 52 subjects are available to authorized Internet users. The data that can be accessed amounts to 38GB. Twenty-five subjects are available upon request and the rest 9 subjects are available only in the MUG laboratory. The subjects were asked to perform the six basic expressions, which are anger, disgust, fear, happiness, sadness, and surprise. MUG database is also considered to test the system performance of facial expression. Here the same parameters are used as those in the CK+ database. A total of 591 images are selected (394 for training and 197 for testing).

In Table 2.7, the confusion matrix shows the classification of different expressions of distance signature. It is observed that the disgust and fear are correctly classified. Whereas anger identifies 29 images perfectly and 2 images are misclassified with disgust and sadness. Happiness recognizes 43 images properly and 2 images are wrongly classified with disgust. Sadness recognizes 28 images perfectly and 1 image is confused with happiness. In the same way, surprise classifies 34 images accurately and 2 images are misclassified with anger and sadness.

Table 2.7 The recognition matrix shows the correct classification of expressions on MUG dataset using distance signature

	Anger	Disgust	Fear	Happiness	Sadness	Surprise
Anger	29	1	0	0	1	0
Disgust	0	30	0	0	0	0
Fear	0	0	26	0	0	0
Happiness	0	2	0	43	0	0
Sadness	0	0	0	1	28	0
Surprise	1	0	0	0	1	34

Table 2.8 The FAR, FRR, and ERR of distance signature on MUG Database

	FAR	FRR	ERR
Anger	0.006	0.064	0.015
Disgust	0.018	0.000	0.015
Fear	0.000	0.000	0.000
Happiness	0.006	0.044	0.015
Sadness	0.011	0.034	0.015
Surprise	0.000	0.055	0.010

The average recognition rate reported is 93.5% for anger, 100% for disgust, 100% for fear, 95.6% for happiness, 96.6% for sadness, and 94.4% for a surprise. The average recognition accuracy of 96.7% with the highest recognition accuracy 100% in case of disgust and sadness and the lowest 66.7% in case of anger is achieved. The average recognition rate of distance signature is 96.7%.

The FAR, FRR, and ERR are used to measure the recognition rate of expressions. The recognition accuracy of the proposed method is measured in terms of the FRR, FAR, and ERR. The FRR, FAR, and ERR of distance signature using MLP for the MUG dataset are shown in Table 2.8.

Table 2.8 indicates the EER of distance signature using MLP. This EER value proved that the distance signatures show the higher recognition accuracy of facial expression for MLP.

2.6.5 Comparative Analyses

The proposed distance signature method is compared with the results obtained from existing arts in the literature [16–19]. A comparison task is presented with the other method. We evaluate our experiments on CK+, JAFFE, MMI, and MUG databases. Table 2.9 summarizes the comparative results with other methods. To efficiently evaluate the performance of our proposed method, it is compared with [17], which is the most recent comprehensive study on expression recognition with remarkable results.

We consider the JAFFE dataset to evaluate the system performance of expression recognition with [17], which shows our proposed procedure recognition of expressions with remarkable results. To measure the system performance of MMI dataset we compare it with and present [16] in Table 2.9. From this table, it is evident that the proposed distance signature performs remarkable recognition in respect of expressions on the MMI database. Our proposed procedures acquired higher classification rate of facial expressions compared to [16–18].

The performance of the FAR for distance signature using MLP on four benchmark datasets such as JAFFE, MMI, CK+, and MUG is shown in Fig. 2.8. The FAR graph

Table 2.9 Testing recognition rate on publicly available databases of six basic expressions with different state-of-the-art methods

	Database	Anger	Disgust	Fear	Happiness	Sadness	Surprise	Avg.
Distance signature	CK+	96.1	95.7	95.8	98.4	95.9	95.8	96.3
[17]	CK+	87.8	93.3	94.3	94.2	96.4	98.4	94.1
[18]	CK+	87	91.5	90.9	96.9	84.5	91.2	90.3
[16]	CK+	76.2	94.1	86.1	96.3	88.2	98.7	91.5
Distance signature	JAFFE	100	100	78.6	85.7	100	100	94
[17]	JAFFE	100	86.2	93.7	96.7	77.4	96.6	91.7
[18]	JAFFE	89.3	90.7	91.1	92.6	90.2	92.3	91.1
Distance signature	MMI	82.8	81	71.4	87.5	100	66.7	81.5
[18]	MMI	80.1	78.2	81.3	83.2	77.1	81	80.1
[16]	MMI	65.6	72.5	72.5	88.2	71.1	93.8	77.4
Distance signature	MUG	93.5	100	100	95.6	96.6	94.4	96.7

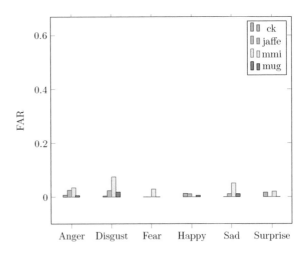

Fig. 2.8 Comparison of FAR of distance signature on CK+, JAFFE, MMI, and MUG databases

Fig. 2.9 Comparison of
FRR of distance signature on
CK+, JAFFE, MMI, and
MUG databases

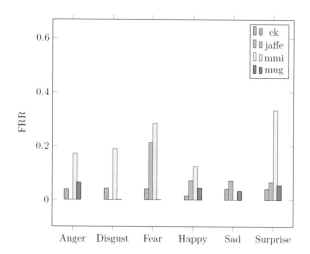

analysis of distance signature yields poor recognition rate in surprise on CK+. MLP-based distance signature performs poor recognition rate in anger on JAFFE. In the same way distance signature also shows poor recognition rate in disgust on MMI and MUG.

The performance analysis of the FRR for distance signature using MLP on four benchmark datasets is shown in Fig. 2.9. The lowest FRR means the highest recognition rate in expressions. The FRR graph analysis of distance signature indicates the promising recognition rate in happiness on CK+. MLP-based distance signature performs poor recognition rate in fear on JAFFE. It also indicates poor recognition rate in surprise and anger on MMI and MUG.

Fig. 2.10 Comparison of
ERR of distance signature on
CK+, JAFFE, MMI, and
MUG databases

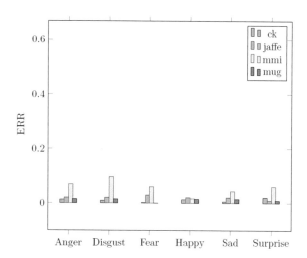

The comparison of ERR for distance signature on four benchmark datasets such as JAFFE, CK+, MMI, and MUG is shown in Fig. 2.10. The ERR graph analysis of distance signature yields the highest recognition rate in fear of CK+. MLP-based distance signature performs promising recognition rate in surprise on JAFFE. It also indicates a promising performance of happiness and fear expressions on MMI and MUG.

2.7 Sum-up Discussion

In this chapter, we explored a distance signature-based facial expression recognition from face images. To evaluate the performance of the proposed system we did consider four benchmark datasets, viz. CK+, JAFFE, MMI, and MUG to test the performance of expressions. The performance of the proposed procedure is validated by the recognition rate and comparison with state-of-the-art reporting. The experimental results indicate the significant performance improvements of facial expression recognition using distance signature.

In the next chapter, we consider the shape signature for recognizing the human emotions. The triangles are formed among the grid and corresponding shape signature is derived from the triangle. This signature is used to extract the features for recognizing human emotions.

References

1. G. Tzimiropoulos, M. Pantic, Optimization problems for fast AAM fitting in-the-wild. In *Proceedings of the IEEE International Conference on Computer Vision* (2013), pp. 593–600
2. X. Zhu, D. Ramanan, Face detection, pose estimation, and landmark localization in the wild. In *Proceedings of the 2012 IEEE Conference on Computer Vision and Pattern Recognition (CVPR)* (IEEE, Washington DC, 2012), pp. 2879–2886
3. Yun Tie, Ling Guan, Automatic landmark point detection and tracking for human facial expressions. EURASIP J. Image Video Process. **2013**(1), 8 (2013)
4. Yan Tong, Yang Wang, Zhiwei Zhu, Qiang Ji, Robust facial feature tracking under varying face pose and facial expression. Pattern Recognit. **40**(11), 3195–3208 (2007)
5. A. Barman, P. Dutta, Facial expression recognition using distance signature feature. In *Advanced Computational and Communication Paradigms* (Springer, Berlin, 2018), pp. 155–163
6. T.Y. Young, *Handbook of Pattern Recognition and Image Processing: Computer Vision*, vol. 2. (Academic Press, Inc., Cambridge, 1994)
7. M. Borda, Fundamentals in information theory and coding–springer 2011. Technical Report, ISBN 978-3-642-20346-6
8. S.N. Sivanandam, S.N. Deepa, *Introduction to Neural Networks Using Matlab 6.0.* (Tata McGraw-Hill Education, New York, 2006)
9. Z. Zhang, M. Lyons, M. Schuster, S. Akamatsu, Comparison between geometry-based and gabor-wavelets-based facial expression recognition using multi-layer perceptron. In *Proceedings of the Third IEEE International Conference on Automatic Face and Gesture Recognition, 1998* (IEEE, Nara, 1998), pp. 454–459

10. P. Lucey, J.F. Cohn, T. Kanade, J. Saragih, Z. Ambadar, I. Matthews, The extended Cohn-Kanade dataset (ck+): a complete dataset for action unit and emotion-specified expression. In *Computer Society Conference on Computer Vision and Pattern Recognition-Workshops* (IEEE, San Francisco, CA, 2010), pp. 94–101

11. M. Lyons, S. Akamatsu, M. Kamachi, J. Gyoba, Coding facial expressions with gabor wavelets. In *Proceedings of the Third IEEE International Conference on Automatic Face and Gesture Recognition, 1998* (IEEE, Nara, 1998), pp. 200–205

12. M.F. Valstar, M. Pantic, Induced disgust, happiness and surprise: an addition to the mmi facial expression database. In *Proceedings of International Conference Language Resources and Evaluation, Workshop on EMOTION*, pp. 65–70, Valletta, Malta, May 2010

13. N. Aifanti, C. Papachristou, A. Delopoulos, The mug facial expression database. In *Procedings of the 11th International Workshop on Image Analysis for Facial Expression Database*, pp. 12–14, Desenzano, Italy, April 2010

14. S. Marcel, M.S. Nixon, S.Z. Li, Handbook of biometric anti-spoofing-trusted biometrics under spoofing attacks, ser. *Advances in Computer Vision and Pattern Recognition* (Springer, London, 2014)

15. J.-M. Cheng, H.-C. Wang, A method of estimating the equal error rate for automatic speaker verification. In *Proceedings of the 2004 International Symposium on Chinese Spoken Language Processing* (IEEE, Hong Kong, 2004), pp. 285–288

16. L. Zhong, Q. Liu, P. Yang, J. Huang, D.N. Metaxas, Learning multiscale active facial patches for expression analysis. *IEEE Trans. Cybern.* **45**(8), 1499–1510 (2015)

17. SL Happy and Aurobinda Routray, Automatic facial expression recognition using features of salient facial patches. IEEE Trans. Affect. Comput. **6**(1), 1–12 (2015)

18. A. Poursaberi, H.A. Noubari, M. Gavrilova, S.N. Yanushkevich, Gauss–Laguerre wavelet textural feature fusion with geometrical information for facial expression identification. *EURASIP J. Image Video Process.* **2012**(1), 1–13 (2012)

19. Lin Zhong, Qingshan Liu, Peng Yang, Bo Liu, Junzhou Huang, and Dimitris N Metaxas. Learning active facial patches for expression analysis. In *Proceddings of the 2012 IEEE Conference on Computer Vision and Pattern Recognition (CVPR)* (IEEE, Washington DC, 2012), pp. 2562–2569

Chapter 3
Shape Signature for Recognizing Human Emotions

3.1 Introduction

In the previous chapter, we discussed how distance signature could be used efficiently as a descriptor for facial expression recognition. After finding the distances from the grid, we see that many triangles are formed within the considered grid. This is another idea of facial expression recognition. In this chapter shape signature-based human emotion recognition system is proposed using Multilayer Perceptron (MLP) and Nonlinear Auto Regressive with eXogenous (NARX). Proper landmark detection and extraction of salient features thereof are challenging tasks in facial expression recognition. In human face components such as eyes, eyebrows, mouth, jaw, etc. regions are crucial in differentiating the expressions. The appearance-based method is applied to the human faces to detect the landmark points. Salient landmark points are marked among the regions of eyes, eyebrows, nose, and mouth. We only consider three points on each eyebrow, four points on each eye, three points on the nose, and four points on the mouth region. These salient landmarks are uses to form a grid with the help of a middle nose landmark point and find out the possible triangles within the grid. Shape signature is derived in a specific order from the triangles and normalized subsequently. The stability index is determined from a normalized shape signature and plays a vital role to recognize the expressions from one face to another. Statistical analysis such as range, moment, skewness, kurtosis, and entropy are calculated from normalized shape factor. The combination of all these features are used as input to MLP and NARX into six basic expressions. Four benchmark databases, i.e. Cohn-Kanade (CK+), Japanese Female Facial Expression (JAFFE), Multi Media Interface (MMI), and Multimedia Understanding Group (MUG) are considered to evaluate the performance of emotion recognition of shape signature feature.

© Springer Nature Singapore Pte Ltd. 2020
P. Dutta and A. Barman, *Human Emotion Recognition from Face Images*,
Cognitive Intelligence and Robotics,
https://doi.org/10.1007/978-981-15-3883-4_3

Organization of This Chapter

This chapter is organized into six parts. In the first part, consisting of Sect. 3.1, we discuss shape signature.

The second part of the chapter explores the proposed framework of shape signature's facial expression recognition. The landmark detection and triangle formation are also discussed here.

The third part of this chapter, consisting of Sect. 3.3, shows the proposed feature extraction mechanism from shape signature. Statistical measures such as moment, range, kurtosis, skewness, and entropy are used to compute the formidable feature set.

The next part, consisting of Sect. 3.4, shows the training of MLP and NARX.

The final part of the chapter discusses the experiment and result analyses on four benchmark databases. The comparison of different expressions is also compared here with state-of-the-art methods.

The last part concludes with a conclusion in Sect. 3.6.

3.2 Proposed Framework of Shape Signature's Emotion Detection

To understand the proposed methodology, here we give a brief description of shape signature-based facial expression recognition. The appearance model is applied to detect the landmark points from a face image. Now salient landmark points are extracted among the eyes, eyebrows, nose, and mouth regions. A grid is formed using the salient landmark points and find the probable triangles within the grid. These triangles form the shape signature. The schematic diagram of shape signature-based facial expression recognition is shown in Fig. 3.1 to understand the step-by-step process of the proposed framework of the emotion recognition system.

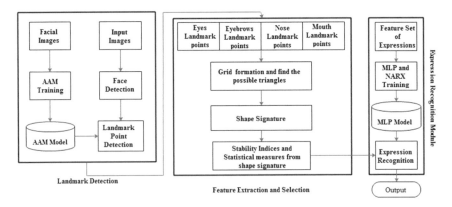

Fig. 3.1 Block diagram of proposed methodology

3.2.1 Landmark Detection Using Active Appearance Model

Exact landmark detection is a challenging task in the field of human emotion recognition. There are many approaches to detect the landmarks on face images. In this chapter, we use the AAM model to detect the landmark points from face images. In the previous chapter, we have discussed AAM in Sect. 2.2.1. Again here we give a brief description of AAM.

Active Appearance Model
AAM is represented by the shape, motion and appearance models. The shape of an independent AAM is defined by a mesh and in particular the vertex locations of the mesh. Mathematically, we define the shape s of an AAM as the coordinates of the v vertices that make up the mesh as

$$s = (x_1, y_1, x_2, y_2, \ldots, x_v, y_v)^T \tag{3.1}$$

AAM allows linear shape variation. This means that the shape s can be expressed as a base shape s_0 plus a linear combination of n shape vectors s_i as

$$s = s_0 + \sum_{i=1}^{n} p_i s_i \tag{3.2}$$

In this expression, the coefficients p_i are the shape parameters. Since we can always perform a linear re-parametrization, wherever necessary we assume that the vectors s_i are orthonormal. AAM is normally computed from hand-labeled training images. The standard approach is to apply Principal Component Analysis (PCA) to the training meshes. The base shape s_0 is the mean shape and the vectors s_0 are the n eigenvectors corresponding to the n largest eigenvalues. Usually, the training meshes are first normalized using a Procrustes analysis before PCA is applied. This step removes variation due to a chosen global shape normalizing transformation so that the resulting PCA is only concerned with local, nonrigid shape deformation.

3.2.2 Triangle Formation

The landmark points are detected on the face images by using the Active Appearance Model (AAM) [1]. A shape model is used during the landmark points detection on the face image. The shape model is created with coordinate points of face images. The eyebrows, eyes, mouth, and nose regions are extracted from face images with the help of the shape model. These regions are considered to extract the prominent landmarks. These salient landmarks are identified as three points on each eyebrow (one is mid-position between two corner points of each eyebrow and remaining two corner points), four points on each eye (two corner points of each eye and remaining

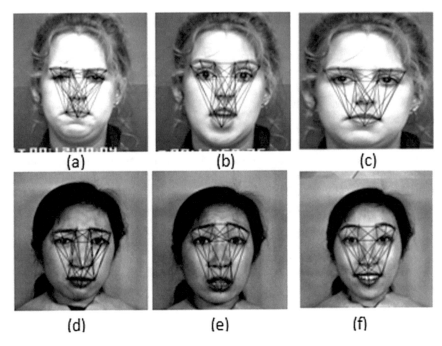

Fig. 3.2 Landmark detection and grid formation on CK+ and JAFFE databases

two points are considered as mid-position of upper and lower eyelid), four points on mouth (two corner points on mouth and remaining two points are identified as mid-position of upper and lower lip), and three points on nose (one is identified as mid-position of two corner points of nose and remaining two are corner points).

The nose region is situated in the mid-position of a face image. As such because of its central geometric location in a human face, the landmarks near the nose region are considered as reference points to form triangles with other landmarks in any facial expression. The triangles are determined accordingly within the grid and any such triangle formed has a specific shape signature as per Eq. 3.12. It may be noted that the shape signature of a specific triangle is sensitive to the facial expression under consideration as depicted in Fig. 3.2. We shall try to exploit this particular property to categorize the expression being considered. Shape information of different such triangles formed in a typical facial grid, considered in a particular sequence, induces a shape signature. These normalized shape signatures are also used to find respective stability indices. In addition, statistical features such as moment, range, skewness, kurtosis, and entropy are computed from normalized shape signature. The combination of extracted features is fed as the input of MLP and NARX to differentiate the expressions into six basic categories.

Each triangle hold the following basic properties:

1. The sum of the angles in a triangle is 180. This is called the angle-sum property.
2. The sum of the lengths of any two sides of a triangle is greater than the length of the third side. Similarly, the difference between the lengths of any two sides of a triangle is less than the length of the third side.
3. The side opposite to the largest angle is the longest side of the triangle and the side opposite to the smallest angle is the shortest side of the triangle.

3.3 Feature Extraction

Prominent facial expression analysis depends upon the proper landmarks selection of the human faces. Extracted discriminative features from the salient landmarks play an important role in facial expression recognition. We shall enhance the different features used in our proposed facial expression recognition system.

3.3.1 Shape Signature

The perimeter of a triangle is the total distance outside the triangle. A triangle has 3 sides whose length may be the same or different. If all the 3 sides of a triangle are equal then it is an equilateral triangle. If 2 sides of a triangle are equal, it is an isosceles triangle. The perimeter of a triangle is the sum of the length of all the 3 sides.

In this section, we present alternative ways of solving triangles by using the half-angle formula. Given a triangle with sides a, b, and c, define as $s = \frac{1}{2}(a + b + c)$. Again we consider as $a + b - c = 2s - 2c = 2(s - c)$.

We know from the cosine theorem

$$\cos(A) = \frac{b^2 + c^2 - a^2}{2bc} \tag{3.3}$$

We also consider $\sin \frac{A}{2}$

$$2 \sin^2 (A/2) = 1 - \cos(A)$$
$$= 1 - \frac{b^2 + c^2 - a^2}{2bc}$$
$$= \frac{(a + b - c)(a - b + c)}{2bc} \tag{3.4}$$
$$= \frac{2(s - b)(s - c}{bc}$$

From the above equation, we calculate

$$\sin\left(\frac{A}{2}\right) = \sqrt{\frac{(s-b)(s-c)}{bc}} \tag{3.5}$$

$$2\cos^2(A/2) = 1 + \cos(A)$$
$$= 1 + \frac{b^2 + c^2 - a^2}{2bc}$$
$$= \frac{(a+b+c)(b+c-a)}{2bc} \tag{3.6}$$
$$= \frac{2s(s-a)}{bc}$$

From the above equation, we calculate

$$\cos\left(\frac{A}{2}\right) = \sqrt{\frac{s(s-a)}{bc}} \tag{3.7}$$

$$\sin(A) = 2\sin\frac{A}{2}\cos\frac{A}{2}$$
$$\sin(A) = \sqrt{(1+\cos(A))(1-\cos(A))} \tag{3.8}$$

Now it derives as from Eq. 3.8

$$\sin(A) = \frac{2}{bc}\sqrt{s(s-a)(s-b)(s-c)} \tag{3.9}$$

The positive square root is always used since A cannot exceed 180. Again by symmetry, there are similar expressions involving the angles B and C. These expressions provide an alternative proof of the sine theorem.

Since the area of a triangle

$$a_r = \frac{1}{2}bc\sin(A)$$
$$a_r = \sqrt{(s(s-a)(s-b)(s-c)} \tag{3.10}$$

By symmetry, there are similar expressions involving the angles B and C. Note that in this expression and all the others for half-angles, the positive square root is always taken. This is because a half-angle of a triangle must always be less than a right angle.

A part of the plane enclosed by a simple closed figure is called a plane region and the measurement of the plane region enclosed is called its area.

A grid is formed over a human face using salient landmarks. The possible triangles are identified within the grid. The perimeter of triangle $p = x + y + z$, where x, y, z are the edges of triangle, $h = p/2$, and area is calculated as $a = \sqrt{h(h-x)(h-y)(h-z)}$. They are computed to determine the shape signature as

$$s_i = \frac{a_i}{p_i^2} \tag{3.11}$$

where index i is used to specify a particular triangle in the face grid. Normalized shape signatures [2] are computed as

$$\mu_i^f = \frac{s_i^f}{\sum_{i=1}^{n} s_i^f} \quad f = 1, 2, \ldots, m \text{ and } i = 1, 2, \ldots, n \tag{3.12}$$

where m represent the total number of images and n represent the total number of shapes. μ_i^f is the shape signature and s_i^f are the shapes of triangles.

3.3.2 Stability Index

The stability index also plays a vital role in the present context. The normalized shape signatures are used to determine the higher-order signature as

$$\gamma^r = \frac{s_i^r}{\sum_{i=1}^{n} s_i^r} \tag{3.13}$$

Here the rth order shape signature is computed for each face image. s_i are the shapes of triangles. In this experiment, we used rth order as $r = 1, 2, \ldots, 8$. We find their rth order signature differences as

$$\Delta s_i^r = \gamma_i^r - \gamma_i^{r-1} \tag{3.14}$$

We set a threshold upon the analysis of the differences in higher-order factors. This tolerance threshold λ follows the condition $\Delta s_i^r \leq \lambda$. Such an order r is treated as a stability index of shape signature.

3.3.3 Range, Moment, Skewness, Kurtosis, and Entropy

The huge number of relevant features are usually found promising in facial expression recognition than the one obtained using a fewer number of features. For this reason, we also consider statistical measures such as range, moment, skewness, kurtosis, and entropy derived from shape signature information. We already discussed it in the previous chapter. The detailed discussions are available in Sect. 2.3.3. Here we mention a brief description of range, moment, skewness, kurtosis, and entropy. The range is calculated from the differences between the maximum and minimum value of the normalized shape signature. The fourth-order moment pair [3] are calculated from normalized shape signature using

$$E_k = \sum_{i=1}^{n} a(i, k) \times v(i) \tag{3.15}$$

where $v = (v_1, v_2, \ldots, v_n)$ is the normalized signature vector and $a(i, k)$ is i raised to power of k, for nonnegative integer values of k; $k = 1, 2, 3, 4$. Asymmetry in the data is measured by skewness [3]. Skewness and kurtosis [4] are calculated as

$$U = \frac{\sum_{i=1}^{n} a(i, 3)^2 \times v(i)}{\sum_{i=1}^{n} a(i, 2)^3 \times v(i)} \text{ and} \tag{3.16}$$

$$V = \frac{\sum_{i=1}^{n} a(i, 4)}{\sum_{i=1}^{m} a(i, 2)^2 \times v(i)} \tag{3.17}$$

where U and V indicate the skewness and kurtosis, respectively. Entropy [5] is calculated as

$$e = -\sum_{i=1}^{n} p_i \log(p_i) \tag{3.18}$$

where p_i contains the histogram count of the shape signature in normalized sense and $\sum_{i=1}^{n} p_i = 1, 0 \leq p_i \leq 1$.

3.4 Classification Using MLP and NARX

A multilayer perceptron is a feedforward type of artificial neural network that maps a set of input features onto a set of appropriate outputs [6]. In the course of the classification task of extracted features, every face image is identified by a vector of 9 elements. These features are used as a Min-Max process matrices by normalizing the minimum and maximum values of each row feature vector. Extracted features are used as input to a multilayer perceptron network and obtain output responses corresponding to minimum errors. A perceptron consists of a number of 9 input nodes, the number of 8 hidden/intermediate nodes, and a number of 6 output nodes. The weights usually excite or inhibit the signal that flows through the edges. The perceptron is found capable of classifying into six basic expressions, viz. happiness, surprise, sadness, anger, fear, and disgust.

NARX [7] neural network is a dynamical neural architecture commonly used for input-output modeling of nonlinear dynamical systems. The network takes as input a window of past input and output values and computes the current output. NARX can deal also with discrete and continuous inputs [8]. The recurrent neural network enables the model to retain information about past inputs and to discover temporal correlations between events that are possibly far away from each other in the data [9]. The NARX model is defined as $w(t) = f(u(t - Du), \ldots, u(t - 1), u(t), w(t - Dw), \ldots, w(t - 1))$, here $u(t)$ and $w(t)$ are the input and output of the network at time t, respectively. Du and Dw indicate time lag of input and output, and f is a nonlinear type function which is approximated by a Multilayer Perceptron (MLP). During training, the NARX recurrent neural network aims to learn optimal weight values by minimizing an objective function engaged in measuring the deviation of the predictions y, from the target outputs, for each training pattern. A typical loss function is the Mean Square Error (MSE) overall training cases. An input image takes $m \times n$ size of a human face and output expression is classified into six basic expressions as indicated in Algorithm 3.1.

The NARX recurrent neural network is a dynamical neural architecture commonly used for input-output modeling of nonlinear dynamical systems. The network takes as input a window of past input and output values and computes the current output. The defining equation for the NARX model is

$$y(t) = f(u(t - D_u), \ldots, u(t - 1), u(t), y(t - D_y), \ldots, y(t - 1)) \qquad (3.19)$$

where $u(t) \in R^N$ and $y(t) \in R^1$ represent the inputs and output of the network at time t, respectively. D_u and D_y are the input and output time lags, and the function f is a nonlinear function approximated by a Multilayer Perceptron (MLP). In this chapter, we shall consider a NARX network with zero input order ($Du = 0$) resulting in the network exploring long-term dependencies of the output signal only. The MLP consists of three layers, namely, the input, hidden, and output layers with recurrent connections from the output to the hidden layer. The architecture of the NARX-RNN can be flattened allowing for the regressed outputs to be concatenated to the exogenous input features and be processed simultaneously. The MLP input at time t is therefore

$$x(t) = [u(t), y(t - D_y), \ldots, y(t - 1)] \qquad (3.20)$$

The hidden layer consists of neurons that compute a nonlinear or linear transformation of the input depending on the activation function used. The hidden states $h(t)$ and network predictions $\bar{y}(t)$ at time t are computed as follows:

$$h(t) = \Psi(W_{hx} \cdot x(t) + b_h) \qquad (3.21)$$

$$\bar{y}(t) = \Gamma(W_{yh} \cdot h(t) + b_y) \qquad (3.22)$$

where W_{hx} and W_{yh} are the input to hidden and hidden to output weight matrices respectively, b_h and b_y are the biases and ψ and Γ are the activation functions which are both set to hyperbolic tangent functions in this work. The hyperbolic tangent was selected for the output activation function to scale the output between -1 and 1 (similar to the external inputs) prior to re-feeding it into the model as delayed output.

3.4.1 NARX Training

During training, the NARX recurrent neural network aims to learn optimal weight values $\theta = [W_{hx}, W_{yh}, b_h, b_y]$ by minimizing a loss (objective) function defined as $J(\theta) = L(\bar{y}; y)$, where L is a distance function that measures the deviation of the predictions, $\bar{y}$, from the target outputs, y, for each training case c. A typical loss function is the Mean Square Error (MSE) defined as

$$j(\theta) = \frac{1}{2m} \sum_c \sum_t (y(t) - \bar{y}(t))^2 \tag{3.23}$$

where m is the total number of time instances over all training cases. A regularization term is added to the loss function to prevent the neural network from over fitting the training data. This is done by scaling the squared weights (excluding the biases) with a user-supplied parameter λ as shown in Eq. 3.24.

$$j(\theta) = j(\theta) + \frac{\lambda}{2m} \sum_j \sum_k (W_{jk})^2 \tag{3.24}$$

Learning of the NARX-RNN parameters can be achieved through backpropagation in conjunction with gradient descent.

3.4.1.1 Gradient Descent

Gradient descent traverses the error surface (defined by a loss function) whose global minimum translates to optimum weights. At each iteration, the algorithm attempts to move toward this minimum through the following update equation:

$$\theta_J = \theta_J - \alpha \frac{\partial}{\partial \theta_J} j(\theta) \tag{3.25}$$

where α is the gradient descent learning rate. The weight gradients provide the direction of the search and the learning rate controls the step size of the search.

The partial derivatives of the loss function with respect to the weights can be calculated through backpropagation. For ease of notation and clarity purposes, the inputs to activation functions in Eqs. 3.26 and 3.27 are annotated as a_1 and a_2, respectively:

$$a_1(t) = W_{hx}.x(t) + b_h \tag{3.26}$$

$$a_2(t) = W_{yh}.h(t) + b_y \qquad (3.27)$$

The partial derivative of the loss function with respect to each layer of the MLP is next computed using the chain rule:

$$\frac{\partial j(\theta)}{\partial y} = y(t) - \bar{y}(t) \qquad (3.28)$$

$$\frac{\partial j(\theta)}{\partial h} = \frac{\partial j(\theta)}{\partial y}.\frac{\partial y}{\partial h} = \frac{\partial j(\theta)}{\partial y}.\mathrm{sech}^2(a_2(t)).W_{yh} \qquad (3.29)$$

From this, the partial derivative of the loss function with respect to each weight matrix is obtained as follows:

$$\frac{\partial j(\theta)}{\partial W_{hx}} = \frac{\partial j(\theta)}{\partial h}.\mathrm{sech}^2(a_1(t)).x(t) \qquad (3.30)$$

$$\frac{\partial j(\theta)}{\partial b_h} = \frac{\partial j(\theta)}{\partial h}.\mathrm{sech}^2(a_1(t)) \qquad (3.31)$$

$$\frac{\partial j(\theta)}{\partial W_{yh}} = \frac{\partial j(\theta)}{\partial y}.\mathrm{sech}^2(a_2(t)).h(t) \qquad (3.32)$$

$$\frac{\partial j(\theta)}{\partial b_y} = \frac{\partial j(\theta)}{\partial y}.\mathrm{sech}^2(a_2(t)) \qquad (3.33)$$

The weight gradients are then summed over all training instances and converted into a single vector for use in the learning rule update Eq. 3.34 of the gradient descent algorithm, that is

$$\frac{\partial}{\partial \theta_J}j(\theta) = \left[\frac{\partial j(\theta)}{\partial W_{hx}} \frac{\partial j(\theta)}{\partial W_{yh}} \frac{\partial j(\theta)}{\partial b_h} \frac{\partial j(\theta)}{\partial b_y}\right] \qquad (3.34)$$

3.5 Experiment and Result

We evaluate shape signature-based facial expression recognition on Cohn-Kanade (CK+) [10], JAFFE [11], MMI [12], and MUG [13] databases. Two different types of neural networks, i.e. MLP and NARX are considered to train and test the performances of each database. The confusion matrices are tabulated to measure the performances of each database. Apart from these the False Rejection Rate (FRR), False Acceptance Rate (FAR), [14] and Error Rate (ERR) are mentioned to the

---

Algorithm 3.1 Proposed Facial Expression Recognition Training Algorithm using Shape Signatures

---

Input: A $m \times n$ human face image expression.
1: AAM fitting is applied to get the landmark points on the face image.
2: Salient landmarks are extracted from Eyebrows, Eyes and Mouth region.
3: Grid is formed out of these landmark points.
4: Find the possible triangles among the grid.
5: Normalize the shape signature.
6: Determine stability indices of shape signature and also compute moment, skewness, kurtosis, and entropy.
7: Combine all these features to get enhanced feature set.
8: This enhanced feature set is fed as input separately to MLP and NARX.
9: Classify the expressions into six basic expressions.
Output: Expression classified into six basic categories.

---

performance of each experiment. We also measure the performance of expression recognition with different state-of-the-art methods.

False accept rate (FAR): A statistic used to measure biometric performance when performing the verification task. The percentage of times a face recognition algorithm, technology, or system falsely accepts an incorrect claim to existence or non-existence of a candidate in the database overall comparisons between a probe and gallery image. The definition of the FAR is mentioned as

$$FAR = \frac{FP}{FP + TN} \tag{3.35}$$

False reject rate (FRR): A statistic used to measure biometric performance when performing the verification task. The percentage of times a face recognition algorithm, technology, or system incorrectly rejects a true claim to existence or non-existence of a match in the gallery, based on the comparison of a biometric probe and biometric template.

$$FRR = \frac{FN}{FN + TP} \tag{3.36}$$

Error rate (ERR) [15] is computed as the division of the between of all incorrect predictions and the total number of items in the database. It is also represented as

$$ERR = \frac{FP + FN}{TP + TN + FP + FN} \tag{3.37}$$

Equal error rate (EER) [16] measures the system recognition accuracy compared to another system (the lower represents better performance) by finding the equal of FRR and FAR. If they are not equal then find the minimum distance between FAR and FRR.

3.5.1 *Experiment on Cohn-Kanade (CK+)*

The shape signature uses a total of 849 images to train and test the performances of the proposed system. In the training phase, the proposed procedure used a total of 566 images for training and remaining 283 images for testing to measure the effectiveness of the facial expression recognition.

In Table 3.1, the confusion matrix shows the recognition performance of expressions into different categories using MLP. The anger classifies 51 images properly and 1 image is misclassified with surprise. The disgust recognizes 47 images properly. The fear recognizes 23 images perfectly and 1 image is confused with happiness. The happiness classifies 64 images properly. The sadness identifies 46 images properly and 3 images are misidentified with surprise and happiness. The surprise classifies 48 images correctly.

For example, if the threshold for a similarity score is set too high in the verification task, then a legitimate identity claim may be rejected (i.e. it might increase the false reject rate (FRR). The parameters of FRR, FAR, and ERR are also used to evaluate the system performances of shape signature using MLP. Table 3.2 shows the evaluated results of FAR, FRR, and ERR. The FAR value of happiness is 0.013 that means it produces a 13/1000 false accept rate. The sadness produces FRR as 0.061. The lower ERR means a higher recognition rate of expressions.

Table 3.3 shows the confusion matrix of the facial expression recognition using NARX. The anger recognizes 51 images properly. The disgust recognizes 47 images

Table 3.1 Shape signature confusion matrix on CK+ database using MLP

	Anger	Disgust	Fear	Happiness	Sadness	Surprise
Anger	51	0	0	0	0	1
Disgust	0	47	0	0	0	0
Fear	0	0	23	1	0	0
Happiness	0	0	0	64	0	0
Sadness	0	0	0	2	46	1
Surprise	0	0	0	0	0	48

Table 3.2 The FAR, FRR, and ERR of shape signature using MLP on CK+ database

	FAR	FRR	ERR
Anger	0.000	0.000	0.000
Disgust	0.000	0.000	0.000
Fear	0.000	0.041	0.003
Happiness	0.013	0.000	0.010
Sadness	0.000	0.061	0.010
Surprise	0.004	0.000	0.003

Table 3.3 Shape signature confusion matrix on CK+ database using NARX

	Anger	Disgust	Fear	Happiness	Sadness	Surprise
Anger	51	0	0	0	0	0
Disgust	0	47	0	0	0	0
Fear	0	0	24	0	0	0
Happiness	0	0	0	64	0	0
Sadness	0	0	0	0	49	0
Surprise	0	0	0	0	0	47

Table 3.4 The FAR, FRR, and ERR of shape signature using NARX on CK+ database

	FAR	FRR	ERR
Anger	0.000	0.000	0.000
Disgust	0.000	0.000	0.000
Fear	0.000	0.000	0.000
Happiness	0.000	0.000	0.000
Sadness	0.000	0.000	0.000
Surprise	0.000	0.004	0.001

properly. The fear identifies 24 images correctly. The happiness classifies 64 images correctly. The sadness classifies 49 images correctly. The surprise identifies 47 images correctly.

The parameters of FAR, FRR, and ERR are also considered to measure the system performances of shape signature using NARX. Table 3.4 shows the evaluated results of FAR, FRR, and ERR. The FAR represents the higher recognition rate of facial expressions. The surprise yields FRR as 0.004. The surprise produces 0.001 as ERR. It also indicates that the system has the highest recognition rate of expressions.

In Fig. 3.3, the FAR of the shape signature is used to compare the recognition performance of different expressions using MLP and NARX. The FAR graph analysis of shape signature yields poor recognition rate in happiness on CK+ using MLP. In the same way, the shape signature shows the poor recognition rate in surprise using NARX.

Figure 3.4 shows the comparison of MLP and NARX of FRR parameter of different expressions. The ERR graph analysis of shape signature yields poor recognition rate in sadness on CK+ using MLP. The shape signature also indicates promising performance in surprise using NARX.

Fig. 3.3 Comparison of FAR of shape signature on CK+ database using MLP and NARX

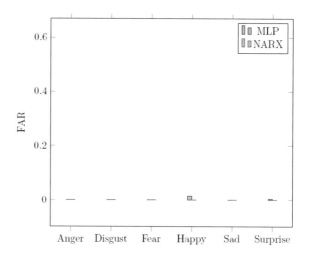

Fig. 3.4 Comparison of FRR of shape signature on CK+ database using MLP and NARX

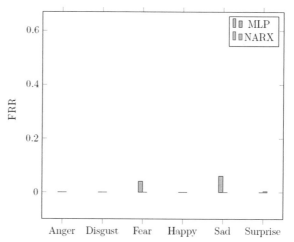

3.5.2 Experiment on JAFFE Database

JAFFE database uses the same procedures as used in the CK+ database. We use a total of 213 images to justify the system performances. A total of 113 images is used for training and the remaining 97 images for testing. Total 97 testing images are divided as 21 for anger, 21 for disgust, 14 for fear, 14 for happiness, 14 for sadness, and 13 for a surprise.

The confusion matrix shows the performance of classification with correctly classified images of different expressions in Table 3.5. The anger identifies 21 images correctly. The disgust recognizes 20 images correctly and 1 image is confused with fear. The fear recognizes 10 images perfectly and 3 images are wrongly classified

Table 3.5 Shape signature confusion matrix on JAFFE database using MLP

	Anger	Disgust	Fear	Happiness	Sadness	Surprise
Anger	21	0	0	0	0	0
Disgust	0	20	1	0	0	0
Fear	2	1	10	1	0	0
Happiness	0	0	0	13	1	0
Sadness	0	0	0	0	13	1
Surprise	0	0	0	0	0	13

Table 3.6 The FAR, FRR, and ERR of shape signature using MLP on JAFFE database

	FAR	FRR	ERR
Anger	0.026	0.000	0.020
Disgust	0.013	0.047	0.020
Fear	0.012	0.028	0.051
Happiness	0.012	0.071	0.020
Sadness	0.012	0.071	0.020
Surprise	0.011	0.000	0.010

with disgust and anger. The happiness classifies 13 images properly and 1 image is confused with sadness. The surprise identifies 13 images properly.

The FAR, FRR, and ERR are considered to evaluate the system performances of a shape signature using MLP. Table 3.6 shows the experimented results of FAR, FRR, and ERR. The FAR value of anger is 0.026 that means it produces a 13/1000 false accept rate. The sadness produces FRR as 0.071. The lowest ERR is 0.010 for surprise and the highest ERR is 0.051 for fear.

Table 3.7 shows the confusion matrix of the facial expression recognition using NARX. The anger recognizes 18 images properly and 3 images are misidentified with disgust. The disgust recognizes 21 images properly. The fear identifies 14 images

Table 3.7 Shape signature confusion matrix on JAFFE database using NARX

	Anger	Disgust	Fear	Happiness	Sadness	Surprise
Anger	18	3	0	0	0	0
Disgust	0	21	0	0	0	0
Fear	0	0	14	0	0	0
Happiness	0	0	0	14	0	0
Sadness	0	0	0	0	14	0
Surprise	0	0	0	0	0	13

Table 3.8 The FAR, FRR, and ERR of shape signature using NARX on JAFFE database

	FAR	FRR	ERR
Anger	0.000	0.142	0.030
Disgust	0.039	0.000	0.030
Fear	0.000	0.000	0.000
Happiness	0.000	0.000	0.000
Sadness	0.000	0.000	0.000
Surprise	0.000	0.000	0.000

Fig. 3.5 Comparison of FAR of shape signature on JAFFE database using MLP and NARX

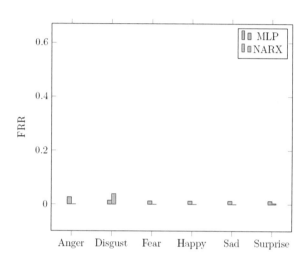

correctly. The happiness classifies 14 images correctly. The sadness classifies 14 images correctly. The surprise identifies 13 images correctly.

The FAR, FRR, and ERR are considered to evaluate the system performances of shape signature using NARX. Table 3.8 shows the evaluated results of FAR, FRR, and ERR. The FAR value of disgust is 0.039 that means it produces a 39/1000 false accept rate. The anger produces FRR as 0.142. The lowest ERR is 0.030 for anger.

In Fig. 3.5, the FAR of the shape signature is used to compare the recognition performance of different expressions using MLP and NARX. The FAR graph analysis of shape signature yields poor recognition rate in anger on JAFFE using MLP. In the same way, the shape signature shows the poor recognition rate in disgust using NARX.

Figure 3.6 shows the comparison of MLP and NARX of the FRR parameter of different expressions. The ERR graph analysis of shape signature yields poor recognition rate in anger on JAFFE using MLP. The shape signature also indicates poor performance of expression in disgust using NARX.

Fig. 3.6 Comparison of
FRR of shape signature on
JAFFE database using MLP
and NARX

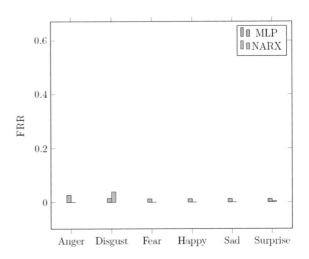

3.5.3 Experiment on MMI Database

MMI database is a more challenging dataset with respect to others to categorize the
expressions into different categories. The proposed procedure uses a total of 325
images to measure the performance of classification. A total of 212 images is used
for training and the remaining 113 images for testing.

The MLP-based confusion matrix shows the performance of classification with
correctly classified images of different expressions in Table 3.9. The anger identifies
26 images correctly and 3 images are mismatched with happiness and sadness. The
disgust recognizes 18 images properly and 3 images are misclassified with happiness
and sadness. The fear recognizes 8 images perfectly and 6 images are mismatched
with the other expressions except for happiness. The happiness classifies 16 images
properly. The sadness identifies 14 images properly and 4 images are misclassified with other expressions except for happiness. The surprise classifies 14 images
properly and 1 image is confused with anger.

Table 3.9 Shape signature confusion matrix on MMI database using MLP

	Anger	Disgust	Fear	Happiness	Sadness	Surprise
Anger	26	0	0	1	2	0
Disgust	0	18	0	1	2	0
Fear	1	2	8	0	1	2
Happiness	0	0	0	16	0	0
Sadness	1	1	1	0	14	1
Surprise	1	0	0	0	0	14

Table 3.10 The FAR, FRR, and ERR of shape signature using MLP on MMI database

	FAR	FRR	ERR
Anger	0.035	0.010	0.053
Disgust	0.032	0.014	0.053
Fear	0.010	0.428	0.061
Happiness	0.020	0.062	0.026
Sadness	0.052	0.222	0.079
Surprise	0.040	0.066	0.044

Table 3.11 Shape signature confusion matrix on MMI database using NARX

	Anger	Disgust	Fear	Happiness	Sadness	Surprise
Anger	28	1	0	0	0	0
Disgust	0	21	0	0	0	0
Fear	0	0	14	0	0	0
Happiness	0	0	0	16	0	0
Sadness	0	0	0	0	17	1
Surprise	0	0	0	0	0	15

The parameters of FAR, FRR, and ERR are evaluated to measure the system performances of shape signature using MLP. Table 3.10 shows the results of FAR, FRR, and ERR. The highest FAR value of sadness is 0.052 that means it produces a 52/1000 false accept rate. Fear produces the highest FRR as 0.428. The lowest ERR is 0.026 for surprise and the highest ERR is 0.079 for fear.

The NARX-based classification results are shown in Table 3.11. The anger recognizes 28 images perfectly and 1 image is misclassified with disgust. The disgust recognizes 21 images properly. The fear recognizes 14 images properly. The happiness classifies 16 images correctly. The sadness identifies 17 images accurately and 1 image is confused with surprise. The surprise identifies 15 images properly.

The FAR, FRR, and ERR are used to evaluate the system performances of shape signature using NARX. Table 3.12 shows the experimented results of FAR, FRR, and ERR. The FAR value of disgust is 0.011 that means it produces a 11/1000 false accept rate. Happiness produces FRR as 0.062. The highest ERR is 0.017 for sadness.

In Fig. 3.7, the FAR of the shape signature is used to compare the recognition performance of different expressions using MLP and NARX. The FAR graph analysis of shape signature yields poor recognition rate in sadness on MMI using MLP. In the same way, shape signature also shows the poor recognition of expression rate in disgust using NARX.

Figure 3.8 shows the comparison of MLP and NARX of the FRR parameter of different expressions. The ERR graph analysis of shape signature yields a poor recognition rate in sadness on MMI using MLP. The shape signature also indicates poor performance of expression in surprise using NARX.

Table 3.12   The FAR, FRR, and ERR of shape signature using NARX on MMI database

	FAR	FRR	ERR
Anger	0.000	0.034	0.008
Disgust	0.011	0.000	0.008
Fear	0.000	0.000	0.000
Happiness	0.000	0.062	0.008
Sadness	0.010	0.055	0.017
Surprise	0.010	0.000	0.008

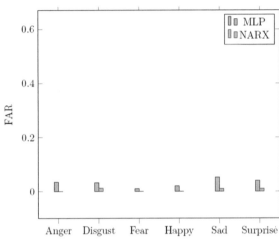

Fig. 3.7   Comparison of FAR of shape signature on MMI database using MLP and NARX

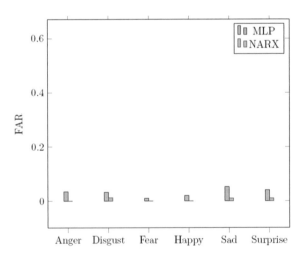

Fig. 3.8   Comparison of FRR of shape signature on MMI database using MLP and NARX

3.5.4   Experiment on MUG Database

MUG database is also evaluated to measure the performance of classification. The proposed procedure uses a total of 591 images to conduct the experiment. The total of 394 images are used for training and the remaining 197 images are used for testing to test the performance of six basic facial expressions.

The MLP-based confusion matrix shows the performance of classification with correctly classified images of different expressions in Table 3.13. The anger classifies 30 images properly and 1 image is confused with sadness. The disgust recognizes 28 images perfectly and 2 images are mismatched into anger. The fear recognizes 26 images correctly. The happiness classifies 43 images properly and 2 images are mismatched with disgust and fear. The sadness recognizes 29 images properly and 1 image is misclassified with anger. The surprise identifies 34 images perfectly and 2 images are wrongly classified into disgust and fear.

The FAR, FRR, and ERR are evaluated to test the system performances of shape signature using MLP. Table 3.14 shows the corresponding results of FAR, FRR, and ERR. The FAR value of anger is 0.012 that means it produces a 12/1000 false accept rate. The highest FRR is 0.066 for disgust. The lowest ERR is 0.005 for fear and the highest ERR is 0.020 for fear.

Table 3.15 shows the confusion matrix of the facial expression recognition using NARX. The anger recognizes 31 images properly. The disgust recognizes 28 images properly and 2 images are confused with fear. The fear identifies 24 images accurately

Table 3.13 Shape signature confusion matrix on MUG database using MLP

	Anger	Disgust	Fear	Happiness	Sadness	Surprise
Anger	30	0	0	0	1	0
Disgust	2	28	0	0	0	0
Fear	0	0	26	0	0	0
Happiness	0	1	1	43	0	0
Sadness	1	0	0	0	29	0
Surprise	0	1	0	1	0	34

Table 3.14 The FAR, FRR, and ERR of shape signature using MLP on MUG database

	FAR	FRR	ERR
Anger	0.012	0.032	0.015
Disgust	0.012	0.066	0.020
Fear	0.005	0.000	0.005
Happiness	0.006	0.044	0.015
Sadness	0.006	0.000	0.005
Surprise	0.000	0.055	0.010

Table 3.15 Shape signature confusion matrix on MUG database using NARX

	Anger	Disgust	Fear	Happiness	Sadness	Surprise
Anger	31	0	0	0	0	0
Disgust	0	28	2	0	0	0
Fear	0	0	24	2	0	0
Happiness	0	0	0	43	2	0
Sadness	0	0	0	0	29	0
Surprise	0	0	0	0	0	36

Table 3.16 The FAR, FRR, and ERR of shape signature using NARX on MUG database

	FAR	FRR	ERR
Anger	0.000	0.000	0.000
Disgust	0.000	0.066	0.010
Fear	0.011	0.076	0.020
Happiness	0.013	0.044	0.020
Sadness	0.012	0.000	0.010
Surprise	0.000	0.000	0.000

and 2 images are misclassified with happiness. The happiness identifies 43 images perfectly and 2 images are misclassified with sadness. The sadness identifies 29 images accurately. The surprise identifies 36 images correctly.

The FAR, FRR, and ERR are considered to evaluate the system performances of shape signature using NARX. Table 3.16 shows the experimented results of FAR, FRR, and ERR. The FAR value of happiness is 0.013 that means it produces a 13/1000 false accept rate. The fear produces the highest FRR as 0.066. The highest ERR is 0.020 for both fear and happiness.

In Fig. 3.9, the FAR of the shape signature is used to compare the recognition performance of different expressions using MLP and NARX. The FAR graph analysis of shape signature yields poor recognition rate in disgust on MUG using MLP. In the same way shape signature also shows the poor recognition of expression rate in sadness using NARX.

Figure 3.10 shows the comparison of MLP and NARX of the FRR parameter of different expressions. The ERR graph analysis of shape signature yields poor recognition rate in disgust on MUG using MLP. The shape signature also indicates poor performance of expression in fear using NARX.

Fig. 3.9 Comparison of
FAR of shape signature on
MUG database using MLP
and NARX

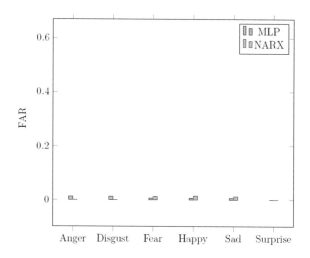

Fig. 3.10 Comparison of
FRR of shape signature on
MUG database using MLP
and NARX

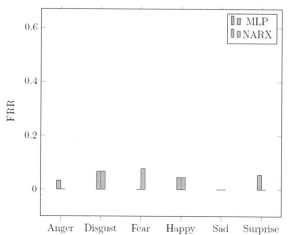

3.5.5 *Comparison of Result with Different State of the Art*

The proposed shape signature technique is compared with the results obtained using existing techniques reported in works of the literature [17–19]. To present a comparison task with the other works of the literature, we confine our experiments to CK+, JAFFE, MMI, and MUG databases.

Table 3.17 shows the results of the shape signature on the CK+ dataset using MLP and NARX. It also summarizes the comparative results with these state-of-the-art methods. The MLP-based shape signature achieves 97.9% as average recognition rate with the highest recognition rate 100% for happiness and the lowest recognition rate 93.8% for sadness. In the same way, NARX also acquires the average recognition rate with the highest recognition accuracy. It is also noticed that our proposed procedures

Table 3.17 Testing recognition rate on publicly available databases of six basic expressions with different state-of-the-art methods

	Database	Anger	Disgust	Fear	Happiness	Sadness	Surprise	Avg.
Shape signature MLP	CK+	98.1	100	95.8	100	93.8	100	97.9
Shape Signature NARX	CK+	100	100	100	100	100	100	100
[18]	CK+	87.8	93.3	94.3	94.2	96.4	98.4	94.1
[19]	CK+	87	91.5	90.9	96.9	84.5	91.2	90.3
[17]	CK+	76.2	94.1	86.1	96.3	88.2	98.7	89.9
Shape Signature MLP	JAFFE	100	95.2	71.4	92.8	92.8	100	92.0
Shape Signature NARX	JAFFE	85.7	100	100	100	100	100	97.6
[18]	JAFFE	77.4	96.6	93.7	96.7	77.4	96.6	91.7
[19]	JAFFE	89.3	90.7	91.1	92.6	90.2	92.3	91.1
Shape Signature MLP	MMI	100	85.7	64.2	100	61.1	80	81.8
Shape Signature NARX	MMI	96.5	100	100	100	94.4	100	98.4
[19]	MMI	80.1	78.2	81.3	83.2	77.1	81	80.1
[17]	MMI	65.6	72.5	72.5	88.2	71.1	93.8	77.4
Shape Signature MLP	MUG	96.7	100	100	100	93.1	100	98.3
Shape Signature NARX	MUG	100	93.3	92.3	95.5	100	100	96.8

acquired a higher average recognition rate of facial expressions than others reported in [17–19]. The NARX network achieved an overwhelming recognition rate of facial expressions than the MLP.

The JAFFE dataset is considered to evaluate the results of the shape signature using MLP and NARX which is shown in Table 3.17. The MLP-based shape signature acquires 92% as average recognition rate with correct recognition rate for anger and the lowest recognition rate 71.4% for sadness. In the same way, NARX also acquires the average recognition rate with the highest recognition accuracy. It also summarizes the comparative results with these state-of-the-art methods. It is also noticed that the proposed shape signature acquired higher average recognition rate of facial expressions than others reported in [18, 19]. The MMI dataset is also considered to evaluate the results of shape signature using MLP and NARX which is shown in Table 3.17. The MLP-based shape signature acquires 81.8% as average recognition rate with the highest recognition rate 100% for anger and the lowest recognition rate 61.1% for sadness. In the same way, NARX also acquires the average recognition rate with the highest recognition accuracy. It also summarizes the comparative results with these state-of-the-art methods. It is also noticed that the proposed shape signature acquired a higher average recognition rate of facial expressions than others reported in [17, 19].

The MUG dataset is also considered to evaluate the results of shape signature using MLP and NARX which is shown in Table 3.17. The MLP-based shape signature acquires 98.3% as average recognition rate with the highest recognition rate for happiness and the lowest recognition rate 92.3% for fear. In the same way, NARX also acquires the average recognition rate with the highest recognition accuracy. From this observation, we conclude that the MLP performs better than the NARX.

The MLP-based comparison of different expressions on four benchmark datasets is shown in Fig. 3.11. In the same way, the NARX-based comparison of different expressions on the same four benchmark datasets is shown in Fig. 3.12.

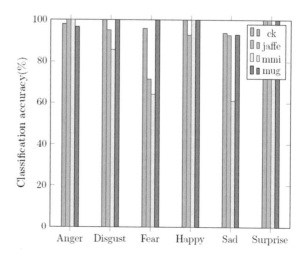

Fig. 3.11 Comparison of expressions of shape signature on CK+, JAFFE, MMI, and MUG databases using MLP

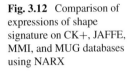

Fig. 3.12 Comparison of expressions of shape signature on CK+, JAFFE, MMI, and MUG databases using NARX

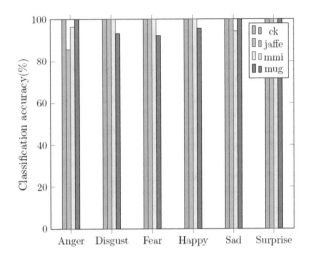

3.6 Sum-up Discussion

This chapter proposed the issue of facial expression recognition using shape signature by using two different networks (MLP and NARX). The effectiveness of the proposed procedure is validated by the recognition performance and comparison with the state-of-the-art reporting. It is also observed that NARX achieved an overwhelming recognition rate of facial expression recognition. The experimental results also indicate significant performance improvements due to the incorporation of distance signature derived from a human face.

In the fourth chapter, a texture signature is considered for recognizing human emotions. Proper landmark detection is a challenging task in facial expression recognition. Triangle formation among the grid is sensitive due to their variations of landmark points from one face to another face of the same expression. This technique deteriorates the performance of emotions. To overcome that problem, a texture region-based facial expression recognition is proposed in the next chapter.

References

1. G. Tzimiropoulos, M. Pantic, Optimization problems for fast aam fitting in-the-wild in *Proceedings of the IEEE International Conference on Computer Vision* (2013), pp. 593–600
2. A. Barman, P. Dutta, Facial expression recognition using shape signature feature, in *2017 Third International Conference on Research in Computational Intelligence and Communication Networks (ICRCICN)* (IEEE, 2017), pp. 174–179
3. T.Y. Young, *Handbook of Pattern Recognition and Image Processing: Computer Vision*, vol. 2, (Academic Press, Inc., 1994)
4. C.H. Chen, D. Stork, Handbook of pattern recognition & computer vision. Int. J. Neural Syst. **5**(3), 257 (1994)

5. M Borda, *Fundamentals in Information Theory and Coding* (Springer, Berlin, 2011). Technical report, ISBN 978-3-642-20346-6
6. Z. Zhang, M. Lyons, M. Schuster, S. Akamatsu, Comparison between geometry-based and gabor-wavelets-based facial expression recognition using multi-layer perceptron, in *Third IEEE International Conference on Automatic Face and Gesture Recognition, 1998. Proceedings* (IEEE, 1998), pp. 454–459
7. H. Jaeger, *Tutorial on Training Recurrent Neural Networks, Covering BPPT, RTRL, EKF and the "Echo State Network" Approach*, vol. 5. GMD-Forschungszentrum Informationstechnik (2002)
8. T. Lin, B.G. Horne, P. Tino, C.L. Giles, Learning long-term dependencies in NARX recurrent neural networks. IEEE Trans. Neural Netw. **7**(6), 1329–1338 (1996)
9. R. Pascanu, T. Mikolov, Y. Bengio, On the difficulty of training recurrent neural networks. ICML **3**(28), 1310–1318 (2013)
10. P. Lucey, J.F. Cohn, T. Kanade, J. Saragih, Z. Ambadar, I. Matthews, The extended cohn-kanade dataset (ck+): A complete dataset for action unit and emotion-specified expression, in *Computer Society Conference on Computer Vision and Pattern Recognition-Workshops* (IEEE, 2010), pp. 94–101
11. M. Lyons, S. Akamatsu, M. Kamachi, J. Gyoba, Coding facial expressions with gabor wavelets, in *Third IEEE International Conference on Automatic Face and Gesture Recognition, 1998. Proceedings* (IEEE, 1998), pp. 200–205
12. M.F. Valstar, M. Pantic, Induced disgust, happiness and surprise: an addition to the mmi facial expression database, in *Proceedings of International Conference Language Resources and Evaluation, Workshop on EMOTION* (Malta, 2010), pp. 65–70
13. N. Aifanti, C. Papachristou, A. Delopoulos. The mug facial expression database, in *Proceedings of the 11th International Workshop on Image Analysis for Facial Expression Database* (Desenzano, Italy, 2010), pp. 12–14
14. L. Introna, H. Nissenbaum, Facial recognition technology a survey of policy and implementation issues (2010)
15. S. Marcel, M.S. Nixon, S. Li, Handbook of biometric anti-spoofing-trusted biometrics under spoofing attacks. *Advances in Computer Vision and Pattern Recognition* (Springer, Berlin, 2014)
16. J.-M. Cheng, H.-C. Wang, A method of estimating the equal error rate for automatic speaker verification, in *2004 International Symposium on Chinese Spoken Language Processing* (IEEE, 2004), pp. 285–288
17. L. Zhong, Q. Liu, P. Yang, J. Huang, D.N. Metaxas, Learning multiscale active facial patches for expression analysis. IEEE Trans. Cybern. **45**(8), 1499–1510 (2015)
18. S.L. Happy, A. Routray, Automatic facial expression recognition using features of salient facial patches. IEEE Trans. Affect. Comput. **6**(1), 1–12 (2015)
19. A. Poursaberi, H.A. Noubari, M. Gavrilova, S.N. Yanushkevich, Gauss–laguerre wavelet textural feature fusion with geometrical information for facial expression identification. EURASIP J. Image Video Process. **2012**(1), 1–13 (2012)

Chapter 4
Texture Signature for Recognizing Human Emotions

4.1 Introduction

In the last two chapters, we discussed how distance and shape information could be used efficiently as a descriptor for facial expression recognition. In this chapter, we propose a texture signature-based human facial expression recognition system. At the same time as done in the last two chapters, Effective landmark detection of a human face offers a crucial role in facial expression tasks. Active Appearance Model (AAM) [1] exploits the texture model to get the landmark on a face image. Salient landmark points are considered from eye, eyebrow, nose, and mouth region and corresponding texture regions are determined. Subsequently, texture features are extracted using Local Binary Pattern (LBP) [2]. Normalized texture signatures supplemented with their respective stability indices are obtained. The raw moment, range, skewness, kurtosis, and entropy are also derived from the normalized signature. These features are used to correctly classify the six expressions of each expressed face images. The experiments are put to test on JAFFE, MMI, CK+, and MUG benchmark facial datasets to justify the effectiveness of the texture descriptor.

Organization of This Chapter
This chapter is structured into five parts. In the first part, consisting of Sect. 4.1, we introduce texture signature useful for human emotion recognition.

The second part of the chapter discusses the proposed system of texture signature. In this chapter, we also elaborate on landmark detection, texture region, and Local Binary Pattern for extracting features.

The third part of this chapter, comprising Sect. 4.3, offers a discussion on the feature extraction mechanism. In this part, we also discuss texture signature apart from the formation and functioning of the stability index. The training process is also discussed in this chapter.

In the next part, Sect. 4.4 shows the result discussion of emotional reflections. This part also makes a detailed discussion about the classification of emotions into different categories.

© Springer Nature Singapore Pte Ltd. 2020
P. Dutta and A. Barman, *Human Emotion Recognition from Face Images*,
Cognitive Intelligence and Robotics,
https://doi.org/10.1007/978-981-15-3883-4_4

The penultimate part of this chapter discusses the experiment and the result analyses on four benchmark databases.

The last section is concluded with sums up discussion in Sect. 4.5.

4.2 Overview of Proposed System

The overview of the schematic diagram is presented in Fig. 4.1. Fast-SIC [1] AAM fitting is used to get the landmark points on a face image. The eyes, eyebrows, nose, and mouth regions of a facial image are discriminative regions to distinguish the expressions. After detection of the landmarks, we have marked about three points on each eyebrow, four points on each eye, three points on the nose, and four points on the mouth. Texture regions are identified using salient landmark points. The normalized evaluation of texture signatures is considered. The higher-order texture signatures are used to find respective stability indices. Statistical range, moment up to fourth order, skewness, kurtosis, and entropy are combined with the texture information signature to supplement the feature set. These salient features classify different expressions into happiness, surprise, anger, fear, disgust, and sadness separately using the NARX classifier.

4.2.1 Landmark Detection

Landmark detection is a challenging task in the field of facial expression recognition. Accurate landmark extracts discriminative features to categorize the expressions into various categories. The appearance model [1] is used to detect the landmarks on the facial images. The detailed discussion is available in the first chapter in Sect. 2.2.1

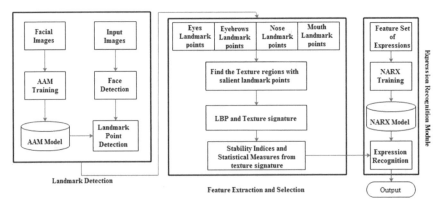

Fig. 4.1 Schematic presentation of the proposed system

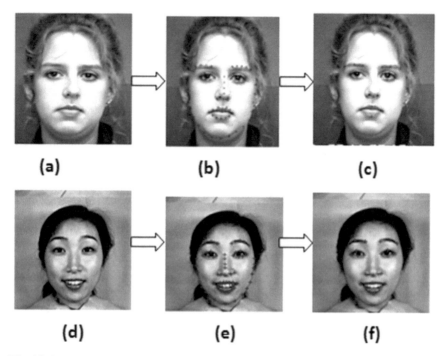

Fig. 4.2 Landmark detection in CK+ for anger: **a** original image **b** AAM fitting model **c** some landmark points and JAFFE for happiness: **d** original image **e** AAM fitting model **f** some landmark points

for the better understanding of AAM. After detection of landmarks, we only consider salient landmarks on eyes, eyebrows, mouthm and nose regions.

Figure 4.2 is considered to show the landmark detection of CK+ and JAFFE databases. The original image is shown in Fig. 4.2a. Appearance model is used on that original image to get the landmarks which is shown in Fig. 4.2b. Salient landmarks are extracted from the appearance-based model as depicted in Fig. 4.2c. In the same way the corresponding original image, AAM fitting model, and salient landmarks of JAFFE are shown in Fig. 4.2d–f.

4.2.2 Texture Region

The active patches are derived from the face image depending upon their elicitation of expressions. These active patches are obtained around eye corner, lip corner, nose corner, and mouth corner region due to their elicitation of expressions. The size of the active facial patches is kept fixed at 9×9. The patches are indexed around their active region as depicted in Fig. 4.3. Active facial patches are dependent on salient

Fig. 4.3 Position of facial patches

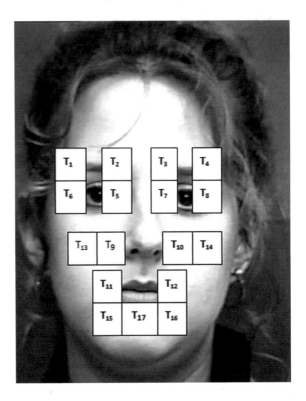

landmarks in [3]. Active patches T_1, T_2, T_3, T_4, T_5, T_6, T_7 and T_8 are directly extracted from eyebrows, eyes, nose, and lip corner, respectively, as depicted in Fig. 4.3. T_9 and T_{10} are the nose corner points. T_{11} and T_{12} are the lip corner points. T_{15} and T_{16} are located just below the lip corner and T_{17} is located between T_{15} and T_{16}. T_{13} and T_{14} are closer to the nose corner points. Now we merge all active facial patches to get a texture region.

The process of texture region identification implies the following sequence of events:

1. Identification of the landmark points using AAM.
2. Prominent landmarks are marked on eyebrows, eyes, mouth, and nose regions.
3. These salient landmarks help to extract the texture regions from facial image.

4.2.3 Local Binary Pattern

The Local Binary Pattern (LBP) operator labels the pixels of an image with decimal numbers, called Local Binary Patterns or LBP codes, which encode the local structure around each pixel. It proceeds thus, as illustrated in Fig. 4.3. Each pixel is compared with its eight neighbors in a 3×3 neighborhood by subtracting the center pixel value; the resulting strictly negative values are encoded with 0 and the others with 1; a binary number is obtained by concatenating all these binary codes in a clockwise direction starting from the top-left one and its corresponding decimal value is used for labeling. The derived binary numbers are referred to as LBP codes.

One limitation of the basic LBP operator is that its small 3×3 neighborhood cannot capture dominant features with large-scale structures. To deal with the texture at different scales, the operator was later generalized to use neighborhoods of different sizes [1]. A local neighborhood is defined as a set of sampling points evenly spaced on a circle which is centered at the pixel to be labeled, and the sampling points that do not fall within the pixels are interpolated using bilinear interpolation, thus allowing for any radius and any number of sampling points in the neighborhood. Figure 4.4 shows some examples of the extended LBP operator, where the notation (p, r) denotes a neighborhood of p sampling points on a circle of radius of r.

$$\text{LBP}_{p,r}(x, y) = \sum_{q=0}^{p-1} s(g_q - g_c)2^q \tag{4.1}$$

here p represents the total number of neighborhoods, the index of the neighbor is represented by q, the neighborhood pixel values of (x, y) are represented by g_q and g_c mentions the surrounding circle pixel neighborhood with a radius r. The function $s(x)$ is written as

$$s(x) = \begin{cases} 1 & x \geq 0 \\ 0 & x < 0 \end{cases}$$

Fig. 4.4 An example of basic LBP

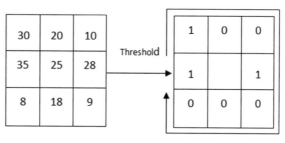

Binary-10010001

Decimal- 145

The histogram of a LBP image LBP(x, y) can be computed as

$$H_k = \sum_{x,y} s(\text{LBP}(x, y)) = k, \quad k = 0, 1, \ldots, p - 1 \qquad (4.2)$$

By the definition above, the basic LBP operator is invariant to monotonic grayscale transformations preserving pixel intensity order in the local neighborhoods. The histogram of LBP labels are calculated over a region that can be exploited as a texture descriptor.

The operator LBP(p, r) produces 2^p different output values, corresponding to 2^p different binary patterns formed by p pixels in the neighborhood. If the image is rotated, these surrounding pixels in each neighborhood will move correspondingly along the perimeter of the circle, resulting in a different LBP value, except patterns with only 1s and 0s.

It has been shown that certain patterns contain more information than others [2]. It is possible to use only a subset of 2^p binary patterns to describe the texture of images. Ojala et al. mentioned these as uniform patterns, denoted $\text{LBP}_{(p,r)}^{U2}$. A Local Binary Pattern is called uniform if it contains at most two bitwise transitions from 0 to 1 or vice versa when the corresponding bit string is considered circular. For instance, 00000000 (0 transitions) and 01110000 (2 transitions) are both uniform whereas 11001001 (4 transitions) and 01010011 (6 transitions). It is observed that the uniform patterns account for around 90% of all the patterns in a (8, 1) neighborhood and around 70% in a (16, 2) neighborhood in texture images [2].

The example of the LBP operator is depicted in Fig. 4.4 for better understanding. The neighboring pixels are substituted with respect to the value of the center pixel. A threshold is chosen to compute the 8th bit binary value and after that, it is converted into a decimal value. Thus $\text{LBP}_{8,1}$ is 145.

4.3 Feature Extraction

The landmarks are identified by AAM fitting model. Landmarks are specific coordinate points on the face images. Prominent landmarks are marked around the nose, eyes, eyebrows, and mouth regions to extract active facial patches. These active facial patches are shown in Fig. 4.3. These active facial patches are identified as $T1$ to $T4$ for eyebrows, $T5$ to $T8$ for eyes, $T9$ to $T10$ indicates corner points of the nose, $T11$ to $T12$ represents the corner points of mouth and $T15$ to $T17$ for points adjacent to the mouth region. Now we merge all the active facial patches to get the texture region of a particular facial image. LBP is used to compute the texture descriptor. This texture descriptor [4] is normalized as

$$\eta_i^F = \frac{H_i^F}{\sum_{i=1}^{n} H_i^F}, \quad F = 1, 2, \ldots, M \text{ and } i = 1, 2, \ldots, n \qquad (4.3)$$

where η_i^F is the texture signature and H_i^F are texture descriptors. M is the total number of facial images and n is the total of texture descriptors.

The feature extraction of texture descriptor implies the following sequence of events:

1. Salient landmarks are identified on facial images.
2. Active facial patches are extracted around the salient landmarks. It is also available in the previous section.
3. The active facial patches are merged to form a texture region.
4. LBP is used on that texture region to get texture descriptors.

4.3.1 Stability Index of Texture Signature

To calculate the stability index, we use a higher-order texture signature. It plays a significant role in facial expression recognition for its different expressive characteristics. The normalized texture is used to find the higher-order signatures. The stability index is defined as

$$\zeta^r = \frac{H_i^r}{\sum_{i=1}^{n} H_i^r} \tag{4.4}$$

rth order signatures are computed from the texture signature of each face image. In this experiment, we consider the order of signature as $r = 10$. Now we calculate the differences among their rth order texture signature as

$$\Delta H_i^r = \zeta_i^r - \zeta_i^{r-1} \tag{4.5}$$

We set a threshold upon the analysis of the differences in higher-order factors. This threshold follows the condition $\Delta \zeta_i^r \in \tau$. This order r is mentioned as a stability index of texture signature.

A few of the images are considered from the MMI dataset for a better understanding of the stability index. Figure 4.5 is chosen to show the stability indices of different expressions corresponding to the MMI database. It is mentioned that stability indices produce different values for various expressions such that anger produces 432 as stability index, surprise produces 436 as stability index, sadness produces 435 as stability index, and happiness produces 426 as stability index. It is also shown in Fig. 4.5 of the MMI dataset.

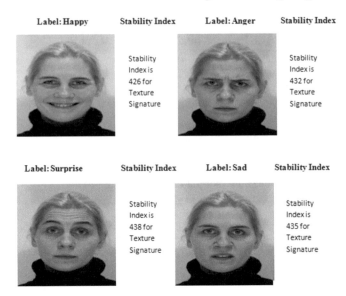

Fig. 4.5 The stability indices are shown for texture signature on MMI database

The stability index of texture descriptor implies the following sequence of events:

1. Normalized texture signatures are computed using Eq. 4.3.
2. Higher-order signatures are calculated from texture signatures using Sect. 4.3.1.
3. We set a threshold upon the analysis of the differences of higher-order factors.
4. The higher order attaining below the preset threshold for the first time is treated as a stability index of texture descriptor for a particular face image.

4.3.2 Statistical Measures of Texture Signature

We discussed statistical measures such as moment, kurtosis, skewness, range, and entropy in Chap. 2, Sect. 2.3.3. It is proved that much number of features give a promising classification of expressions than the fewer number of features. For this reason, we also compute range, moment, skewness, kurtosis, and entropy from texture signature to get a feature set.

The proposed texture feature extraction is shown in Algorithm 4.1. According to this algorithm first, the landmark points are identified using an Active Appearance Model. After that salient landmark points are considered among eyes, eyebrows, nose, and mouth regions. These salient landmark points compute the texture regions and subsequently find the Local Binary Pattern to get texture signature. The stability index and statistical analysis are computed from this texture signature.

Algorithm 4.1 Proposed Training Algorithm of Facial Expression Recognition

---

Input: An $m \times n$ human face image expression.
  AAM fitting is applied to get the landmark points on the face image.
2: Salient landmarks are extracted from Eyebrows, Eyes and Mouth region.
  Grid and texture regions are formed out of these landmark points.
4: Normalize texture feature to get texture signature.
  Determine stability indices of texture signature using equation and also compute moment, skew-ness, kurtosis and entropy.
6: Combine all these features to get an enhanced feature set.
  This enhanced feature set is fed as input to NARX.
8: **Output**: Expression classified into six basic categories.

4.3.3   Training Using Nonlinear Auto Regressive with eXogenous Input

The NARX [5] recurrent neural network is a dynamical neural network architecture normally used for input-output modeling of nonlinear dynamical systems. The network receives as input a window of past input and output values and calculates the current output. The NARX model can be defined as $y(t) = f(w(t - Dw), \ldots, w(t - 1), w(t), y(t - Dy), \ldots, y(t - 1))$, here $w(t)$ and $y(t)$ are the network input and output respectively at time t, respectively. Dw and Dy represent input and output time lags, and f is a nonlinear function which is approximated by a Multilayer Perceptron (MLP) [6]. During training, NARX network aims to learn optimal weight values by minimizing a objective function [7]. For each training pattern, Mean Square Error (MSE) function measures the deviation of the predictions y, from the target outputs. In Algorithm 4.1, we elaborate the proposed training algorithm for NARX.

4.4   Result and Discussion on Texture Signature

The proposed system is evaluated on instances from Cohn-Kanade (CK+) [8], Japanese Female Facial Expressions (JAFFE) [9], MUG [10], and MMI [11] benchmark databases. As discussed earlier, landmark detection was done on the face image while texture signatures are used for feature extraction. These features are used for the classification of expressions into different categories by the NARX network.

4.4.1   Experimental Result on the CK+

The CK+ database [8] has both male and female facial expressions having six basic emotions. In the training phase, NARX is applied on a total of 713 images of CK+ database to conduct the training and remaining 391 images for testing in order to

measure the performance of the CK+ database. In this experiment, the proposed
system has been selected 393 images of different expressions. There are divides as
anger (72), fear (43), disgust (54), sadness (71), happiness (84), and surprise (67)
among the total facial images.

Table 4.1 illustrates the overall performance of the recognition accuracy of the
texture signature. Anger recognizes 71 images properly and 1 image is confused
with sadness. Disgust identifies 53 images correctly and 1 image is confused with
fear. Fear recognizes 41 images properly and 1 image is misclassified with happiness.
Happiness identifies 83 images correctly and 1 image is misidentified with disgust.
Sadness recognizes 70 images properly and 1 image is misidentified with surprise.
Surprise expression is classified correctly.

We also consider false rejection rate (FRR), false acceptance rate (FAR), and
error rate (ERR) to measure the system performance in Table 4.2. Error rate (ERR)
is computed as the division of the number of all incorrect predictions and a total
number of the database. It is also shown as Error Rate (ERR)=False Positive (FP) +
False Negative (FN)/(True Positive (TP) + True Negative (TN) + False Positive (FP)
+ False Negative (FN)).

Table 4.1 The confusion matrix of texture signature on CK+ database using NARX

	Anger	Disgust	Fear	Happiness	Sadness	Surprise
Anger	71	0	0	0	1	0
Disgust	0	53	1	0	0	0
Fear	0	0	42	1	0	0
Happiness	0	1	0	83	0	0
Sadness	0	0	0	0	70	1
Surprise	0	0	0	0	0	67

Table 4.2 The FAR, FRR, and ERR of texture signature on CK+ database

	FAR	FRR	ERR
Anger	0.000	0.013	0.002
Disgust	0.003	0.018	0.005
Fear	0.002	0.023	0.005
Happiness	0.003	0.011	0.005
Sadness	0.003	0.014	0.005
Surprise	0.003	0.000	0.002

4.4.2 Experimental Result on the JAFFE

The JAFFE [9] database contains 213 gray-level images of seven facial expressions (six basic + neutral) of 10 different females. A total of 116 images of the JAFFE database are used for training and the remaining 95 images are used to test the performance of expressions.

Table 4.3 shows the performance of the expressions recognition. Anger identifies 18 images accurately and 3 images are mismatched with disgust. Disgust identifies 18 images perfectly and 2 images are misidentified with fear. Fear recognizes 12 images properly and 2 images are confused with happiness. Happiness recognizes 13 images perfectly and 1 image is misidentified with sadness. Sadness recognizes 12 images perfectly and 2 images are a mismatched surprise. The surprise recognizes correctly.

To measure the system performance we also consider false acceptance rate (FAR), false rejection rate (FRR), and error rate (ERR). The FRR, FAR, and ERR are considered to show the performance of facial expression recognition as shown in Table 4.4.

Table 4.3 The confusion matrix of texture signature on JAFFE database using NARX

	Anger	Disgust	Fear	Happiness	Sadness	Surprise
Anger	18	3	0	0	0	0
Disgust	0	18	2	0	0	0
Fear	0	0	12	2	0	0
Happiness	0	0	0	13	1	0
Sadness	0	0	0	0	12	2
Surprise	0	0	0	0	0	12

Table 4.4 The FAR, FRR, and ERR of texture signature on JAFFE database

	FAR	FRR	ERR
Anger	0.000	0.142	0.031
Disgust	0.040	0.100	0.052
Fear	0.024	0.142	0.042
Happiness	0.024	0.071	0.031
Sadness	0.012	0.142	0.031
Surprise	0.024	0.000	0.021

4.4.3   Experiment on MMI Database

MMI database offers more challenging instances in facial expression analysis compared to others. The same set of parameters is used in the MMI database, which is used in the CK+ database. A total of 493 images have been labeled with six basic expressions of frontal exposure (out of the 313 images for training and the remaining 177 images for testing).

The confusion matrix of texture signature using NARX is provided in Table 4.5. Anger recognizes 36 images properly and 4 images are misclassified with sadness. Disgust classifies 37 images perfectly and 2 images are mismatched with anger and fear. Fear recognizes 23 images perfectly and 2 images are misidentified with happiness. Happiness identifies 22 images accurately and 2 images are misidentified with sadness. Sadness recognizes 28 images properly and 1 image is mismatched with happiness. Surprise expression is classified correctly.

To measure the system performance, we also consider false rejection rate (FRR), false acceptance rate (FAR), and error rate (ERR). The FRR, FAR, and ERR are indicated in Table 4.6 to show the performance of facial expression recognition.

Table 4.5 The confusion matrix of texture signature on MMI database using NARX

	Anger	Disgust	Fear	Happiness	Sadness	Surprise
Anger	36	4	0	0	0	0
Disgust	1	37	1	0	0	0
Fear	0	0	23	2	0	0
Happiness	0	0	0	22	2	0
Sadness	0	0	0	1	28	1
Surprise	0	0	0	0	0	20

Table 4.6 The FAR, FRR, and ERR of texture signature on MMI database

	FAR	FRR	ERR
Anger	0.007	0.100	0.028
Disgust	0.028	0.051	0.033
Fear	0.006	0.080	0.016
Happiness	0.019	0.083	0.028
Sadness	0.013	0.066	0.022
Surprise	0.006	0.000	0.005

4.4.4 Experiment on MUG Database

MUG [10] database is also used to evaluate the system performance of recognition of facial expressions. From the MUG database we used a total of 297 images for training and the remaining 139 images were used to evaluate the performance of the network.

In Table 4.7, the confusion matrix tabulates the performance of different expressions. Anger classifies 17 images properly and 1 image is misclassified with disgust. Disgust identifies 29 images properly and 2 images are misidentified with fear and happiness. Fear recognizes 14 images properly. Happiness identifies 28 images perfectly and 2 images are mismatched with sadness. Sadness recognizes 20 images properly and 1 image is confused surprise. The surprise expression recognizes correctly.

We consider false rejection rate (FRR), false acceptance rate (FAR), and error rate (ERR) to measure the system performance. The FRR, FAR, and ERR are indicated in Table 4.8 to show the performance of facial expression recognition.

Table 4.7 The confusion matrix of texture signature on MUG database using NARX

	Anger	Disgust	Fear	Happiness	Sadness	Surprise
Anger	17	1	0	0	0	1
Disgust	0	29	1	1	0	0
Fear	0	0	14	0	0	0
Happiness	0	0	0	28	2	0
Sadness	0	0	0	0	20	1
Surprise	0	0	0	0	0	24

Table 4.8 The FAR, FRR, and ERR of texture signature on MUG database

	FAR	FRR	ERR
Anger	0.000	0.105	0.014
Disgust	0.009	0.064	0.021
Fear	0.008	0.000	0.007
Happiness	0.009	0.066	0.021
Sadness	0.016	0.047	0.021
Surprise	0.017	0.000	0.014

4.4.5   Performance Measure with State of the Art

Table 4.9 is considered to measure the performance of expression recognition on four benchmark databases. The NARX got 98.6% average classification accuracy on CK+ with a maximum recognition rate of 100% in case of surprise and minimum classification accuracy 97.7% in case of fear. The proposed texture signature methods are compared with the results obtained in the literature [3, 12–15]. Texture-based approach in Table 4.9 acquired 98.6, 98.1, 97.7, 98.8, 98.6, and 100% for anger, disgust, fear, happiness, sadness, and surprise on CK+ database using NARX which could beat the obtained recognition rate in [3].

To present a comparison task with the other literature, we confine our experiments to JAFFE database. Table 4.9 summarizes the comparative results with other state-of-the-art methods. The NARX got 90.0% average classification accuracy on the JAFFE with a maximum classification accuracy 100% in case of surprise and minimum classification accuracy 85.7% in case of anger.

We also evaluate the experiments on the MMI dataset. Table 4.9 summarizes the comparative results with other state-of-the-art methods. The average recognition rate of 95.5% is obtained using NARX with a maximum recognition rate of 100% in case of surprise and minimum classification accuracy 93.3% in case of sadness.

Table 4.9 Testing performance on publicly available databases with different state-of-the-art methods

	Database	Anger	Disgust	Fear	Happiness	Sadness	Surprise	Average
Texture signature on NARX	CK+	98.6	98.1	97.7	98.8	98.6	100	98.6
[3]	CK+	87.8	93.3	94.3	94.2	96.4	98.4	94.1
[15]	CK+	87.1	90.2	92	98.1	91.4	100	93.1
[13]	CK+	87	91.5	90.9	96.9	84.5	91.2	90.3
[12]	CK+	76.2	94.1	86.1	96.3	88.2	98.7	91.5
Texture signature on NARX	JAFFE	85.7	90.0	85.7	92.9	85.7	100	90.0
[3]	JAFFE	100	86.2	93.7	96.7	77.4	96.6	91.7
[15]	JAFFE	96.6	90	93.7	93.5	93.5	90	92.8
[13]	JAFFE	89.3	90.7	91.1	92.6	90.2	92.3	91.1
Texture signature on NARX	MMI	97.5	94.9	96	91.7	93.3	100	95.5
[13]	MMI	80.1	78.2	81.3	83.2	77.1	81	80.1
[12]	MMI	65.6	72.5	72.5	88.2	71.1	93.8	77.4
[14]	MMI	50.2	79.8	67.1	82.9	60.2	88.5	71.4
Texture signature on NARX	MUG	94.7	96.8	92.9	93.3	95.2	100	95.7

Fig. 4.6 Comparison of
FAR on CK+, JAFFE, MMI,
and MUG databases

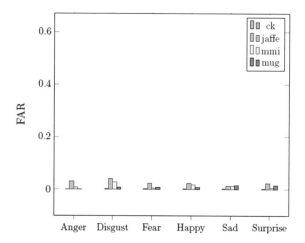

MUG database is also considered to confine the comparison task. Table 4.9 summarizes the comparative results with other state-of-the-art methods. The average
classification of 95.7% is obtained using NARX with a maximum recognition rate of
100% in case of surprise and minimum classification accuracy 93.3% in case of happiness. The proposed system achieves an overwhelming recognition rate compared
to the other approaches.

The performance of the FAR for texture signature on four benchmark datasets
such as CK+, JAFFE, MUG, and MMI is shown in Fig. 4.6. The FAR graph analysis
of texture signature yields a poor recognition rate in surprise on CK+. NARX-based
texture signature yields a less promising recognition rate in disgust on JAFFE. In the
same way, distance signature also shows poor recognition rate in disgust and surprise
on MMI and MUG.

The performance analysis of the FRR for distance signature using MLP on four
benchmark datasets is shown in Fig. 4.7. The lowest FRR means the highest recognition rate in expressions. The FRR graph analysis of texture signature indicates the
promising recognition rate in surprise on CK+. NARX-based texture signature indicates poor recognition rate in sadness on JAFFE. It also indicates a poor recognition
rate in anger on MMI and MUG.

The comparison of ERR for distance signature on four benchmark datasets such
as CK+, MMI, JAFFE, and MUG is shown in Fig. 4.8. The ERR graph analysis of
texture signature yields the highest recognition rate in anger on CK+. NARX-based
texture signature indicates poor recognition rate in disgust on JAFFE. It also indicates
poor performance in sadness on MMI and MUG.

Fig. 4.7 Comparison of
FRR on CK+, JAFFE, MMI,
and MUG databases

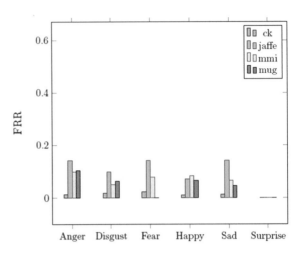

Fig. 4.8 Comparison of
ERR on CK+, JAFFE, MMI,
and MUG databases

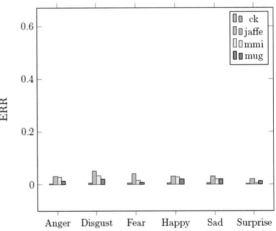

4.5   Discussion

This chapter proposed the issue of facial expression recognition of texture signature
using NARX-based neural network. The effectiveness of the proposed procedure
is validated by the recognition rate of different expressions and comparison with
the state-of-the-art performance. The FAR, FRR, and ERR are used to measure the
performance of the proposed procedure. The experimental results also explain the
significant improvements in performance due to the incorporation of texture signature
associated with a human face.

The distance and shape signatures are discussed in Chaps. 2 and 3 for recognizing the emotions from the human face. Individual signature performs well in recognizing emotions. In the next chapter, we merge the individual distance and shape signatures to form a combined Distance-Shape (D-S) signature. This signature achieves an overwhelming recognition rate of emotions than the individual distance and shape signature.

References

1. G. Tzimiropoulos, M. Pantic, Optimization problems for fast AAM fitting in-the-wild, in *Proceedings of the IEEE International Conference on Computer Vision* (2013), pp. 593–600
2. T. Ojala, M. Pietikäinen, D. Harwood, A comparative study of texture measures with classification based on featured distributions. Pattern Recognit. 29(1), 51–59 (1996)
3. S.L. Happy, A. Routray, Automatic facial expression recognition using features of salient facial patches. IEEE Trans. Affect. Comput. 6(1), 1–12 (2015)
4. A. Barman, P. Dutta, Texture signature based facial expression recognition using NARX, in *2017 IEEE Calcutta Conference (CALCON)* (IEEE, 2017), pp. 6–10
5. H. Jaeger, *Tutorial on training recurrent neural networks, covering BPPT, RTRL, EKF and the "echo state network" approach*, vol. 5 (GMD-Forschungszentrum Informationstechnik, 2002)
6. T. Lin, B.G. Horne, P. Tino, C. Lee Giles, Learning long-term dependencies in NARX recurrent neural networks. IEEE Trans. Neural Netw. 7(6), 1329–1338 (1996)
7. R. Pascanu, T. Mikolov, Y. Bengio, On the difficulty of training recurrent neural networks. ICML 3(28), 1310–1318 (2013)
8. P. Lucey, J.F. Cohn, T. Kanade, J. Saragih, Z. Ambadar, I. Matthews, The extended Cohn-Kanade dataset (CK+): a complete dataset for action unit and emotion-specified expression, in *Computer Society Conference on Computer Vision and Pattern Recognition-Workshops* (IEEE, 2010), pp. 94–101
9. M. Lyons, S. Akamatsu, M. Kamachi, J. Gyoba, Coding facial expressions with Gabor wavelets, in *Proceedings of the Third IEEE International Conference on Automatic Face and Gesture Recognition* (IEEE, 1998), pp. 200–205
10. N. Aifanti, C. Papachristou, A. Delopoulos, The MUG facial expression database, in *Proceedings of the 11th International Workshop on Image Analysis for Facial Expression Database*, Desenzano, Italy, April (2010), pp. 12–14
11. M.F. Valstar, M. Pantic, Induced disgust, happiness and surprise: an addition to the mmi facial expression database, in *Proceedings of International Conference on Language Resources and Evaluation, Workshop on EMOTION*, Malta, May (2010), pp. 65–70
12. L. Zhong, Q. Liu, P. Yang, J. Huang, D.N. Metaxas, Learning multiscale active facial patches for expression analysis. IEEE Trans. Cybern. 45(8), 1499–1510 (2015)
13. A. Poursaberi, H.A. Noubari, M. Gavrilova, S.N. Yanushkevich, Gauss–Laguerre wavelet textural feature fusion with geometrical information for facial expression identification. EURASIP J. Image Video Process. 2012(1), 1–13 (2012)
14. L. Zhong, Q. Liu, P. Yang, B. Liu, J. Huang, D.N. Metaxas, Learning active facial patches for expression analysis, in *2012 IEEE Conference on Computer Vision and Pattern Recognition (CVPR)* (IEEE, 2012), pp. 2562–2569
15. L. Zhang, D. Tjondronegoro, Facial expression recognition using facial movement features. IEEE Trans. Affect. Comput. 2(4), 219–229 (2011)

Chapter 5
Distance-Shape Signature Duo for Determination of Human Emotion

5.1 Introduction

Previous three chapters contain three feature descriptors individually distance signature, shape signature, and texture signature. In course of Distance-Shape (D-S) signature, respective stability indices and statistical measures supplement the signature features with a view to enhance the performance of the task of facial expression classification. Incorporation of these supplementary features is duly justified through extensive study and analyses of results obtained thereon.

While appreciating the usefulness of individual signature features in a marginal sense, the question coming up next is whether the joint contribution of the signature descriptors discussed in the previous chapters is in a portion to offer even more impressive performance. Accordingly, in this chapter we explore as to how is the merge of distance and shape signature going to work. In fact, features such as distance signature, shape signature, corresponding stability indices of each signature and also statistical analyses, viz. moment, kurtosis, skewness, etc. are formed a feature set. These features are used as input to Multilayer Perceptron (MLP) for the training and subsequent testing in a supervised learning mode of facial expression recognition. Proper landmarks detection on human faces occurs to be the most challenging task in feature extraction that we use and make successful in facial expression recognition. The face region of a human such as a mouth, jaw, eyes, and eyebrows, etc. show a vital role in separating from one expression to another expression of the same person. The appearance-based method is applied to the human face images to detect the landmarks. Salient landmarks are marked among the region of nose and mouth, eyes, and eyebrows. The consideration of the landmark points among the regions is three points on the eyebrow, four points on each eye, three points on the nose, and four points on the mouth region. These detected landmarks connect each other to form a grid. Now distances are computed within the grid and subsequently find the triangles from the grid. The distance signature is computed from the predefined relative distances and it will be normalized. In the same way, identified

P. Dutta and A. Barman, *Human Emotion Recognition from Face Images*, Cognitive Intelligence and Robotics, https://doi.org/10.1007/978-981-15-3883-4_5

triangles are used to compute the shape signature. Subsequently, the stability index is computed individually from the normalized distance signature and shape signature. It plays an important role in a face image for the recognition of facial expressions into different categories. Statistical measures such as moment, range, skewness, entropy, and kurtosis are computed from each normalized signature (distance signature and shape signature) duo. Now all features are merged to form a discriminating feature set. This feature set is used as input to the multilayer perceptron for the classification of expressions into different categories. It is also shown that the merged Distance-Shape (D-S) signature-based facial expression recognition system gives a promising recognition rate of classification of expressed emotions than the individual signature (distance and shape signature).

Organization of This Chapter
This chapter is organized into five parts. In the first part, consisting of Sect. 5.1, we discuss introduction and schematic diagram of human emotions recognition.

The second part of the Sect. 5.2 explores landmark detection using the AAM model. This part also shows the discussion about grid formation, feature extraction mechanism, and combined distance and texture signatures.

The third part of this chapter, consisting of Sect. 5.3, shows the discussion on emotion recognition using MLP.

The final part of the chapter discusses the experiment and result evaluation on four benchmark databases.

The chapter concludes with a conclusion in Sect. 5.5.

5.2 Schematic Diagram of Facial Expression Recognition

Figure 5.1 shows the proposed methodology of a facial expression using distance signature and shape signature features. First, a shape model is considered on a face image. Secondly, the Active Appearance Model (AAM) [1] is used to apply on face images to detect the prominent landmark points. Salient landmark points are marked on the mouth, eyes, nose, and eyebrows region to identify the valuable feature set. These salient landmark points are used to form a grid. The relative distances are computed among every pair of landmark points within the grid and normalized. Normalized distances are called distance signature. The landmark of mid-position of the nose landmark is used as a reference point to constitute triangles with the other prominent extracted landmarks for any expressed emotion. The triangles are formed from the grid and any such formed triangle has a specific property called shape signature. These triangles are very sensitive due to their variation of emotions. The triangles are considered to compute the normalized shape signature. Other formidable features such as stability indices are measured from both normalized signature (distance and shape signatures). Subsequently, statistical parameters such as moment, range, entropy, kurtosis, and skewness are computed to get a more comprehensive feature set of individual distance and shape signatures. Now individual distance and

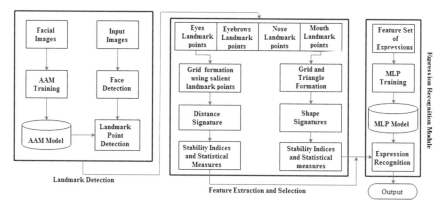

Fig. 5.1 Block diagram of proposed methodology

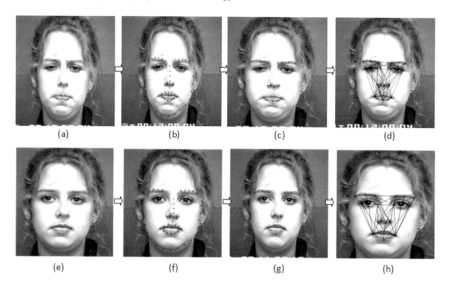

Fig. 5.2 Details of emotion recognition

shape features are merged to form a combined Distance-Shape signature. The individual and combined features are used as input to Multilayer Perceptron (MLP) to classify the expressions into six basic categories. To understand the flow graph, we consider Fig. 5.2 which shows the step-by-step mechanism of feature extraction from human faces.

5.2.1   Landmark Detection and Grid Formation

The Fast-SIC AAM [1] is used to determine the landmark points from a face image. The explanation of the AAM is available in Chap. 2, Sect. 2.2.1. Salient landmark points are extracted among the mouth eyes, nose, and eyebrows regions to form a grid. The formation of grid is discussed in Chap. 2, Sect. 2.2.2. The corresponding Figs. 2.3, 2.4, and 2.5 of the Chap. 2 are considered as examples of the landmark point detection and grid formation.

5.2.2   Feature Extraction

The feature extraction mechanisms are available in facial expression recognition such as a holistic and geometric features approach. Feature extraction plays a cardinal role to classify expressions. Proper feature extraction from human face images relies on the accurate selection of facial landmark points. The extraction of formidable features from salient landmarks is vital to recognize facial expressions. In this chapter, we use two different mechanisms for emotion recognition. Firstly, the distance signature is used to recognize emotions. Secondly, the shape signature is considered to recognize the emotions. After extraction of both distance and shape signatures, we consider a merged distance and shape signatures (D-S) to recognize the emotions of face images.

5.2.3   Formation of Distance-Shape (D-S) Signature

Distance signature is obtained using Eq. 2.4. In the same way, shape signature is also obtained using Eq. 3.12. Individual features such as distance and shape features are merged to form a Distance-Shape (D-S) signature feature for facial expression recognition. Stability indices are determined from both distance and shape signature to get prominent features. Many numbers of features yield a promising recognition rate of facial expression than a smaller number of features. For this reason, statistical measures such as moment, range, kurtosis, skewness, and entropy are computed from both distance and shape signatures. The distance feature extraction mechanism is explained in Algorithm 5.1. In the same way, shape signature feature extraction is elaborated in Algorithm 5.2. Now we combine both distance and shape signature features to constitute a merged Distance-Shape (D-S) signature [2] for emotion recognition. After extraction of both signatures, we investigated an experiment on a combination of distance and shape signatures and noticed that the combination of signatures offers promising features than the individual signature.

Algorithm 5.1 : *Distance Feature Extraction(D)*

1: **begin**
2:    Identify the landmark points l_i using AAM [1].
3:    The eyes, nose, mouth and eyebrows regions are used to extract salient landmark points $l_i (i = 1, 2, \ldots, 21)$.
4:    These salient landmark points l_i are joined with each other to constitute a grid.
5:    Distances ($d_i where\ i = 1, 2, \ldots, n$) are calculated from the grid.
6:    Normalize the distances using Eq. 2.4 to obtain distance signature (β_i).
7:    Find stability index $(\beta_i^r)^f$ from distance signature using Eq. 2.5 and corresponding differences of higher-order signatures are calculated using Eq. 2.6.
8:    Calculate range, moment [$l_{k1} (where\ k = 1, 2, 3, 4)$], skewness ($u$) and kurtosis ($q$) using Eqs. 2.7, 2.8 and 2.9.
9:    Also calculate entropy (En) from distance signature using Eq. 2.10.
10:    $D \leftarrow [range, (\beta_i^r), l_k, u, q, En]$.
11:    Return D.
12: **end**

Algorithm 5.2 : *Shape Feature Extraction(S)*

1: **begin**
2:    Identify the landmark points l_i using AAM [1].
3:    The eyes, nose, mouth and eyebrows regions are used to extract salient landmark points $l_i (i = 1, 2, \ldots, 21)$.
4:    These salient landmark points l_i are joined with each other to constitute a grid.
5:    Find the triangles and also calculate the s_{i2} using Eq. 3.11.
6:    Normalize the shape using Eq. 3.12 to obtain shape signature (μ_i).
7:    Find stability index (γ_i^r) from shape signature using Eq. 3.13 and corresponding differences of higher-order signatures are calculated using Eq. 3.14.
8:    Calculate range, moment [$E_k (where\ k = 1, 2, 3, 4)$], skewness ($U$) and kurtosis ($V$) using Eqs. 3.15, 3.16 and 3.17.
9:    Also calculate entropy (e) from shape signature using Eq. 3.18.
10:    $S \leftarrow [range, (\mu_i^r), E_k, U, V, e]$.
11:    Return S.
12: **end**

5.3 Feature Classification by MLP Training

There are many approaches to recognize emotions such as Support Vector Machine (SVM), Deep Learning, etc. We use MLP to recognize the emotions. The distance and shape signatures are used to extract features set which are represented by a vector of 9 elements each. Now combined Distance-Shape signature (D-S) is represented by a vector of 18 elements for each face image. The Min-Max process is used to normalize extracted features. It calculates the differences between in minimum and maximum values of each row feature vector. These features are fed as input to MLP to produce the output result with negligible errors. The diagram of the MLP network is indicated in Fig. 5.3 for the understanding of the training process. The training is completed by reducing of the Mean Square Error (MSE) as $e_k = 1/2 \sum (t_k - y_k)^2$ for different emotions. The number of output neurons is indicated by k of the MLP. There are four steps in the training algorithm: weights initialization, feedforward,

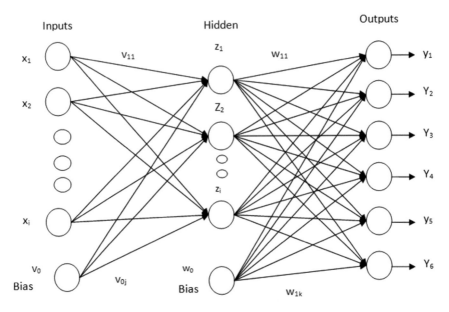

Fig. 5.3 Diagram of Multilayer Perceptron (MLP)

backpropagation of errors, and updations of biases and weights. In the first step, some small random values are assigned for the wights of input. Input unit x_i ($i = 1, \ldots, n$), n represents the number of inputs information and sends the input information to all hidden units z_j. Now the biases and weights are denoted as v_o and w_o. Each hidden unit computes the response using ($tanh$) activation and transmits its response z_j to each output unit. The activation function $tanh$ is used to compute the output of each unit. At the time of error backpropagation, every output unit measures the errors from the difference of y_k and t_k. Depending on these errors, the term δ_k ($k = 1, \ldots, m$) is calculated at the output unit y_k and sent back to all units in the previous layer. In this experiment, m represents the total number of output (here it is set as six). Similarly, the term δ_j ($j = 1, \ldots, p$) is computed for each hidden unit z_j, where p represents the number of hidden units. In the last step, biases and weights are modified through a δ factor. A threshold and learning rate are represented by ζ and η, respectively. The training is stopped when satisfying the error of $e \leq \zeta$. Step-by-step procedure of MLP algorithm which is a feedforward, backpropagation of error, supervised training is shown in Algorithm 5.3. At the time of testing, six basic emotions are assigned to the maximal value of the neuron outputs. The testing is performed to measure the classification rate of expressions of the proposed system.

Algorithm 5.3 Classification of MLP Algorithm

1: Initialize weights with small random values.

2: While stopping condition is false, do step 3–10.

3: For each training sample do steps 4–9.

4: Each input unit x_i ($i = 1, ..., n$) sends out signal into hidden units.

5: Each hidden unit z_j ($j = 1, .., p$) sums its weighted input signal as $z_i n_j = v_{oj} + \sum_{i=1}^{n} x_i v_{ij}$ and subjected to tanh activation to compute the output signals as $z_j = f(z_i n_j)$ (f is *tanh* activation function).

6: Each output unit y_k ($k = 1, .., m$) sums its weighted input signal as $y_{ink} = w_{ok} + \sum_{j=1}^{m} x_i w_{jk}$ and linear activation is applied to compute the output signals as $y_k = f(y_i n_j)$ (f is linear activation function).

7: Each output unit (y_k, $k = 1, ..., m$) receives a target (t_k, $k = 1, ..., m$) pattern corresponding to an input sample, error information is derived as $\delta_k = (t_k - y_k) f(y_i n_k)$.

8: Each hidden unit (z_j, $j = 1, .., n$) computes error information as $\delta_j = \delta_{inj} f(z_i n_j)$

9: Each output unit (y_k, $k = 1, .., m$) updates its bias and wight as $\Delta w_{jk} = \eta \delta_k z_j$ and $\Delta w_{ok} = \eta \delta_k$ where ($j = 1, ..., p$) and hidden unit (z_j, $j = 1, ..., p$) updates its bias and weight as $\Delta v_{ij} = \eta \delta_j x_i$ and $\Delta v_{oj} = \eta \delta_j$ where ($i = 1, .., n$).

10: Test the stopping condition. The stopping condition may be the calculated error being less than a preassigned threshold limit. On termination the minimization of the error is achieved.

5.4 Experiment on Four Benchmark Databases and Result Analysis

The signature-based (distance and shape) facial expression recognition is used individually and in a combination of both Distance-Shape (D-S) signature on four benchmark datasets, i.e. Cohn-Kanade (CK+) [3], MMI [4], JAFFE [5], and MUG [6] databases. Each database is considered to show the training process and also considered to show the effectiveness of testing performance of expressions. Table 5.1 shows the recognition rate of expressions of MLP training on different datasets. We also measure the results with different state of the art in order to justify the effectiveness of our proposed method.

Table 5.1 Training procedure on CK+ database using distance and shape signatures

Proposed approach	Images	Hidden unit	Avg. recognition rate	Time (s)
Distance signature	566	6	98.6	0.08
Shape signature	566	6	99.3	0.10

5.4.1 Experiment and Result on CK+ Database

The Cohn-Kanade (CK+) dataset is a collection of various university students of different age groups. This dataset is divided into 65% female, 15% African-American, and 3% Asian or Latino images. The extracted features are used as input to MLP to justify the system performance of expressed emotion.

The dataset has been divided into a training set and a test set to compute the system performance of facial expressions. A total of 849 images are considered, out of the 566 images used for training and the remaining 283 images used for testing. The MLP uses 566 images to train network with 6 hidden units. The network takes 0.08 s to converge to the error. The distance signature achieves 98.6% as an average recognition rate of expressions. In the same way, the MLP network uses 566 images to train the network with 6 hidden units. The network takes 0.10 s to converge to error. Shape signature achieves 99.3% as an average recognition rate of expressions. We consider the ζ and η as 0.01 on the basis of experimentation and the recognition rate of facial expressions is shown in Table 5.1. During the testing, test images are not necessarily used in the training phase. For that reason, it is also called a person's independent procedure. The proposed individual signature (distance signature and shape signature) and combined D-S signature use a total of 283 images to measure the system performances. The dataset is divided as 51 for anger, 24 for fear, 47 for disgust, 64 for happiness, 49 for sadness, and 48 for surprise.

We consider the recognition matrix in Table 5.2 to show the performance of the distance signature. The anger expression classified 49 images perfectly and 2 images are misclassified with surprise. The disgust expression is classified into 45 images accurately but 2 images are misclassified with happiness and anger. The fear expression is classified into 23 images properly and 1 image is mismatched with happiness. The happiness expression recognized 63 images properly and 1 image is mismatched with anger. The sadness expression identified 47 images perfectly and 2 images are mismatched with surprise. The surprise expression recognized 46 images properly and 2 images are misclassified with disgust and happiness. The overall classification accuracy of the distance signature is 96.3%. The highest recognition rate of expression is obtained as 98.4% for happiness and the lowest recognition rate of expression is obtained as 95.7% for disgust which is indicated in Table 5.31.

Table 5.2 The recognition matrix of distance signature on CK+ dataset

	Anger	Disgust	Fear	Happiness	Sadness	Surprise
Anger	49	0	0	0	0	2
Disgust	1	45	0	1	0	0
Fear	0	0	23	1	0	0
Happiness	1	0	0	63	0	0
Sadness	0	0	0	0	47	2
Surprise	0	1	0	1	0	46

The parameter of False Acceptance Rate (FAR), False Rejection Rate (FAR), and Error Rate (ERR) are also considered to measure the system performances of the distance signature using MLP. Table 5.3 shows the evaluated results of FAR, FRR, and ERR. The FAR represents the higher recognition rate of facial expressions in sadness. The system produces the highest recognition rate of expression when the system has the lowest FRR values. The sadness yields FRR as 0.040. The disgust produces 0.007 as ERR.

The recognition matrix of shape signature is used to show a recognition rate of facial expression which is available in Table 5.4. The anger expression is classified into 51 images perfectly and 2 images are mismatched with happiness. The disgust expression is classified into 47 images correctly. The fear expression is classified into 23 images accurately and 1 image is misidentified with sadness. The happiness expression is classified into 64 images perfectly. The sadness expression is classified into 46 images accurately and 1 image is misclassified with surprise. The surprise expression is classified into 48 images correctly. As can be observed anger, disgust, happiness, and surprise report correct recognition and remaining expressions such as anger, fear, and sadness are misclassified. The average classification of the shape signature is 98.3% with the highest recognition rate for anger, disgust, happiness, and surprise expressions and the lowest recognition rate is 93.9% for sadness as depicted in Table 5.31.

The accuracy of the proposed procedure is also measured in terms of FRR, FAR, and ERR. The system performance of FAR, FRR, and ERR of shape signature using MLP for CK+ dataset is indicated in Table 5.5. The FAR value of happiness is 0.013

Table 5.3 The FAR, FRR, and ERR of distance signature on CK+ database

	FAR	FRR	ERR
Anger	0.008	0.039	0.014
Disgust	0.004	0.042	0.010
Fear	0	0.041	0.003
Happiness	0.013	0.015	0.014
Sadness	0.000	0.040	0.007
Surprise	0.017	0.041	0.021

Table 5.4 The recognition matrix of shape signature on CK+ dataset

	Anger	Disgust	Fear	Happiness	Sadness	Surprise
Anger	51	0	2	0	0	0
Disgust	0	47	0	0	0	0
Fear	0	0	23	1	0	0
Happiness	0	0	0	64	0	0
Sadness	0	0	0	2	46	1
Surprise	0	0	0	0	0	48

Table 5.5 The MLP-based shape signature's FAR, FRR, and ERR on CK+ dataset

	FAR	FRR	ERR
Anger	0	0	0
Disgust	0	0	0
Fear	0	0.041	0.035
Happiness	0.013	0.000	0.010
Sadness	0	0.061	0.010
Surprise	0.004	0	0.035

Table 5.6 Training procedure on JAFFE dataset using distance and shape signatures

Proposed approach	Images	Hidden unit	Avg. recognition rate	Time (s)
Distance signature	116	6	96.6	0.10
Shape signature	116	6	96.6	0.12

which means it produces a 13/1000 false accept rate. The lowest FRR means it yields promising recognition of expressions. The fear produces the FRR as 0.041. The ERR is 0.010 for fear (Table 5.5).

5.4.2 Experiment and Result on JAFFE Dataset

The JAFFE [5] dataset has 213 gray level images of 10 Japanese females with seven expressions (six basic + one neutral). The expressions are represented as anger, disgust, sadness, happiness, fear, and surprise. The JAFFE dataset is divided into two parts, one for the training set and another one for test set. The MLP uses 116 images to train network with 6 hidden units. The network takes 0.10 s to converge to the error. The distance signature achieves 98.6% as an average recognition rate of expressions. Shape signature gets 99.3% as an average recognition rate of expressions. A total of 213 images are considered to measure the system performance of expression recognition. The total images are divided as 116 for training and the remaining 97 for testing. The notations ζ and η have been selected based on the system experimentation and they are assigned to 0.001. The network gets a 96.6% recognition rate of facial expression during the training. The proposed system uses a total of 97 images to measure the system performance of expressed emotion.

In Table 5.7, the recognition matrix shows the classification of different expressions of distance signature. From this table, we observe that anger, disgust, sadness, and surprise expressions are recognized accurately. The fear expression is classified into 11 images perfectly but 3 images are misidentified with disgust and anger. The

Table 5.7 The recognition matrix of distance signature on JAFFE dataset

	Anger	Disgust	Fear	Happiness	Sadness	Surprise
Anger	19	0	2	0	0	0
Disgust	0	20	0	0	0	0
Fear	1	1	11	1	0	0
Happiness	0	2	0	14	0	0
Sadness	0	0	0	0	14	0
Surprise	0	0	0	0	0	14

average classification performance of the distance signature is 94% with the correct recognition rate for five expressions and the lowest recognition rate is 78.6% for fear as depicted in Table 5.31.

The parameters of FAR, FRR, and ERR are also considered to measure the system performances of distance signature using MLP on JAFFE. Table 5.8 shows the evaluated results of FAR, FRR, and ERR. The FAR represents the higher recognition rate of facial expressions in sadness, and surprise. The system produces the highest recognition rate of expression when the system has the lowest FRR values. The happiness, sadness, and surprise indicate the accurate rate of expressions. The fear shows the ERR value as 0.051.

Table 5.8 The MLP-based distance signature's FAR, FRR, and ERR on JAFFE dataset

	FAR	FRR	ERR
Anger	0.013	0.095	0.030
Disgust	0.013	0	0.010
Fear	0.024	0.214	0.051
Happiness	0.012	0.000	0.010
Sadness	0	0	0
Surprise	0	0	0

Table 5.9 The recognition matrix of shape signature on JAFFE dataset

	Anger	Disgust	Fear	Happiness	Sadness	Surprise
Anger	21	0	0	0	0	0
Disgust	0	20	0	0	0	0
Fear	1	1	11	1	0	0
Happiness	0	0	0	14	0	0
Sadness	0	0	0	0	14	0
Surprise	0	0	0	0	0	14

Table 5.10 The MLP-based shape signature's FAR, FRR, and ERR on JAFFE dataset

	FAR	FRR	ERR
Anger	0.026	0	0.020
Disgust	0.013	0	0.010
Fear	0	0.021	0.030
Happiness	0	0	0
Sadness	0	0	0
Surprise	0	0	0

Table 5.11 Training procedure on MMI database using distance and shape signatures

Proposed procedure	Database	No. of images	Hidden unit	Avg. recognition rate	Time (s)
Distance signature	MMI	212	7	92.5	0.06
Shape signature	MMI	212	7	90.1	0.09

The recognition matrix of shape signature is shown in Table 5.9. It is observed that the disgust, happiness, sadness and surprise expressions are recognized accurately. The anger expression is classified into 19 images perfectly and 2 images are mismatched with fear. The fear expression classifies 11 images correctly but 3 images are misclassified with anger, disgust, and happiness. The average recognition rate of the shape signature is 94.9% as reported in Table 5.31.

The accuracy of the proposed procedure is also measured in terms of FRR, FAR, and ERR. The system performance of FRR, FAR, and ERR of shape signature using MLP for the JAFFE dataset is indicated in Table 5.10. The FAR value of anger is 0.013 that means it produces a 13/1000 false accept rate. The lowest FRR means it yields promising recognition of expressions. The fear produces the FRR as 0.021. The ERR is 0.030 for fear.

5.4.3 Experiment and Result on MMI Database

The MMI dataset has face images of research staff members and students. They are between 19 and 62 years. In this dataset, 44% of subjects are female, having either a South American or Asian ethnic background. To conduct the experiment on this dataset we use a total of 325 images (212 for training and 113 for testing) for both distance and shape signature features. Table 5.11 shows the accuracy of training for both distance and shape signatures using MLP. The MLP network takes 0.10 s to converge to the error for distance signature. In the same way, it takes 0.12 s to converge to the error for shape signature. The proposed system applies a total of 113 images to test the system performance of facial expressions. MMI is a more

Table 5.12 The recognition matrix of distance signature on MMI dataset

	Anger	Disgust	Fear	Happiness	Sadness	Surprise
Anger	24	3	2	0	0	0
Disgust	0	17	0	0	3	1
Fear	2	1	10	0	0	1
Happiness	0	2	0	14	0	0
Sadness	0	0	0	0	18	0
Surprise	1	1	1	0	2	10

Table 5.13 The FAR, FRR, and ERR of distance signature on MMI database using MLP

	FAR	FRR	ERR
Anger	0.035	0.172	0.070
Disgust	0.076	0.190	0.097
Fear	0.030	0.285	0.061
Happiness	0	0.125	0.017
Sadness	0.052	0	0.044
Surprise	0.020	0.333	0.061

challenging dataset for facial expression recognition with respect to CK+ and JAFFE. First, the subjects consist of heterogeneous expressions. Different subjects show the expressed pose of the same person in a different manner. Second, a few poses have accessories such as mustache, glasses, headcloth, etc.

In Table 5.12, the recognition matrix shows the classification of distance signature on MMI. The anger expression classifies 24 images accurately and 5 images are in misclassification with disgust and fear. The disgust expression is classified into 17 images perfectly and 4 images are misclassified with sadness and surprise. The fear expression is classified into 10 images correctly and 4 images are misclassified. The happiness expression is classified into 14 images perfectly and 2 images are confused with disgust. The sadness expression is classified into 18 images accurately. The surprise expression recognized 10 images correctly and 5 images are in misclassification. The fear and surprise are in worst misclassification with anger, disgust, sadness, and surprise. The average recognition rate of the distance signature is 81.5%.

The parameters of FAR, FRR, and ERR are also considered to measure the system performances of distance signature using MLP on the MMI dataset. Table 5.13 shows the evaluated results of FAR, FRR, and ERR. The FAR represents the higher recognition rate of facial expressions in happiness. The system produces the highest recognition rate of expression when the system has the lowest FRR values. The sadness indicates the accurate classification rate of expression but other emotions have poor a classification rate. The anger the ERR value as 0.070.

Table 5.14 The confusion matrix on MMI database using shape signature

	Anger	Disgust	Fear	Happiness	Sadness	Surprise
Anger	29	0	0	0	0	0
Disgust	0	18	0	1	1	1
Fear	0	1	9	0	2	2
Happiness	0	0	0	16	0	0
Sadness	0	4	1	1	11	1
Surprise	0	1	1	0	1	12

Table 5.15 The MLP-based shape signature's FAR, FRR, and ERR on MMI dataset

	FAR	FRR	ERR
Anger	0	0	0
Disgust	0.065	0.142	0.079
Fear	0.020	0.357	0.061
Happiness	0.020	0	0.017
Sadness	0.042	0.388	0.097
Surprise	0.040	0.200	0.061

The recognition matrix of shape signature is indicated in Table 5.14. This table shows the best recognition rate of expressions on anger, disgust, happiness, and sadness. The anger expression is classified into 29 images correctly. The disgust expression is classified into 18 images rightly and 3 images are in mismatch with happiness, sadness and surprise. The fear expression is classified into 9 images correctly and 5 images are wrongly classified. The happiness expression is classified into 16 images perfectly. The sadness expression is classified into 11 images accurately and 7 images are misclassified. The surprise expression is classified into 12 images duly and 3 images are misclassified. The overall recognition rate of the shape signature is 81.8% as shown in Table 5.31. The highest recognition rate of expression of shape signature is 100% for anger and happiness. The lowest recognition rate of shape signature on the MMI database is 61.1% for sadness.

The accuracy of the proposed procedure is also measured in terms of FRR, FAR, and ERR. The system performance of FRR, FAR, and ERR of shape signature using MLP for the MMI dataset is indicated in Table 5.15. The FAR value of disgust is 0.065 that means it produces a 65/1000 false accept rate. The lowest FRR means it yields promising recognition of expressions. The disgust produces the FRR as 0.142. The ERR is 0.079 for disgust (Table 5.15).

Table 5.16 Training procedure on MUG database using distance and shape signatures

Proposed procedure	Database	No. of images	Hidden unit	Avg. recognition rate	Time (s)
D-S signature	MUG	212	10	95.3	0.15
Distance signature	MUG	394	7	98.5	0.05
Shape signature	MUG	394	7	98.0	0.08

5.4.4 Experiment and Result on MUG Dataset

MUG [6] database is also applied to examine the recognition rate of facial expression recognition. In this method the same set of parameters are applied which were used in CK+, JAFFE, and MMI datasets. A total of 591 images are used to measure system performance. The dataset is divided as training and testing set (out of the 394 for training and remaining 197 for testing). The MLP uses 394 images during the training of the MUG database of distance signature and achieves 98.5% average accuracy of expressions with 7 hidden units. It takes 0.05 s to converge to the network error. In the same way, when we perform training of shape signature, it achieves 98% average accuracy of expressions with 7 hidden units. It takes 0.08 s to converge to the network error.

The testing result of the shape signature is shown in Table 5.17. The confusion matrix of distance signature shows the recognition of various expressions. It is observed that disgust and fear are classified correctly. The anger expression recognized rightly 29 images but 2 images are in a mismatch with disgust and sadness. The happiness expression is classified correctly into 43 images and 2 images are in a mismatch with disgust. The sadness expression is classified into 28 images accurately and 1 image is mismatched with happiness. The surprise expression recognized 34 images perfectly and 2 images are misclassified. The average performance of the distance signature is 96.7% as presented in Table 5.31. The highest recognition rate of expression of distance signature is 100% for anger and happiness. The lowest recognition rate of expression of distance signature on the MUG database is 61.1% for sadness.

Table 5.17 The recognition matrix on MUG database using distance signature

	Anger	Disgust	Fear	Happiness	Sadness	Surprise
Anger	29	1	0	0	1	0
Disgust	0	30	0	0	0	0
Fear	0	0	26	0	0	0
Happiness	0	2	0	43	0	0
Sadness	0	0	0	1	28	0
Surprise	1	0	0	0	1	34

The parameters of FAR, FRR, and ERR are also considered to measure the system performances of distance signature using MLP on the MUG dataset. Table 5.18 shows the evaluated results of FAR, FRR, and ERR. The FAR represents the higher recognition rate of facial expressions in fear. The system produces the highest recognition rate of expression when the system has the lowest FRR values. Disgust and fear indicate the accurate classification rate of expression. The anger shows the ERR value as 0.015.

The testing result of the shape signature is shown in Table 5.19 which shows the correct classification of fear and sadness. The expressions of anger, disgust, happiness, and surprise are got promising recognition rates of expressions. There are also some instances of mismatch being observed with other emotions such as surprise being mismatched with disgust and happiness. The average recognition rate of shape signature is 96.7% which is shown in Table 5.31. The highest recognition rate of expression of shape signature is 100% for disgust and happiness. The lowest recognition rate of expression of shape signature on the MUG database is 93.1% for sadness.

The performance of the proposed approach is also measured in terms of FRR, FAR, and ERR. The system performance of FRR, FAR, and ERR of shape signature using MLP for the MUG dataset is indicated in Table 5.20. The FAR value of disgust is 0.012 that means it produces a 12/1000 false accept rate. The lowest FRR means it yields promising recognition of expressions. The disgust produces the FRR as 0.066. The ERR is 0.020 for disgust (Table 5.20).

Table 5.18 The FAR, FRR, and ERR of distance signature on MUG database using MLP

	FAR	FRR	ERR
Anger	0.006	0.064	0.015
Disgust	0.018	0	0.015
Fear	0	0	0
Happiness	0.006	0.044	0.015
Sadness	0.011	0.034	0.015
Surprise	0	0.055	0.010

Table 5.19 The confusion matrix on MUG database using shape signature

	Anger	Disgust	Fear	Happiness	Sadness	Surprise
Anger	30	0	0	0	1	0
Disgust	2	28	0	0	0	0
Fear	0	0	26	0	0	0
Happiness	0	1	1	43	0	0
Sadness	0	0	0	0	29	0
Surprise	0	1	0	1	0	34

Table 5.20 The MLP-based shape signature's FAR, FRR, and ERR on MUG dataset

	FAR	FRR	ERR
Anger	0.012	0.032	0.015
Disgust	0.012	0.066	0.020
Fear	0.005	0.000	0.005
Happiness	0.006	0.044	0.015
Sadness	0.006	0.000	0.005
Surprise	0.000	0.055	0.010

Table 5.21 Training procedure on CK+, JAFFE, MMI, and MUG databases using combination of distance and shape signature

Proposed approach	Dataset	Images	Hidden unit	Avg. classification rate	Time (s)
D-S signature	CK+	566	10	100	0.16
D-S signature	JAFFE	116	10	97.9	0.14
D-S signature	MMI	212	10	95.3	0.15
D-S signature	MUG	394	10	99.0	0.14

5.4.5 Experiment and Result of D-S Signature on CK+, JAFFE, MMI, and MUG Databases

Two signatures (distance signature and shape signature) are combined jointly to form a Distance-Shape (D-S) signature. This D-S signature is used on the four benchmark datasets to conduct the experiment and also validate the recognition rate of emotions in Table 5.21. The MLP uses 394 images during the training on the CK+ dataset of D-S signature and achieves startling 100% average accuracy of expressions with 10 hidden units. It takes 0.16 s to converge to the network error. In the same way, when we perform training on JAFFE of D-S signature, it achieves 97.9% average accuracy of expressions with 10 hidden units. It takes 0.14 s to converge to the network error. The combination of the D-S signature achieves a 95.3% average recognition rate of expressions during the training on MMI with 10 hidden units and a 99% average recognition rate of expressions during the training on MUG with 10 hidden units.

We provide Table 5.22 to show the average classification of facial expressions for training. During testing, the average classification of the D-S signature on the CK+ dataset is mentioned in Table 5.23. From this table, it appears that all expressions are classified correctly. It is also noticed that the combination of the D-S signature is accomplished better than the individual distance and shape signatures.

The FAR, FRR, and ERR are considered to evaluate the system performances of D-S signature on CK+. Table 5.24 shows the evaluated results of FRR, FAR, and ERR. The FRR, FAR, and ERR show the accurate recognition of all expressions.

Table 5.22 Training recognition matrix of D-S signature on CK+ dataset

	Anger	Disgust	Fear	Happiness	Sadness	Surprise
Anger	102	0	0	0	0	0
Disgust	0	94	0	0	0	0
Fear	0	0	48	0	0	0
Happiness	0	0	0	128	0	0
Sadness	0	0	0	0	98	0
Surprise	0	0	0	0	0	96

Table 5.23 The confusion matrix on CK+ database using D-S signature

	Anger	Disgust	Fear	Happiness	Sadness	Surprise
Anger	51	0	0	0	0	0
Disgust	0	47	0	0	0	0
Fear	0	0	24	0	0	0
Happiness	0	0	0	64	0	0
Sadness	0	0	0	0	49	0
Surprise	0	0	0	0	0	48

Table 5.24 The FAR, FRR, and ERR of D-S signature on CK+ database

	FAR	FRR	ERR
Anger	0	0	0
Disgust	0	0	0
Fear	0	0	0
Happiness	0	0	0
Sadness	0	0	0
Surprise	0	0	0

The recognition matrix in Table 5.25 presents the classification rate of expressions on JAFFE dataset. The anger, disgust, happiness, sadness, and surprise expressions are classified correctly. Whereas the fear expression is classified into 11 images accurately and 3 images are in misclassification with disgust and anger. The average classification of facial expression for the D-S signature on the JAFFE database is 96.4%. It is also noticed that the combination of the D-S signature performs an overwhelming recognition rate on JAFFE.

The accuracy of the proposed procedure is also measured in terms of FRR, FAR, and ERR. The system performance of FRR, FAR, and ERR of D-S signature using MLP for the JAFFE dataset are indicated in Table 5.26. The FAR values of fear, happiness, sadness, and surprise are 0.000 that means it produces a correct classification. The FRR values show the misclassification with the correct classification.

Table 5.25   The confusion matrix on JAFFE database using D-S signature

	Anger	Disgust	Fear	Happiness	Sadness	Surprise
Anger	21	0	0	0	0	0
Disgsut	0	20	0	0	0	0
Fear	2	1	11	0	0	0
Happiness	0	0	0	14	0	0
Sadness	0	0	0	0	14	0
Surprise	0	0	0	0	0	14

Table 5.26   The FAR, FRR, and ERR of D-S signature on JAFFE database

	FAR	FRR	ERR
Anger	0.026	0	0.020
Disgust	0.039	0	0.030
Fear	0	0.021	0.030
Happiness	0	0.142	0.020
Sadness	0	0	0
Surprise	0	0	0

Table 5.27   The recognition matrix of D-S signature on MMI dataset

	Anger	Disgust	Fear	Happiness	Sadness	Surprise
Anger	29	0	0	0	0	0
Disgust	0	18	0	1	1	1
Fear	0	1	9	0	2	2
Happiness	0	0	0	45	0	0
Sadness	0	4	1	1	11	1
Surprise	0	1	1	0	1	12

The highest misclassification in happiness. The ERR values also indicate the correct classification rate of expressions with misclassification.

The classification of the D-S signature on the MMI database is mentioned in Table 5.27. The anger expression is classified correctly. The fear expression recognized 9 images rightly and 5 images are in a mismatch with disgust, sadness, and surprise. In the same way, the sad expression recognized 11 images perfectly and 7 images are confused with disgust, fear, happiness, and disgust. It is observed that the fear and sad belong to the most difficult for the correct classification of facial expressions with the other expressions. The average classification of expressions for the MMI dataset is 81.9%.

Table 5.28 The FAR, FRR, and ERR of D-S signature on MMI database

	FAR	FRR	ERR
Anger	0	0	0
Disgust	0.065	0.142	0.079
Fear	0.020	0.357	0.061
Happiness	0.020	0.000	0.177
Sadness	0.042	0.388	0.097
Surprise	0.040	0.200	0.061

Table 5.29 The recognition matrix of D-S signature on MUG dataset

	Anger	Disgust	Fear	Happiness	Sadness	Surprise
Anger	30	1	0	0	0	0
Disgust	0	30	0	0	0	0
Fear	0	0	25	0	1	0
Happiness	0	0	0	45	0	0
Sadness	1	0	0	1	27	0
Surprise	0	0	0	0	0	36

The accuracy of the proposed procedure is also measured in terms of FRR, FAR, and ERR. The system performance of FAR, FRR, and ERR of the D-S signature using MLP for MMI dataset is indicated in Table 5.28. The FAR value of anger is 0.000 that means it produces a correct classification. The FRR values show the misclassification with the correct classification. The highest misclassification occurred in sadness. The ERR values also indicate the correct classification rate of expressions with misclassification.

Table 5.29 shows the performance of facial expression for the D-S signature on the MUG dataset. The expressions disgust, happiness, and surprise acquire an accurate recognition rate. The anger expression recognized 30 images accurately and 1 image is confused with disgust. The average recognition rate of expressions is 97.7%. It is also noticed that the combination of the D-S signature achieves an overwhelming recognition rate of expressions.

The performance of the proposed method is measured in terms of the FRR, FAR, and ERR. The values of FAR, FRR, and ERR of D-S signature using MLP for the MUG dataset are tabulated in Table 5.30. The FAR value of anger is 0.006 that means it produces a 6/1000 as a false accept rate. The disgust produces FRR as 0.000. It indicates the accurate classification of emotions. The ERR is 0.010 for anger.

Table 5.30 The FAR, FRR, and ERR of D-S signature on MUG database

	FAR	FRR	ERR
Anger	0.006	0.032	0.010
Disgust	0.006	0.000	0.005
Fear	0	0.038	0.005
Happiness	0.006	0.000	0.005
Sadness	0.006	0.069	0.015
Surprise	0	0	0

5.4.6   Performance Comparison of FRR, FAR, and ERR of Distance, Shape, and D-S Signatures

The comparison of the FAR for distance, shape, and D-S signatures using MLP on CK+ is shown in Fig. 5.4. The FAR graph analysis of distance signature yields a poor recognition rate in surprise. The FAR graph analysis of shape signature shows less promising performance in happiness. From this graph analysis, we also conclude that the combined D-S signature yields a promising recognition rate compared to the individual signature.

The comparison of the FRR for distance, shape, and D-S signatures using MLP on CK+ is shown in Fig. 5.5. The FRR graph analysis of shape signature yields poor recognition rate in disgust. The FRR graph analysis of the shape signature performs a poor recognition rate in sadness. It is also shown that the combined D-S signature indicates a promising recognition rate than the individual signature.

Fig. 5.4 FAR of CK+ using MLP

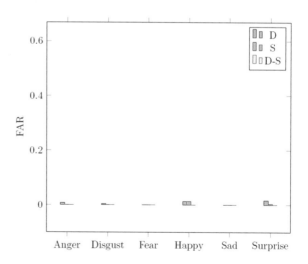

Fig. 5.5 FRR of CK+ using
MLP

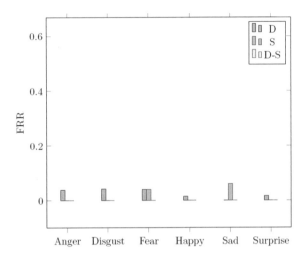

Fig. 5.6 The MLP-based
ERR of CK+

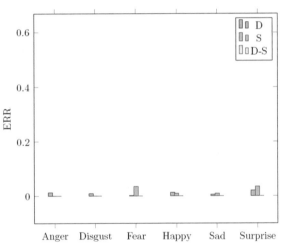

The comparison of the ERR for distance, shape, and D-S signatures using MLP
on CK+ is shown in Fig. 5.6. The ERR graph analysis of distance signature yields a
poor recognition rate in disgust. The ERR graph analysis of shape signature shows
the less promising performance in fear. From this graph analysis, it is also shown
that the combined D-S signature yields a promising recognition rate in individual
expressions.

The performance of FAR for distance, shape, and D-S signatures using MLP on
the JAFFE dataset is shown in Fig. 5.7. The FAR graph analysis of distance signature
yields a poor recognition rate in fear. The FAR graph analysis of shape signature
shows the less promising recognition rate in anger. From this graph analysis, we also
conclude that the combined D-S signature produces poor FAR in anger and disgust.

Fig. 5.7 FAR of JAFFE
using MLP

Fig. 5.7 FAR of JAFFE
using MLP

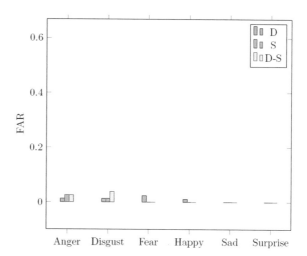

Fig. 5.8 FRR of JAFFE
using MLP

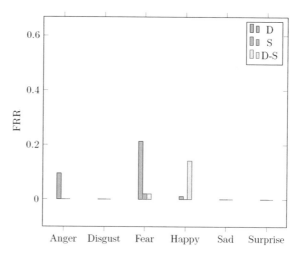

The comparison of the FRR for distance, shape, and D-S signatures using MLP on the JAFFE dataset is shown in Fig. 5.8. The FRR graph analysis of distance signature indicates a poor recognition rate in fear. The FRR graph analysis of shape signature performs the poor classification rate of expressions in fear. A combined D-S signature performs a less promising recognition rate in happiness. It is also shown that the combined D-S signature indicates a promising recognition rate in surprise expression.

The comparison of the ERR for distance, shape, and D-S signatures using MLP on the JAFFE dataset is shown in Fig. 5.9. The ERR graph analysis of distance signature shows a poor recognition rate in fear. The ERR graph analysis of shape signature

Fig. 5.9 ERR of JAFFE
using MLP

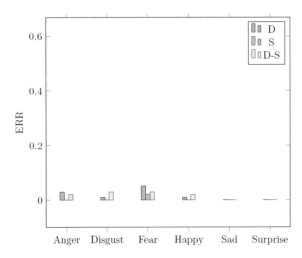

Fig. 5.10 FAR of MMI
using MLP

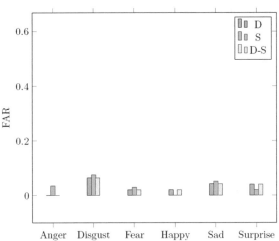

indicates the less promising recognition rate in fear. From this graph analysis, it
is also shown that the combined D-S signature yields a higher recognition rate in
sadness and surprise expressions.

The performance of the FAR for distance, shape, and D-S signatures using MLP on
the MMI dataset is shown in Fig. 5.10. The FAR graph analysis of distance signature
yields a poor recognition rate in disgust. The FAR graph analysis of shape signature
shows the less promising recognition rate in disgust. From this graph analysis, we
also observe that the combined D-S signature yields a promising recognition rate in
anger.

The comparison of the FRR for distance, shape, and D-S signatures using MLP on
the MMI dataset is shown in Fig. 5.11. The FRR graph analysis of distance signature
yields a poor recognition rate in surprise expression. The FRR graph analysis of

Fig. 5.11 FRR of MMI
using MLP

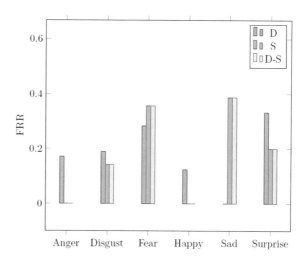

Fig. 5.12 ERR of MMI
using MLP

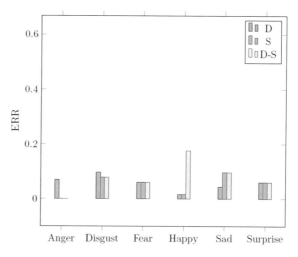

shape signature performs the poor recognition rate of expressions in disgust, sadness and surprise. It is also shown that the combined D-S signature indicates a poor performance in disgust, fear, sadness, and surprise expressions.

The comparison of the ERR for distance, shape, and D-S signatures using MLP on the MMI dataset is shown in Fig. 5.12. The ERR graph analysis of distance signature yields a poor recognition rate in anger. The ERR graph analysis of shape signature shows the less promising performance in disgust, fear, happiness, sadness, and surprise. From this graph analysis, it is also shown that the combined D-S signature performs a less promising recognition rate in happiness.

The performance of the FAR for distance, shape, and D-S signatures using MLP on the MUG dataset is shown in Fig. 5.13. The FAR graph analysis of distance signature

Fig. 5.13 FAR of MUG
using MLP

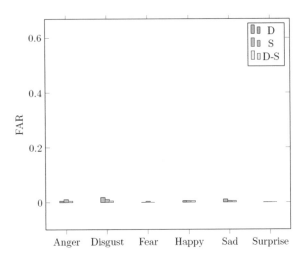

Fig. 5.13 FAR of MUG
using MLP

Fig. 5.14 FRR of MUG
using MLP

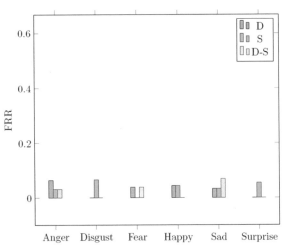

yields a poor recognition rate in disgust. The FAR graph analysis of shape signature shows the less promising recognition rate in disgust. From this graph analysis, we also observe that the combined D-S signature yields a promising recognition rate in surprise.

The comparison of the FRR for distance, shape, and D-S signatures using MLP on the MUG dataset is shown in Fig. 5.14. The FRR graph analysis of distance signature yields a poor recognition rate in anger. The FRR graph analysis of shape signature performs the poor recognition rate of expressions in disgust. It is also shown that the combined D-S signature indicates a less promising recognition rate in sadness.

The comparison of the ERR for distance, shape, and D-S signatures using MLP on the MUG dataset is shown in Fig. 5.15. The ERR graph analysis of distance signature

Fig. 5.15 ERR of MUG using MLP

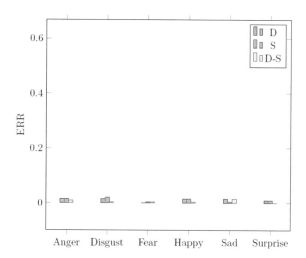

yields a poor recognition rate in anger. The ERR graph analysis of shape signature shows the less promising performance in disgust. From this graph analysis, it is also shown that the D-S signature yields a higher recognition rate in surprise.

5.4.7 Comparison with Different State of the Art

The proposed individual signature (distance and shape) and combined D-S signature are used to compare the results with the state of the art in the literature [7–11]. The comparison task will be difficult due to insufficient knowledge of data and explained mechanisms considered by other literature. We prove the validity of our proposed experiment on four benchmark CK+, JAFFE, MMI, and MUG datasets to show a comparison task with the other literature. Table 5.31 shows the summarization of the comparative results with the other literature. In the present scope, we achieve an overall classification accuracy of 100% emotion recognition for combined D-S signature on the CK+ dataset which is better than the average acquired result as mentioned in [8]. It is also observed that our proposed system achieves a higher classification rate of emotion recognition with respect to the other literature in [7–9]. Individual signature (distance or shape signature) also shows promising results of emotion recognition on the CK+ dataset.

JAFFE database is considered to measure the system performance of distance, shape, and D-S signatures with respect to other methods. The distance signature achieves a 94% average recognition rate with a less promising recognition rate for fear. Shape signature yields 94.9% as an average recognition rate with poor recognition rate for fear. In the same way, the combined D-S signature shows the average recognition rate as 96.4 with less promising recognition rate for fear. It is also shown that the combined D-S signature performs an overwhelming recognition rate com-

Table 5.31 Recognition rate of expressions on four benchmark databases of six basic expressions with different state-of-the-art methods

Signature	Dataset	Anger	Disgust	Fear	Happiness	Sadness	Surprise	Avg.
Distance	CK+	96.1	95.7	95.8	98.4	95.9	95.8	96.3
Shape	CK+	100	100	95.8	100	93.9	100	98.3
D-S	CK+	100	100	100	100	100	100	100
[8]	CK+	87.8	93.3	94.3	94.2	96.4	98.4	94.1
[11]	CK+	87.1	90.2	92	98.1	91.4	100	93.1
[9]	CK+	87	91.5	90.9	96.9	84.5	91.2	90.3
[7]	CK+	76.2	94.1	86.1	96.3	88.2	98.7	89.9
Distance	JAFFE	100	100	78.6	85.7	100	100	94
Shape	JAFFE	90.5	100	78.6	100	100	100	94.9
D-S	JAFFE	100	100	78.6	100	100	100	96.4
[8]	JAFFE	100	86.2	93.7	96.7	77.4	96.6	91.7
[11]	JAFFE	96.6	90	93.7	93.5	93.5	90	92.8
[9]	JAFFE	89.3	90.7	91.1	92.6	90.2	92.3	91.1
Distance	MMI	82.8	81	71.4	87.5	100	66.7	81.5
Shape	MMI	100	85.7	64.3	100	61.1	80	81.8
D-S	MMI	100	85.7	64.3	100	61.1	80	81.9
[9]	MMI	80.1	78.2	81.3	83.2	77.1	81	80.1
[7]	MMI	65.6	72.5	72.5	88.2	71.1	93.8	77.4
[10]	MMI	50.2	79.8	67.1	82.9	60.2	88.5	71.4
Distance	MUG	93.5	100	100	95.6	96.6	94.4	96.7
Shape	MUG	96.8	93.3	100	95.6	100	94.4	96.7
D-S	MUG	96.8	100	96.2	100	93.1	100	97.7

pared to the individual signature. Our proposed procedures achieve a higher recognition rate of emotions with respect to the other literature in [8, 9, 11]. Individual signature (distance or shape signature) indicates an overwhelming recognition rate of emotions on the JAFFE dataset.

MMI database is also evaluated to measure the system performance of distance, shape, and D-S signatures with respect to other methods. The distance signature achieves an 81.5% average recognition rate with less promising recognition rate for a surprise. Shape signature yields 81.8% as an average recognition rate with a poor recognition rate for sadness. In the same way, combined D-S signature shows the average recognition rate as 81.9 with less promising recognition rate for sadness. The merged D-S signature performs an overwhelming recognition rate compared to the individual signature. Our proposed approaches achieve a higher classification rate of emotion recognition than reported by others available in [7, 9, 10]. Individual signature (distance or shape signature) indicates an overwhelming recognition rate of emotions on the MMI dataset.

Fig. 5.16 Comparison of recognition rate of expression with other approach

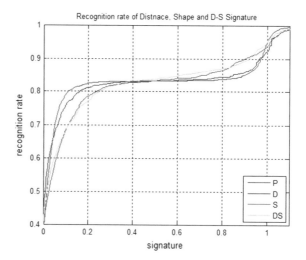

MUG database is also evaluated to measure the system performance of distance, shape, and D-S signatures with respect to other methods. The distance signature achieves a 96.7% average recognition rate with a less promising recognition rate for anger. Shape signature yields 96.7% as an average recognition rate with poor recognition rate for disgust. In the same way, the merged D-S signature shows the average recognition rate as 97.7 with less promising recognition rate for sadness. It is also observed that the combined D-S signature performs an overwhelming recognition rate compared to the individual signature. Individual signature (distance or shape signature) indicates an overwhelming recognition rate of emotions on the MUG dataset.

We consider Fig. 5.16 to present a comparison of performance recognition with other approaches. Hence we use for the sake of convenience some notations, viz. D for distance signature, S for shape signature, and D-S for a combination of distance and shape signature. We also consider patch-based facial expression recognition as P for another method [8]. From this plot, we show that merged signature (D-S) gets a promising classification rate. It is also noticed that individual distance (D) and shape (S) signatures perform better than the patch-based (P) facial expression recognition. Table 5.31 mentions the average classification of emotion recognition with the state-of-the-art methods. From this observation, we show that the merged D-S signature obtains an overwhelming classification rate of different emotions.

5.5 Sum-up Discussion

In this chapter we proposed an expression recognition system using various approaches, viz. distance signature, shape signature, and merged D-S signature. The successfulness of the proposed system is experimented by the recognition rate of expressions and estimates of the similarities with state-of-the-art literature. The evaluated results show the improved performances due to the incorporation of the combined D-S signature than the individual signature (distance and shape). Distance signature and shape signature-based facial expression recognition system improves the recognition of expressions than the other state-of-the-art methods. It is also notified that the D-S signature outperforms than the individual distance signature and shape signature. This also justifies that the coupling of two signatures ensures performance enhancement.

In the next chapter, we consider distance and texture signatures to form a distance-texture (D-T) signature to classify the expressions from human face images using different neural networks such as MLP, NARX, and RBF. We already introduce facial expression recognition using individual distance, shape, and texture signature features in Chaps. 2, 3 and 4. After introducing the individual feature, we consider a merged Distance-Texture (D-T) signature for recognizing expressions from benchmark datasets. The D-T signature is evaluated on benchmark datasets to measure the system performances. It is also considered to measure the comparison with respect to individual distance, shape, and texture signatures and also combined D-S signature feature.

References

1. G. Tzimiropoulos, M. Pantic, Optimization problems for fast AAM fitting in-the-wild, in *Proceedings of the IEEE International Conference on Computer Vision* (2013), pp. 593–600
2. A. Barman, P. Dutta, Facial expression recognition using distance and shape signature features. Pattern Recognit. Lett. (2017)
3. P. Lucey, J.F. Cohn, T. Kanade, J. Saragih, Z. Ambadar, I. Matthews, The extended Cohn-Kanade dataset (CK+): a complete dataset for action unit and emotion-specified expression, in *Computer Society Conference on Computer Vision and Pattern Recognition-Workshops* (IEEE, 2010), pp. 94–101
4. M.F. Valstar, M. Pantic, Induced disgust, happiness and surprise: an addition to the mmi facial expression database, in *Proceedings of International Conference on Language Resources and Evaluation, Workshop on EMOTION* Malta, May (2010), pp. 65–70
5. M. Lyons, S. Akamatsu, M. Kamachi, J. Gyoba, Coding facial expressions with Gabor wavelets, in *Proceedings of the Third IEEE International Conference on Automatic Face and Gesture Recognition* (IEEE, 1998), pp. 200–205
6. N. Aifanti, C. Papachristou, A. Delopoulos, The MUG facial expression database, in *Proceedings of the 11th International Workshop on Image Analysis for Facial Expression Database*, Desenzano, Italy, April (2010), pp. 12–14
7. L. Zhong, Q. Liu, P. Yang, J. Huang, D.N. Metaxas, Learning multiscale active facial patches for expression analysis. IEEE Trans. Cybern. **45**(8), 1499–1510 (2015)

8. SL Happy and Aurobinda Routray, Automatic facial expression recognition using features of salient facial patches. IEEE Trans. Affect. Comput. **6**(1), 1–12 (2015)
9. A. Poursaberi, H.A. Noubari, M. Gavrilova, S.N. Yanushkevich, Gauss–Laguerre wavelet textural feature fusion with geometrical information for facial expression identification. EURASIP J. Image Video Process. **2012**(1), 1–13 (2012)
10. L. Zhong, Q. Liu, P. Yang, B. Liu, J. Huang, D.N. Metaxas, Learning active facial patches for expression analysis, in *2012 IEEE Conference on Computer Vision and Pattern Recognition (CVPR)* (IEEE, 2012), pp. 2562–2569
11. Ligang Zhang, Dian Tjondronegoro, Facial expression recognition using facial movement features. IEEE Trans. Affect. Comput. **2**(4), 219–229 (2011)

Chapter 6
Distance-Texture Signature Duo for Determination of Human Emotion

6.1 Introduction

Previous Chaps. 2, 3 and 4 consist of three feature descriptors individually distance signature, shape signature and texture signature and Chap. 5 considered as combined descriptor such as distance and shape signature (D-S). In course of Distance-Texture (S-T) signature, respective stability indices and statistical measures supplement the signature features with a view to enhance the performance task of facial expression classification. Incorporation of these supplementary features is duly justified through extensive study and analysis of results obtained thereon.

While appreciating the usefulness of individual signature features in a marginal sense, the question coming up next is whether the join contribution of the signature descriptors discussed in the previous chapters is in a portion to offer even more impressive performance. Accordingly, in this chapter, we propose an individual signature (Distance and Texture signature) and merged D-T signature (Distance-Texture) based approach for emotion recognition. Effective landmark detection plays a vital role during facial expression recognition. Active Appearance Model (AAM) [1] is used to identify the landmark points from a face image. After identification of the landmarks, few of them are marked on the mouth, nose, eyes, and eyebrows regions. A grid and texture regions are formed with the help of marked landmarks. The euclidean finds the distances among all possible pair combinations of the grid. The Local Binary Pattern (LBP) [2, 3] is used to find the texture descriptor through the identified landmarks. Normalized distance and texture signatures are used to compute stability indices. The statistical measures (such as raw moment, range, entropy, skewness, and kurtosis) are computed from both normalized signatures to enhance the feature set. These prominent features are applied to recognize facial expressions. The experiments are evaluated on four benchmark datasets (such as CK+, JAFFE, MMI, and MUG) to measure the system performance.

© Springer Nature Singapore Pte Ltd. 2020
P. Dutta and A. Barman, *Human Emotion Recognition from Face Images*,
Cognitive Intelligence and Robotics,
https://doi.org/10.1007/978-981-15-3883-4_6

The contributions of this chapter are:

1. Grid formation: The appearance model is applied on a face image to identify the landmarks and few of them are used to extract the salient landmarks from the mouth, nose, eyes, and eyebrows. A grid is formed with the help of extracted landmarks.
2. Formation of Texture region: Texture regions are formed with the extracted landmarks from the mouth, nose, eyes, and eyebrows regions. These regions serve a crucial role to identify the expression.
3. Distance and Texture signature: A grid is considered to compute the distance signature and subsequently texture signature is also measured from the regions of texture. Extracted signatures are used individually and merged Distance-Texture (D-T) to detect the prominent features for expression identification.
4. Stability index: It is a discriminative feature for expression identification.
5. Statistical measures (i.e. moment, range, entropy, kurtosis, and skewness) are also computed from both individual and combined D-T signatures to supplement as an enhanced feature set for facial expression recognition.

Organization of this Chapter

This chapter is organized into six parts. In the beginning part, an introduction is elaborated on the individual signature of human emotion.

The second part of the chapter shows the overview of the proposed emotion recognition of distance, texture, and combined Distance-Texture (D-T) signature features. In this part, we also discuss landmark detection and grid formation. A texture region formation is also mentioned here and correspondingly local binary patterns are extracted. A stability index plays an important role for recognizing the expressions. Statistical measures such as range, moment, skewness, kurtosis, and entropy are considered to calculate the formidable feature set.

The third part of this chapter, consisting of Sect. 6.3. Feature selection and classification of emotions are explored here. Three separate networks such as Multilayer Perceptron (MLP), Nonlinear Auto Regressive with eXogenous input (NARX), and Radial Basis Function (RBF) are used to train and test the performances of emotions.

The next part, consisting of Sect. 6.4 which shows the result and evaluation on four benchmark datasets such as CK+, JAFFE, MMI, and MUG. The experimental results on individual datasets are shown here.

A separate discussion is available in Sect. 6.5 which explores the performances of each benchmark datasets.

The last chapter concludes with a conclusion in Sect. 6.6.

6.2 Proposed System of Emotion Recognition

The overview of the proposed system is indicated in Fig. 6.1. The appearance model [4] is very useful on a face image to detect the proper landmarks. The regions of the mouth, nose, eyes, and eyebrows, etc. are sensitive due to their variations of

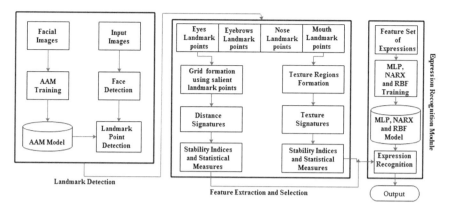

Fig. 6.1 Proposed block diagram of facial expression recognition

expressions. These salient landmarks are identified by four points on the mouth, three points on each eyebrow, three points on the nose, and four points on each eye as mentioned in Fig. 6.2. A grid is formed with 21 landmark points and Euclidean distances are measured among the pairwise of landmark points grid and also identify the texture region. It is mentioned that the order of the relative distances plays a significant role at the time of forming distance signature. The normalized distance and texture signatures are used to enhance the feature set of facial expression recognition. The stability indices are computed from the considerable order of signatures (distance and texture). Statistical parameters, i.e. moment, range, entropy, skewness, and kurtosis are also computed from both signatures to enhance the feature set for facial expression. These features fed as input to three different neural networks to classify expressions such as disgust, sadness anger, surprise, fear, and happiness.

6.2.1   Facial Grid Formation Using Detected Landmark

The landmark identification approaches are available in [5, 6] during different facial expressions. Most of the landmarks hold common properties for various expressions and few of them play a crucial role in differentiating the various expressions of the same person. The facial landmark detection is achieved by AAM which is available in Chap. 2 of Sect. 2.2.1. In the same way, grid formation discussion is also elaborated in Chap. 2 of Sect. 2.2.2. The landmark detection framework and grid formation in CK+ is shown in Fig. 6.2 for easy understanding. In the same away, the corresponding JAFFE database is also considered to show the landmark detection and grid formation in Fig. 6.3.

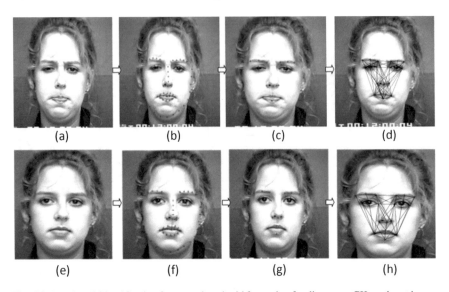

Fig. 6.2 Landmark identification framework and grid formation for disgust on CK+: **a** input image, **b** AAM model, **c** detected landmarks and **d** grid formation, and landmark identification framework and grid for sadness on CK+: **e** input image, **f** AAM model, **g** detected landmarks and **h** grid formation

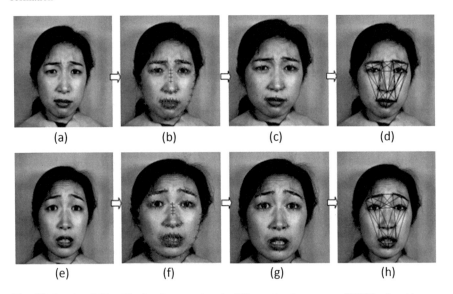

Fig. 6.3 Landmark identification framework and grid formation for anger on JAFFE: **a** input image, **b** AAM model, **c** detected landmarks and **d** grid formation, and landmark identification framework and grid formation for surprise on JAFFE: **e** input image, **f** AAM model, **g** detected landmarks and **h** grid formation

Fig. 6.4 Detected regions of facial patches

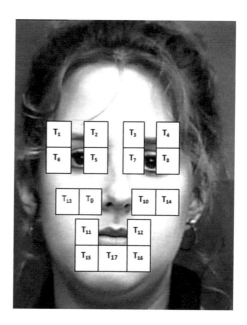

6.2.2 Texture Region

The idea of the active patches of facial images is available in [7]. For example, the corner points of the eye have a decisive role to distinguish the different expressions from one expression to another. If we consider the sadness and surprising emotions, wrinkles of the nose are sufficient to separate the expressed emotions. During the variation of expressions, active regions are extracted from a face image. The active patches of expressed images are identified at mouth corner regions, eye corner, and nose corner due to their variation of emotions and also discussed in the fourth chapter of Sect. 4.2.2. After combining the active facial patches, the LBP is used to extract the texture region from a face image. The detailed discussion of LBP is available in the fourth chapter of Sect. 4.2.3. Here we show a Fig. 6.4 that extract the facial patches from a face image.

6.2.3 Feature Extraction

The individual distance and texture signature play an important role in recognizing the facial expression from four benchmark datasets. Now we combine this individual signature to form a duo signature as Distance-Texture (D-T) [8] to recognize the expressions and also measure the performances of D-T signature. The individual distance and texture signatures are explained in the second and fourth chapters. The normalized distance signature is computed using Eq. 2.3. In the same way, normalized texture signature computed using Eq. 4.3.

6.2.4   Stability Index from Distance Signature and Texture Signature

Another formidable feature is extracted from the justified order signature (distance signature and texture signature) called the stability index. Higher order signatures are considered to compute the stability indices for each face image. The individual stability index plays a crucial role in recognizing expressions. Now we combine both stability indices of distance and texture signature to measure the system accuracy. The definition of the stability indices for individual signature is elaborated in the second and fourth chapters. These discussions are also available in Sects. 2.5 and 4.3.1. The determination of stability index consists of the following events:

1. Normalized distance and texture signatures are computed among the grid of face images.
2. The distance and texture are used to compute the order signatures.
3. A threshold is chosen upon the examination of the differences in justified order factors of individual signature.
4. The higher order attaining below the preset threshold for the first time is mentioned as a stability index of that particular face image.

6.2.5   Statistical Measures from Distance and Texture Signature

We consider a huge number of features for increasing the effectiveness of the emotion recognition system. In this regard statistical approaches such as range, kurtosis, moments, entropy, and skewness are measured from both normalized distance and texture signatures. The detailed discussion of the statistical measures is available in the second chapter of Sect. 2.3.3. These statistical measures play an indispensable role to identify the expression for both individual signatures. The statistical measures are joined from both individual and combined signature to form a combined feature set for recognizing the expressions.

6.3   Feature Selection and Classification

The features set are captured from both individual signature and merged D-T signature for facial expression recognition using Eqs. 2.3 and 4.3. The performance of the proposed system is evaluated on four datasets, i.e. CK+, MMI, MUG, and JAFFE. The recognition rate of the proposed system is shown in Table 6.1.
Why we don't consider the only distance signature and texture signature:

1. The distance and texture signatures result are shown in Table 6.1.

Table 6.1 Recognition rate on CK+ dataset using only distance signature and texture signature

Signature	Anger	Disgust	Fear	Happiness	Sadness	Surprise	Average
Only distance using MLP	84.7	87.0	72.1	100	100	87.0	88.4
Only distance using NARX	97.2	98.1	90.7	100	94.4	94.0	95.7
Only distance using RBF	98.6	94.4	93.0	96.4	90.1	94.2	94.4
Only texture using MLP	79.2	88.9	72.1	92.9	90.1	88.4	85.3
Only texture using NARX	94.4	90.7	88.4	96.4	93.0	94.1	92.8
Only texture using RBF	95.8	87.0	79.1	96.4	91.5	95.7	90.9

2. From this table, we observe that the only distance and texture signatures yield a poor recognition rate.
3. Enhanced individual distance signature and texture signature yield promising recognition rate of expressions.

Only distance signature and relevant distance signature and subsequently only texture signature and relevant texture signature are used for the comparison of the recognition rate of the proposed system. The experiment is evaluated only on the CK+ dataset for distance signature and texture signature. A comparison is performed between two Tables 6.1 and 6.11. From this observation, we indicate that the enhanced distance signature and texture signature are performed superior to the only distance signature and texture signature. This is the main reason for considering enhanced distance signature and texture signature such as kurtosis, entropy, moment, range, and skewness to obtain a discriminative feature set. The stability index is an indispensable feature to show the variation of different expressions obtained as per Eqs. 2.5 and 4.4. Statistical parameters such as moment, entropy, range, skewness, and kurtosis are supplemented to feature set for enhancing the accuracy of the facial expressions recognition. Each extracted feature is merged together to form a relevant distance signature and texture signature for classifying the emotions. The merged Distance-Texture (D-T) signature is also used for classifying the emotions after considering individual signature. The dimension of each signature is a 9-dimensional vector. Feature extraction approaches for the relevant distance signature and texture signature are indicated in Algorithm 6.1 and 6.2. The combined D-T signature consists of 18 elements of vector space. The proposed training procedure is indicated in Algorithm 6.3 for classifying the emotions.

Algorithm 6.1 : *Distance Feature Extraction*(D)

1: **begin**
2:     Identify the landmark points l_i using AAM [4].
3:     The nose, eyes, mouth and eyebrows regions are used to extract salient landmark points
       $l_i (i = 1, 2, \ldots, 21)$.
4:     These salient landmark points l_i are linked with each other to form a grid.
5:     Distances ($d_i where\ i = 1, 2, \ldots, n$) are calculated from the grid.
6:     Normalize the distances using Eq. 2.4 to obtain distance signature (β_i).
7:     Find stability index ($\beta_i^r)^f$ from distance signature using Eq. 2.5 and corresponding differences
       of higher order signatures are calculated using Eq. 2.6.
8:     Calculate range, moment [$l_{k1}(where\ k = 1, 2, 3, 4)$], skewness ($u$) and kurtosis ($q$) using
       Eqs. 2.7, 2.8 and 2.9.
9:     Also calculate entropy (En) from distance signature using Eq. 2.10.
10:     $D \leftarrow [range, (\beta_i^r), l_k, u, q, En]$.
11:     Return D.
12: **end**

Algorithm 6.2 : *Texture Feature Extraction*(B)

1: **begin**
2:     Detect the landmark points l_i using AAM [4].
3:     Consider the eyes, nose, mouth and eyebrows regions to extract salient landmark points
       $l_i (i = 1, 2, \ldots, 21)$.
4:     These salient landmark points l_i help to find texture regions T_i ($i = 1, 2, \ldots, 17$) and combine
       all regions to get texture feature using Eqs. 4.1 and 4.2.
5:     Normalize the texture feature using Eq. 4.3 to form texture signature η_i.
6:     Find stability index (ζ_i^r) from texture signature using Eq. 4.4 and corresponding differences
       of higher order signatures are calculated using Eq. 4.5.
7:     Calculate range, moment [$l_k(where\ k = 1, 2, 3, 4)$], skewness ($u$) and kurtosis ($q$) using Eqs.
       2.7, 2.8 and 2.9.
8:     Also calculate entropy (En) from distance signature using Eq. 2.10.
9:     $T \leftarrow [range, (\zeta_i^r), l_k, u, q, En]$.
10:     Return T.
11: **end**

Algorithm 6.3 : *Training Algorithm Facial Expression Recognition*($Images$)

1: **begin**
2:     Assign L = number of images
3:     **for** $i = 1\ to\ L$ **do**
4:         obtain i^{th} distance or texture signatures.
5:     **end for**
6:     Assign expression label of ith images to y_i.
7:     Use all training features X and expression labels Y to train networks MLP, NARX and RBF.
8: **end**

6.3.1   Training Procedure of Multilayer Perceptron

The dimension of the relevant distance and texture signatures is indicated by 9 elements of each vector. In the same way, the dimension of the combined D-T signature is represented by 18 elements of each vector. A Min-Max process is used to normalize both signatures. After normalizing individual signature (distance and texture) and merged D-T signatures are fed as the input of MLP for classifying the emotions. The training is stopped when a Mean Square Error (MSE) [9] $e_k = 1/2 \sum (t_k - y_k)^2$ is minimum for different emotions. Here y_k and t_k indicate the desired response and target where the range of k is 6 for the MLP. There are four steps in training: weights initialization, Feedforward, Backpropagation, and modification of the biases and weights. During the initialization of the weights, small values are assigned. We consider the x_i ($i = 1, \ldots, n$) as input unit, here n is the input number of information and sends this information to each hidden node z_j ($j = 1, 2, \ldots, 8$). The wights and biases are represented by v_o and w_o. The output of each hidden unit is calculated by an activation function tanh. After computing, the output of hidden unit z_j sends to every output unit. The last layer computes the output using linear activation. At the moment of backpropagation of errors, each output node computes the associated error as the difference of the desired y_k with the target value t_k. This error is used to calculate the factor δ_k ($k = 1, \ldots, m$) at the output y_k. It sends back to all the previous layer units. Here, m represents the output units ($m = 6$). Similarly, δ_j ($j = 1, \ldots, p$) is computed for every hidden unit z_j, the number of hidden units is $p = 8$. The biases and weights are modified by $the\delta$ factor in the last step. The notations ζ and η are considered as threshold and learning rate. The training will be stopped when it satisfies the condition $e_k \leq \zeta$. During the testing, Six emotions are assigned a maximum value based on the output of each expression.

6.3.2   Radial Basis Function Training Mechanism

The radial basis function (RBF) network [10] has three layers such as input, hidden, and output. The total numbers of input and output neurons are assigned by n and m. The hypothetical connection is formed between the input and hidden units. The weighted connection is formed at output layers. A Gaussian function is used as activation to compute the output for important characteristics. The RBF network converges first of the training over the other such as forward and backward network. The distance signature and texture signature are computed from the training set after labeling each expression. For a test image, first features are extracted from the testing set and then these features are applied on a trained network to measure the accuracy of the expression recognition.

   The explanation of the training procedure of RBF in mentioned here. In the first step, small random values are assigned to the initial node. Each input unit x_i ($i = 1, \ldots, n$) transmits the information to each hidden unit, here n represents the input feature number. Now every node calculates the radial basis function. The input feature is selected to find centers. A radial basis function is used to transform the input feature in hidden layer: $v_i(x_i) = \exp(-\frac{1}{2\sigma_i^2}||x_{ji} - X_{ji}||^2)$. Here $||.||$ represents a input norm mentioned as usually Euclidean distance, X_{ji} represents the input variables center of the RBF unit, σ_i indicates the width of ith input and x_{ji} represents input pattern of the jth variable. The output layer weights are assigned to small random values. The network produces the output as

$$y_{ne} = \sum_{i=1}^{h} w_{im} v_i(x_i + w_o) \qquad (6.1)$$

where hidden layer are represented by h, y_{ne} indicates the output of mth node at output layer for the nth coming pattern, w_{im} represents the weight between ith RBF unit and mth output node and w_o represents the bias at nth output node. The training will be stooped when the error is below the threshold ζ.

6.3.3   Training Using Nonlinear Auto Regressive with eXogenous Input

The NARX recurrent [11] network is a type of nonlinear dynamical network architecture. The nonlinear dynamical systems are a type of input-output modeling. It is also appropriate for continuous and discrete inputs [12]. The recurrent network activates the model to keep information about past inputs and it also finds the temporal correlations between events that are possibly far away from each other in the data [13]. The recurrent network also faces a vanishing gradients problem [13] at the time of learning. In this training, such kind of problem is neglected. The network feeds as input depending on the window of past input and output values and calculates the running output. It is also defined as

$$\mathbf{y}(t) = f(u(t - Du), \ldots, u(t - 1), u(t), y(t - Dy), \ldots, y(t - 1)) \qquad (6.2)$$

where the notations $u(t)$ and $y(t)$ represent inputs and outputs of the network at time t. Du and Dy indicates the time lags of the input and output and f represents a nonlinear function. This function is estimated by backpropagation through time (BPTT) [11]. The idea of the BPTT is available in the article [11]. The BPTT has three labels such as input, hidden, and output. It also has recurrent links from the output unit to the hidden unit. The hidden unit calculates the output using a nonlinear or linear function. The hidden unit $\mathbf{h}(t)$ and output unit $\mathbf{y}(t)$ are derived at time t as

$$\mathbf{h}(t) = \phi(\mathbf{w_{hx}}x(t)) + b_h \text{ and } \mathbf{y}(t) = \gamma(\mathbf{w_{yh}}h(t)) + b_y \qquad (6.3)$$

where $\mathbf{w_{hx}}$ and $\mathbf{w_{yh}}$ represent weight matrices of the input-to-hidden and hidden-to-output respectively, b_h and b_y indicate biases and ϕ and γ represent the hyperbolic tangent activation functions in hidden unit. A linear activation function is used in the output unit. The hyperbolic tangent is used at the output activation to scale the output between -1 and 1 prior to feeding it into the model as delayed output. The NARX recurrent training network tries to optimize the weight values by minimizing an objective function.

6.3.4 Convolutional Neural Network Training

The training mechanism of a convolutional neural network (CNN) is mentioned here. The network takes the input size as 6×6 feature and computes the outputs at each unit of emotion. The CNN diagram consists of 2 convolutional layers, 2 pooling layers, and 1 fully connected layer. The first label is called the convolution layer, which uses a kernel size of 3×3 and produces outputs of an expressed image size of 4×4. It is maintained by a max-pooling layer with a kernel size of 2×2. The kernel is used to downsize the image size to half. In a similar way, again a convolution layer is used for the feature and is maintained by another max-pooling for downsizing. The output is passed through a fully connected layer that has 12 neurons. The functionality of the fully connected layer is the same as MLP. This type of neural network has assigned to six output nodes. The output nodes are fully linked to the previous layer.

6.4 Result and Evaluation

The suggested methodology is experimented on four benchmark datasets such as CK+ [14], MMI [15], JAFFE [16], and MUG [17] to measure the system performance of emotion recognition. The individual signature such as distance and texture and combined Distance-Texture signature are fed as the input of MLP, RBF, NARX, and CNN for recognition of facial expressions.

6.4.1 Evaluated Result on the CK+ Dataset

The CK+ [14] dataset has six basic expressions of both male and female images. The basic expressions are mentioned as fear, anger, disgust, surprise, happiness, and sadness. We compute the output with respect to the target of a network at the time of training. At the same time, weights and biases are modified for better approximation of results. We choose 713 images of CK+ dataset for training and 393 images for testing. Three different networks (MLP, RBF, and NARX) use 8 hidden units during training. The accuracy of expression recognition is validated at the time of testing.

The desired output compares with the target of a particular node using MSE. Each network identifies the emotions into six categories. These expressions are mentioned as fear (43), anger (72), sadness (71), disgust (54), surprise (67), and Happiness (84) at the time of performance testing of expressions. This dataset is also called a person independent where each test expressions are not available in the training dataset.

The Expression Recognition of Distance Signature Using MLP

The expression recognition of distance signature using MLP is shown in Table 6.2. Anger classifies 71 images accurately and 1 image is confused with surprise. Disgust recognizes 54 images correctly. Fear identifies 42 images rightly and 1 image is in misclassification with surprise. Happiness recognizes 80 images absolutely and 4 images are in a mismatch with disgust and fear. Sadness indicates 65 images accurately and 6 images are in misclassification with disgust, fear, and happiness. Surprise recognizes 64 images accurately and 5 images are misclassified with disgust and fear.

The Expression Recognition of Distance Signature Using NARX

The classification of distance signature using NARX is shown in Table 6.3. Anger identifies 71 images accurately and 1 image is misidentified with disgust. Disgust classifies 53 images correctly and 1 image is confused with fear. Fear recognizes 42 images properly and 1 image is misidentified with happiness. Happiness identifies 83 images accurately and 1 image is confused as sadness. Sadness identifies 69 images perfectly and 2 images are misidentified with surprise. Surprise classifies 69 images accurately.

Table 6.2 The expression recognition of distance signature using MLP on CK+

	Anger	Disgust	Fear	Happiness	Sadness	Surprise
Anger	71	0	0	0	0	1
Disgust	0	54	0	0	0	0
Fear	0	0	42	0	0	1
Happiness	0	2	2	80	0	0
Sadness	0	2	3	1	65	0
Surprise	0	1	4	0	0	64

Table 6.3 The expression recognition of distance signature on CK+ database using NARX

	Anger	Disgust	Fear	Happiness	Sadness	Surprise
Anger	71	1	0	0	0	0
Disgust	0	53	1	0	0	0
Fear	0	0	42	1	0	0
Happiness	0	0	0	83	1	0
Sadness	0	0	0	0	69	2
Surprise	0	0	0	0	0	69

Table 6.4   The confusion matrix of distance signature on CK+ database using RBF

	Anger	Disgust	Fear	Happiness	Sadness	Surprise
Anger	72	0	0	0	0	0
Disgust	0	53	1	0	0	0
Fear	0	0	43	0	0	0
Happiness	0	0	0	84	0	0
Sadness	0	0	4	0	67	0
Surprise	0	0	0	0	0	69

Table 6.5   The expression recognition of texture signature using MLP on CK+

	Anger	Disgust	Fear	Happiness	Sadness	Surprise
Anger	64	0	2	3	1	2
Disgust	1	52	1	0	0	0
Fear	2	0	35	1	2	3
Happiness	6	0	4	72	0	2
Sadness	0	1	0	0	69	1
Surprise	1	0	3	2	1	62

The Expression Recognition of Distance Signature Using RBF

The classification of distance signature using RBF is indicated in Table 6.4. Anger recognizes 72 images accurately. Disgust classifies 53 images rightly and 1 image is confused as fear. Fear recognizes 43 images accurately. Happiness classifies 84 images accurately. Sadness identifies 67 images rightly and 4 images are in a mismatch as fear. Surprise recognizes 69 images accurately.

The Expression Recognition of Texture Signature Using MLP

The Table 6.5 shows the expression recognition of texture signature using MLP. Anger recognizes 64 images rightly and 8 images are misidentified as fear, happiness, sadness, and surprise. Disgust identifies 52 images accurately and 2 images are misidentified as anger and fear. Fear recognizes 35 images perfectly and 8 images are confused as anger, happiness, surprise, and sadness. Happiness identifies 72 images perfectly and 12 images are misclassified as anger, disgust, and fear. Sadness indicates 69 images properly and 2 images are mismatched as disgust and surprise. Surprise detects 62 images rightly and 7 images are in a mismatch with anger, happiness, sadness, and fear.

The Expression Recognition of Texture Signature Using NARX

The recognition of texture signature using NARX is shown in Table 6.6. Anger identifies 71 images accurately and 1 image is mismatched as disgust. Disgust recognizes 53 images perfectly and 1 image is confused as fear. Fear recognizes 42 images accurately and 1 image is misidentified with happiness. Happiness identifies 83 images

Table 6.6 The expression recognition of texture signature using NARX on CK+

	Anger	Disgust	Fear	Happiness	Sadness	Surprise
Anger	71	1	0	0	0	0
Disgust	0	53	1	0	0	0
Fear	0	0	42	1	0	0
Happiness	0	0	0	83	1	0
Sadness	0	0	0	0	70	1
Surprise	0	0	0	0	0	69

Table 6.7 The expression recognition of texture signature using RBF on CK+

	Anger	Disgust	Fear	Happiness	Sadness	Surprise
Anger	72	0	0	0	0	0
Disgsut	0	53	1	0	0	0
Fear	0	0	43	0	0	0
Happiness	0	0	0	84	0	0
Sadness	0	0	4	0	67	0
Surprise	0	0	0	0	0	69

accurately and 1 image is mismatched as sadness. Sadness identifies 70 images accurately and 2 images are misidentified with surprise. Surprise recognizes 69 images accurately.

The Expression Recognition of Texture Signature Using RBF

The RBF-based recognition of texture signature is shown in Table 6.7. Anger recognizes 72 images accurately. Disgust classifies 53 images properly and 1 image is confused with fear. Fear recognizes 43 images accurately. Happiness classifies 84 images accurately. Sadness identifies 67 images rightly and 4 images are mismatched with fear. Surprise identifies 69 images accurately.

The Expression Recognition of D-T Signature Using MLP

The Table 6.8 shows the classification of D-T signature using MLP. Anger classifies 71 images correctly and 1 image is confused with disgust. Disgust identifies 54 images accurately. Fear recognizes 42 images properly and 1 image is misclassified with disgust. Happiness identifies 79 images perfectly and 5 images are mismatched as anger, disgust, and fear. Sadness indicates 70 images properly and 1 image is confused with disgust. Surprise recognizes 68 images perfectly and 1 image in a mismatch with anger.

The Expression Recognition of D-T Signature Using NARX

The expression recognition of D-T signature using NARX is shown in Table 6.9. Anger recognizes 72 images accurately. Disgust classifies 52 images accurately and

Table 6.8   The expression recognition of D-T signature on CK+ database using MLP

	Anger	Disgust	Fear	Happiness	Sadness	Surprise
Anger	71	1	0	0	0	0
Disgust	0	54	0	0	0	0
Fear	0	1	42	0	0	0
Happiness	3	1	1	79	0	0
Sadness	0	1	0	0	70	0
Surprise	1	0	0	0	0	68

Table 6.9   The expression recognition of D-T signature using NARX on CK+

	Anger	Disgust	Fear	Happiness	Sadness	Surprise
Anger	72	0	0	0	0	0
Disgust	0	52	2	0	0	0
Fear	0	0	42	1	0	0
Happiness	0	0	0	84	0	0
Sadness	0	0	0	0	70	1
Surprise	0	0	0	0	0	69

Table 6.10   The expression recognition of D-T signature on CK+ database using RBF

	Anger	Disgust	Fear	Happiness	Sadness	Surprise
Anger	72	0	0	0	0	0
Disgust	0	54	0	0	0	0
Fear	0	0	43	0	0	0
Happiness	0	0	0	84	0	0
Sadness	0	0	5	0	66	0
Surprise	0	0	1	0	0	68

2 images are mismatched as fear. Fear indicates 42 images correctly and 1 image is misidentified with happiness. Happiness detects 84 images accurately. Sadness identifies 70 images accurately and 1 image is misidentified with surprise. Surprise identifies 69 images accurately.

The Expression Recognition of D-T Signature Using RBF

The expression recognition of D-T signature using RBF is mentioned in Table 6.10. Anger identifies 72 images accurately. Disgust classifies 54 images correctly. Fear recognizes 43 images accurately. Happiness recognizes 84 images accurately. Sadness classifies 66 images correctly and 5 images are mismatched as fear. Surprise classifies 68 images accurately and 1 image is confused with fear.

Recognition Rate on CK+ of Distance, Texture, and D-T Signatures Using MLP, NARX, and RBF

Three different MLP, RBF, and NARX networks are used on distance signature to show the facial expression recognition in Table 6.11. The distance signature using MLP acquires an overall recognition accuracy of 95.9% with the highest recognition rate of 100% for disgust and lowest recognition rate of 91.5% for sadness. At the time of training, it takes 360 iterations with 15 s to minimize the MSE. NARX recognizes 71 emotions perfectly as anger and 1 emotion is mismatched with disgust. The texture signature using NARX gets an overall recognition rate of 98.4% with the highest recognition rate of 100% for surprise and the lowest recognition rate of 97.2% for sadness. It takes 371 iterations with 12 s to minimize the MSE. RBF identifies 72 images for anger. The distance signature using RBF gets an overall recognition rate of 98.7% with the highest detection rate of 100% accuracy for anger, fear, happiness, and surprise, and lowest recognition rate of 94.4% for sadness. It takes 375 iterations with 18 s to minimize the MSE. The MLP, RBF, and NARX have produced the average classification accuracies of 95.9%, 98.4, and 98.7% for distance signature. From these statements, it is noticed that the RBF-based distance signature produced better results compare to the other two networks.

The performance of the texture signature on the CK+ dataset using MLP, RBF, and NARX networks is shown in Table 6.11. Average recognition rate of texture signature is mentioned in Table 6.70. The overall recognition rate of 89.9% was achieved using MLP with the highest recognition rate of 96.3% for disgust and the

Table 6.11 Recognition rate on CK+ with different state-of-the-art methods

	Anger	Disgust	Fear	Happiness	Sadness	Surprise	Avg.
Distance signature on MLP	98.6	100	97.3	95.2	91.5	92.8	95.9
Distance signature on NARX	98.6	98.1	97.7	98.8	97.2	100	98.4
Distance signature on RBF	100	98.1	100	100	94.4	100	98.7
Texture signature on MLP	88.9	96.3	81.4	85.7	97.2	89.9	89.9
Texture signature on NARX	98.6	98.1	97.7	98.8	98.6	100	98.6
Texture signature on RBF	98.6	90.7	83.7	100	95.8	100	94.8
D-T signature on MLP	98.6	100	97.7	94	98.6	98.6	97.9
D-T signature on NARX	98.6	96.3	97.7	98.8	98.6	100	98.3
D-T signature on RBF	100	100	100	100	93	98.6	98.6
[18]	87.8	93.3	94.3	94.2	96.4	98.4	94.1
[19]	87.1	90.2	92	98.1	91.4	100	93.1
[20]	87	91.5	90.9	96.9	84.5	91.2	90.3
[7]	71.3	95.3	81.1	95.4	88.2	98.2	88.2

lowest recognition rate of 81.4% for fear. The texture signature runs 345 iterations with 14 s to minimize the MSE. The overall recognition rate of 98.8% is got using NARX with the highest recognition rate of 100% for surprise and the lowest accuracy of 97.7% for fear. The texture signature using NARX runs 360 iterations with 16 s to minimize the MSE. In this way, RBF has obtained an overall recognition rate of 94.8% with the highest recognition rate of 100% for happiness and surprise and the lowest recognition rate of 83.7% for fear. The texture signature using RBF runs 365 iterations with 17 s to converge to the MSE. From these considerations, it is noticed that the texture signature using NARX achieved a promising recognition rate of emotions.

The recognition rate of D-T signature is available in Table 6.11 using MLP, RBF, and NARX networks. The overall recognition rate of 97.9% is obtained using MLP with the highest recognition rate of 100% for disgust and the lowest recognition rate of 94% for happiness. The overall recognition rate of 98.3% is obtained using NARX with the highest recognition rate of 100% for surprise and the lowest recognition rate of 96.3% for disgust. The RBF has got an average recognition rate of 98.6% with the highest recognition rate of 100% for anger, fear, disgust, and happiness and the lowest recognition rate of 93% for sadness. From these results, it is noticed that D-T signature using RBF achieved promising classification rate of emotions. The MLP, NARX, and RBF networks take 22, 21, and 23 s, respectively, to minimize the MSE with 410, 407, and 445 iterations.

Recall and F-measure on CK+ Database of Distance, Texture, and D-T Signatures Using MLP, NARX, and RBF

True positive and true negatives are the observations that are correctly predicted. We want to minimize false positives and false negatives. These terms are a bit confusing. So lets take each term one by one and understand it fully.

True Positives (TP): These are the correctly predicted positive values which mean that the value of actual class is yes and the value of predicted class is also yes. Example, if an actual class value indicates that this passenger survived and predicted class tells you the same thing.

True Negatives (TN): These are the correctly predicted negative values which mean that the value of the actual class is no and value of the predicted class is also no. Example, if actual class says this passenger did not survive and predicted class tells you the same thing.

False positives and false negatives: These values occur when your actual class contradicts with the predicted class.

False Positives (FP): When actual class is no and the predicted class is yes. Example, if actual class says this passenger did not survive but predicted class tells you that this passenger will survive.

False Negatives (FN): When actual class is yes but predicted class in no. Example, if actual class value indicates that this passenger survived and predicted class tells you that passenger will die.

Recall (Sensitivity):

Recall is the ratio of correctly predicted positive observations to all observations in actual class—yes. Recall = TP/TP+FN

F-measure:

F-measure is the weighted average of Precision and Recall. Therefore, this score takes both false positives and false negatives into account. Intuitively it is not as easy to understand as accuracy, but F1 is usually more useful than accuracy, especially if you have an uneven class distribution. Accuracy works best if false positives and false negatives have a similar cost. If the cost of false positives and false negatives are very different, it's better to look at both Precision and Recall.

F-measure $= 2 * (\text{Recall} * \text{Precision})/(\text{Recall} + \text{Precision})$

Table 6.12 shows the recall and F-measure of distance signature of MLP, RBF, and NARX networks. The performance of recall and f-measure is shown in Table 6.13 of texture signature. In the same way, the corresponding recall and f-measure of

Table 6.12 The performance measure of distance signature on CK+ dataset using recall and F-measure

| | Distance | | | | | |
| | MLP | | NARX | | RBF | |
	Recall	F-measure	Recall	F-measure	Recall	F-measure
Anger	0.98	0.99	0.98	0.99	1	1
Disgust	1	0.95	0.98	0.98	0.98	0.99
Fear	0.97	0.89	0.97	0.97	1	0.94
Happiness	0.95	0.96	0.98	0.98	1	1
Sadness	0.91	0.95	0.97	0.97	0.94	0.97
Surprise	0.92	0.94	1	0.98	1	1

Table 6.13 The performance measure of texture signature on CK+ dataset using recall and F-measure

| | Texture | | | | | |
| | MLP | | NARX | | RBF | |
	Recall	F-measure	Recall	F-measure	Recall	F-measure
Anger	0.88	0.87	0.98	0.99	0.98	0.98
Disgust	0.96	0.97	0.98	0.98	0.90	0.95
Fear	0.81	0.79	0.97	0.97	0.83	0.91
Happiness	0.85	0.88	0.98	0.98	1	0.96
Sadness	0.97	0.95	0.98	0.98	0.95	0.96
Surprise	0.89	0.89	1	0.99	1	0.95

D-T signature are indicated in Table 6.14. From these Tables, we observe that the combined D-T signatures yield promising recall and f-measure than the individual signature.

6.4.1.1   Result Evaluation of CNN on CK+ Dataset

A CNN has been evaluated on distance, texture, and D-T signatures to test the performance of expression recognition. The recognition rate of distance signature is mentioned in Table 6.15. Anger identifies 58 images rightly and 14 images are in a mismatch with disgust and surprise. The disgust recognizes 39 images properly and 15 images are misclassified with anger, sadness, and surprise. Fear identifies 38 images accurately and 5 images are mismatched with anger, happiness, and sadness. Happiness indicates 78 images properly and 6 images are misidentified with anger, disgust and surprise. Sadness recognizes 51 images properly and 20 images are in misclassification with anger, happiness, disgust, and surprise. Surprise identifies 57 images perfectly and 12 images are in a mismatch with anger, fear, and sadness.

The recognition matrix of texture signature is shown in Table 6.16. Anger recognizes 48 images correctly and large number of images are in a mismatch with disgust, happiness, sadness, and surprise. Disgust recognizes 42 images properly and 12 images are misidentified with all expressions except disgust. Fear identifies 15

Table 6.14   The performance measure of D-T signature on CK+ dataset using recall and F-measure

| | D-T | | | | | |
| | MLP | | NARX | | RBF | |
	Recall	F-measure	Recall	F-measure	Recall	F-measure
Anger	0.98	0.96	0.98	0.99	1	1
Disgust	1	0.96	0.96	0.97	1	1
Fear	0.97	0.97	0.97	0.96	1	0.93
Happiness	0.94	96	0.98	0.98	1	1
Sadness	0.98	0.99	0.98	0.98	0.92	0.96
Surprise	0.98	0.99	1	0.99	0.98	0.99

Table 6.15   The recognition rate of distance signature on CK+ database using CNN

	Anger	Disgust	Fear	Happiness	Sadness	Surprise
Anger	58	9	0	0	0	5
Disgust	2	39	0	10	1	2
Fear	2	0	38	1	2	0
Happiness	3	2	0	78	0	1
Sadness	2	0	5	2	51	11
Surprise	4	0	1	0	7	57

Table 6.16 The recognition rate of texture signature on CK+ database using CNN

	Anger	Disgust	Fear	Happiness	Sadness	Surprise
Anger	48	8	0	5	4	7
Disgust	3	42	1	4	3	1
Fear	6	5	11	15	3	3
Happiness	10	4	3	63	0	4
Sadness	7	7	2	4	39	12
Surprise	8	5	5	1	1	49

Table 6.17 The recognition rate of D-T signature on CK+ database using CNN

	Anger	Disgust	Fear	Happiness	Sadness	Surprise
Anger	66	1	0	0	3	2
Disgust	0	48	1	3	1	1
Fear	0	0	38	4	1	0
Happiness	0	1	5	77	0	1
Sadness	1	1	3	2	62	2
Surprise	1	0	0	0	3	65

Table 6.18 Testing performance on CK+ dataset with CNN

	Anger	Disgust	Fear	Happiness	Sadness	Surprise	Avg.
Distance signature	80.6	72.2	88.4	92.9	71.8	82.6	81.7
Texture signature	66.7	77.8	25.6	75	54.9	71	64.1
D-T signature	91.7	88.9	88.4	91.7	87.3	94.2	90.6

images accurately and 27 images are misclassified with remaining expressions. Happiness identifies 63 images correctly and 21 images are confused with all expressions except sadness. Sadness recognizes 39 images properly and 32 images are misclassified with remaining expressions. Surprise identifies 49 images correctly and large number of images are in misclassification with different expressions.

The recognition rate of texture signature is shown in Table 6.17. Anger recognizes 66 images properly and 6 images are misclassified with disgust, sadness, and surprise. Disgust detect 48 images perfectly and 6 images are mismatched with all expressions except anger. Fear identifies 38 images accurately and 5 images are misclassified with happiness and sadness. Happiness recognizes 77 images accurately and 7 images are misclassified with disgust, fear, and surprise. Sadness recognizes 62 images properly and 9 images are misclassified with remaining expressions. Surprise identifies 65 images perfectly and 4 images are misidentified with anger and sadness.

Table 6.18 shows the recognition of the distance, texture, and D-T signatures on the CK+ dataset using CNN. The overall classification rate of distance signature using CNN is available in Table 6.18. Distance signature obtains an average recognition rate of 81.7% with the highest recognition rate of 92.9% for happiness and the lowest recognition rate of 71.8% for sadness. The texture signature recognizes 48 images accurately as anger and 24 images are in a mismatch with happiness, disgust, sadness, and surprise. The texture signature gets an average recognition rate of 64.1% with the highest recognition rate of 77.8% for disgust and the lowest recognition rate of 25.6% in case of fear. D-T signature identifies 66 images properly for anger and 6 images are misidentified with disgust, sadness, and surprise. D-T signature obtains an average recognition rate of 90.6% with the highest recognition rate of 94.2% for sadness and the lowest recognition rate of 88.4% in case of fear. From these results, it is noticed that the D-T signature yields a promising result.

The performance of recalls of CNN on CK+ dataset is shown for distance signature as anger $= 0.80$, disgust $= 0.72$, fear $= 0.88$, happiness $= 0.92$, sadness $= 0.71$, and surprise $= 0.82$ and F-measures is mentioned as anger $= 0.81$, disgust $= 0.75$, fear $= 0.87$, happiness $= 0.89$, sadness $= 0.77$, and surprise $= 0.78$. The performance of recall and F-measure is also shown as for texture signature (Recall: anger $= 0.66$, disgust $= 0.77$, fear $= 0.25$, happiness $= 0.75$, sadness $= 0.54$, and surprise $= 0.71$ and F-measure: anger $= 0.62$, disgust $= 0.67$, fear $= 0.33$, happiness $= 0.71$, sadness $= 0.64$, and surprise $= 0.67$). The performance of recall and F-measure is mentioned as for D-T signature (Recall: anger $= 0.91$, disgust $= 0.88$, fear $= 0.88$, happiness $= 0.91$, sadness $= 0.87$, and surprise $= 0.94$ and F-measure: anger $= 0.94$, disgust $= 0.91$, fear $= 0.84$, happiness $= 0.90$, sadness $= 0.87$, and surprise $= 0.92$).

6.4.2   Result Evaluation on the JAFFE Dataset

The JAFFE [16] dataset has 213 images of seven facial expressions. It consists of different female images. During training and testing, the network chooses the same set of parameters used in the CK+ dataset. A detail discussion is available in Sects. 4.1 to 4.3. We consider a total of 116 images for the JAFFE dataset to conduct training and 97 images are utilized for testing to measure the recognition rate of expressions. The testing dataset is mentioned as fear (14), anger (21), disgust (20), happiness (14), surprise (14), and sadness (14).

The Recognition of Distance Signature Using MLP

The recognition of distance signature using MLP is shown in Table 6.19. Anger identifies 21 images accurately. Disgust recognizes 20 images properly. In the same way, happiness, sadness, and surprise recognize accurately. Fear identifies 11 images properly and 3 images are misidentified with disgust and anger.

The Recognition of Distance Signature Using NARX

The recognition of distance signature using NARX is shown in Table 6.20. Anger recognizes 20 images accurately and 1 image is misidentified with disgust. Disgust recognizes 20 images accurately. Fear recognizes 12 images perfectly and 2 images

Table 6.19 The recognition of distance signature on JAFFE dataset using MLP

	Anger	Disgust	Fear	Happiness	Sadness	Surprise
Anger	21	0	0	0	0	0
Disgust	0	20	0	0	0	0
Fear	2	1	11	0	0	0
Happiness	0	0	0	14	0	0
Sadness	0	0	2	0	12	0
Surprise	0	0	0	0	0	14

Table 6.20 The classification of distance signature on JAFFE dataset using NARX

	Anger	Disgust	Fear	Happiness	Sadness	Surprise
Anger	20	1	0	0	0	0
Disgust	0	20	0	0	0	0
Fear	0	0	12	2	0	0
Happiness	0	0	0	12	2	0
Sadness	0	0	0	0	14	0
Surprise	0	0	0	0	0	14

Table 6.21 The classification of distance signature on JAFFE dataset using RBF

	Anger	Disgust	Fear	Happiness	Sadness	Surprise
Anger	21	0	0	0	0	0
Disgust	0	20	0	0	0	0
Fear	2	1	11	0	0	0
Happiness	0	0	0	14	0	0
Sadness	0	0	0	0	14	0
Surprise	0	0	0	0	0	14

are confused with happiness. Happiness detects 12 images rightly and 2 images are in a mismatch with sadness. The sadness and surprise expressions identify accurately.

The Recognition of Distance Signature Using RBF

The classification of distance signature using NARX is indicated in Table 6.21. The anger, as well as disgust expressions, recognize properly. Fear recognizes 11 images properly and 3 images are in a mismatch with disgust and anger. Happiness detects 12 images accurately and 2 images are misidentified with sadness. The happiness, sadness, and surprise expressions recognize accurately.

The Recognition of Texture Signature Using MLP

The confusion matrix of texture signature using NARX is shown in Table 6.22. Anger recognizes 21 images accurately. Disgust classifies 15 images properly and 5 images are in a mismatch with surprise. Fear recognizes 13 images accurately and 1 image is

Table 6.22 The classification of texture signature on JAFFE database using MLP

	Anger	Disgust	Fear	Happiness	Sadness	Surprise
Anger	21	0	0	0	0	0
Disgust	0	15	0	0	0	5
Fear	0	0	13	0	0	1
Happiness	0	0	0	14	0	0
Sadness	0	0	0	1	13	0
Surprise	0	0	0	0	0	14

Table 6.23 The classification of texture signature on JAFFE dataset using NARX

	Anger	Disgust	Fear	Happiness	Sadness	Surprise
Anger	18	3	0	0	0	0
Disgust	0	18	2	0	0	0
Fear	0	0	12	2	0	0
Happiness	0	0	0	13	1	0
Sadness	0	0	0	0	12	2
Surprise	0	0	0	0	0	14

misidentified with surprise. Happiness recognizes 14 images accurately. The sadness identifies 13 images perfectly and 1 image is mismatched with happiness. Surprise identifies accurately.

The Recognition of Texture Signature Using NARX

The confusion matrix of texture signature using NARX is shown in Table 6.23. Anger recognizes 18 images accurately and 3 images are misidentified with disgust. Disgust recognizes 18 images perfectly and 2 images are confused with fear. Fear recognizes 12 images properly and 2 images are misidentified with happiness. Happiness identifies 13 images perfectly and 1 image is misclassified with sadness. The sadness identifies 12 images accurately and 2 images are misidentified with surprise. Surprise identifies 14 images accurately.

The Recognition of Texture Signature Using RBF

The recognition matrix of texture signature using RBF is shown in Table 6.24. Anger recognizes 21 images accurately. Disgust classifies 19 images perfectly and 1 image is misidentified with surprise. Fear recognizes 14 images properly. Happiness recognizes 12 images perfectly and 2 images are misidentified with surprise. The sadness identifies 13 images accurately and 1 image is mismatched with disgust. Surprise identifies 13 images accurately and 1 image is confused with disgust.

The Classification of D-T Signature Using MLP

The MLP-based recognition matrix of D-T signature is shown in Table 6.25. Anger recognizes 21 images accurately. Disgust classifies 19 images correctly. Fear rec-

Table 6.24 The classification of RBF-based texture signature on JAFFE database

	Anger	Disgust	Fear	Happiness	Sadness	Surprise
Anger	21	0	0	0	0	0
Disgust	0	19	0	0	0	1
Fear	0	0	14	0	0	0
Happiness	0	0	0	12	0	2
Sadness	0	1	0	0	13	0
Surprise	0	1	0	0	0	13

Table 6.25 The classification of MLP-based D-T signature on JAFFE dataset

	Anger	Disgust	Fear	Happiness	Sadness	Surprise
Anger	21	0	0	0	0	0
Disgust	0	20	0	0	0	0
Fear	0	0	14	0	0	0
Happiness	0	0	0	14	0	0
Sadness	0	0	0	4	10	0
Surprise	0	0	0	0	0	14

Table 6.26 The classification of NARX-based D-T signature on JAFFE dataset

	Anger	Disgust	Fear	Happiness	Sadness	Surprise
Anger	20	1	0	0	0	0
Disgust	0	19	1	0	0	0
Fear	0	0	12	2	0	0
Happiness	0	0	0	13	1	0
Sadness	0	0	0	0	12	2
Surprise	0	0	0	0	0	14

ognizes 14 images properly. Happiness classifies 14 images correctly. The sadness recognizes 10 images perfectly and 4 images are misclassified with happiness. Surprise expression identifies 14 images accurately (Table 6.25).

The Classification of D-T Signature Using NARX

The NARX-based recognition matrix of D-T signature is shown in Table 6.26. Anger indicates 20 images accurately and 1 image is mismatched with disgust. Disgust classifies 20 images correctly. Fear recognizes 12 images properly. Happiness classifies 13 images rightly and 1 image is misidentified with sadness. The sadness recognizes 12 images perfectly and 2 images are mismatched with disgust. Surprise expression detects 14 images accurately.

Table 6.27   The classification of D-T signature on JAFFE database using RBF

	Anger	Disgust	Fear	Happiness	Sadness	Surprise
Anger	21	0	0	0	0	0
Disgust	0	20	0	0	0	0
Fear	0	0	14	0	0	0
Happiness	0	0	0	14	0	0
Sadness	0	0	0	2	12	0
Surprise	0	0	0	0	0	14

Table 6.28   Recognition rate on JAFFE database database with different state-of-the-art methods

	Anger	Disgust	Fear	Happiness	Sadness	Surprise	Avg.
Distance signature on MLP	100	100	78.6	100	85.7	100	94.1
Distance signature on NARX	95.2	100	85.7	85.7	100	100	93.2
Distance signature on RBF	100	100	78.6	100	100	100	96.4
Texture signature on MLP	100	75	92.9	100	92.9	100	93.5
Texture signature on NARX	85.7	90	85.7	92.9	85.7	100	90
Texture signature on RBF	100	95	100	85.7	92.9	92.9	94.4
D-T signature on MLP	100	100	100	100	71.4	100	95.2
D-T signature on NARX	95.2	95	85.7	92.9	85.7	100	92.4
D-T signature on RBF	100	100	100	100	85.7	100	97.6
[18]	100	86.2	93.7	96.7	77.4	96.6	91.7
[19]	96.6	90	93.7	93.5	93.5	90	92.8
[20]	89.3	90.7	91.1	92.6	90.2	92.3	91.1

The Recognition of D-T Signature Using RBF

The RBF-based recognition matrix of D-T signature is shown in Table 6.27. Anger identifies 21 images accurately. Disgust classifies 20 images correctly. Fear recognizes 14 images properly. Happiness classifies 14 images correctly. The sadness identifies 12 images properly and 2 images are in a mismatch with happiness. Surprise recognizes 14 images accurately.

Recognition Rate on JAFFE Dataset of Distance, Texture, and D-T Signatures Using MLP, RBF, and NARX

Table 6.28 shows the recognition rate of the distance signature for the JAFFE dataset using MLP, NARX, and RBF. An average classification rate of distance signature is mentioned in Table 6.28. An overall recognition rate of 94.1% is achieved by MLP with the highest recognition rate of 100% for anger, happiness, and disgust and the lowest recognition rate of 78.6% for fear. MLP runs 369 iterations in 17 s to minimize the MSE. An average recognition rate of 93.2% is achieved by NARX with the highest recognition rate of 100% for disgust, surprise, and sadness and the lowest recognition rate of 85.7% for fear. The NARX runs 378 iterations in 18 s to minimize the MSE. The RBF has obtained an overall recognition rate of 96.4% with the highest recognition rate of 100% for five expressions and the lowest recognition rate of 78.6% for fear. The RBF runs 380 iterations in 19 s to minimize the MSE. From these results, it is noticed that the distance signature obtained overwhelming recognition using RBF.

Table 6.28 indicates the recognition rate of texture signature using MLP, RBF, and NARX networks. The overall classification rate of texture signature is mentioned in Table 6.28. The overall recognition rate of 93.5% is achieved by MLP with the highest recognition rate of 100% for anger, happiness, and surprise and the lowest recognition rate of 75% for fear. The texture signature runs 355 iterations in 15 s to minimize the MSE using MLP. The overall recognition rate of 90% is achieved by NARX with the highest recognition rate of 100% for surprise and the lowest recognition rate of 85.7% for anger, sadness, and fear. The texture signature runs 370 iterations in 17 s to minimize the MSE using NARX. The RBF has obtained an average recognition rate of 94.4% with the highest recognition rate of 100% for anger and fear and the lowest recognition rate of 85.7% for happiness. The texture signature runs 380 iterations in 18 s to minimize the MSE using RBF. These observations show that the texture signature obtained a promising recognition rate of expression.

Table 6.28 shows the recognition rate of merged D-T signature using MLP, RBF, and NARX. An average recognition rate of 95.2% is got by MLP with the highest recognition rate of 100% for anger, disgust, happiness, fear, and surprise and the lowest recognition rate of 71.4% for sadness. The D-T signature runs 435 iterations in 23 s to minimize the MSE using MLP. The overall recognition rate of 92.4% is achieved by NARX with the highest recognition rate of 100% for surprise and the lowest recognition rate of 85.7% for fear. The D-T signature runs 427 iterations in 22 s to minimize the MSE using NARX. RBF has got an overall recognition rate of 97.6% with the highest recognition rate of 100% for anger, fear, disgust, surprise, and happiness and the lowest recognition rate of 85.7% for sadness. The D-T signature runs 449 iterations in 24 s to minimize the MSE using RBF. These results show that the combined D-T signature obtained an overwhelming classification rate of emotions.

Recall and F-measure on JAFFE Database of Distance, Texture, and D-T Signatures Using MLP, RBF, and NARX

Table 6.29 indicates the recall and F-measure of distance signature using MLP, RBF, and NARX. The performance of recall and F-measure for texture signature is shown in Table 6.30. In the same way, the corresponding recall and f-measure of the D-T signature are shown in Table 6.31. From the above Tables we observe that the individual signature performs a good recognition rate of expressions but when we consider merged D-T signature yields an overwhelming classification rate of emotions.

Table 6.29   The performance measure of distance signature on JAFFE

	Distance					
	MLP		NARX		RBF	
	Recall	F-measure	Recall	F-measure	Recall	F-measure
Anger	1	0.95	0.95	0.97	1	0.95
Disgust	1	0.97	1	0.97	1	0.97
Fear	0.78	0.81	0.85	0.92	0.88	0.92
Happiness	1	1	0.85	0.85	1	1
Sadness	0.87	0.92	1	0.93	1	1
Surprise	1	1	1	1	1	1

Table 6.30   The performance measure of texture signature on JAFFE

	Texture					
	MLP		NARX		RBF	
	Recall	F-measure	Recall	F-measure	Recall	F-measure
Anger	1	1	0.85	0.92	1	1
Disgust	0.75	0.85	0.90	0.87	0.95	0.92
Fear	0.96	0.85	0.85	0.97	1	1
Happiness	1	0.96	0.92	0.89	0.85	0.92
Sadness	0.92	0.96	0.85	0.88	0.92	0.96
Surprise	1	0.82	1	0.92	0.92	0.86

Table 6.31   The performance measure of D-T signature on JAFFE

	D-T					
	MLP		NARX		RBF	
	Recall	F-measure	Recall	F-measure	Recall	F-measure
Anger	1	1	0.95	0.99	1	1
Disgust	1	1	0.95	0.97	1	1
Fear	1	1	0.85	0.96	1	1
Happiness	1	0.87	0.92	0.98	1	0.93
Sadness	0.71	0.83	0.85	0.85	0.92	0.92
Surprise	1	1	1	1	1	1

6.4.2.1   Experimental Result of CNN on JAFFE Database

The distance, texture, and D-T signatures of the JAFFE dataset are considered to measure the performance of expression recognition using CNN. The recognition matrix of distance signature is shown in Table 6.32. Anger identifies 21 images correctly with no misclassification. The disgust recognizes 19 images rightly and 1 image is

Table 6.32 The recognition matrix of distance signature on JAFFE dataset using CNN

	Anger	Disgust	Fear	Happiness	Sadness	Surprise
Anger	21	0	0	0	0	0
Disgust	0	19	0	0	1	0
Fear	0	1	13	0	0	0
Happiness	3	0	0	11	0	0
Sadness	0	4	0	0	10	0
Surprise	1	0	1	0	2	10

Table 6.33 The recognition matrix of texture signature on JAFFE dataset using CNN

	Anger	Disgust	Fear	Happiness	Sadness	Surprise
Anger	15	1	2	0	3	0
Disgust	2	15	1	0	2	0
Fear	0	0	13	0	0	1
Happiness	1	3	0	8	2	0
Sadness	0	3	1	1	9	0
Surprise	0	2	2	1	2	7

in a mismatch with sadness. Fear identifies 13 images accurately and 1 image is confused with disgust. Happiness indicates 11 images properly and 3 images are misidentified with anger. Sadness recognizes 10 images positively and 4 images are in misclassification with anger. Surprise identifies 10 images properly and 4 images are misidentified with anger, fear, and sadness.

The recognition matrix of texture signature is shown in Table 6.33. Anger identifies 15 images perfectly and 6 images are mismatched with disgust, fear, and sadness. Disgust detects 15 images properly and 5 images are in misclassification with anger, fear, and sadness. Fear identifies 13 images accurately and 1 image is mismatched with surprise. Happiness identifies 8 images properly and 4 images are in a mismatch with anger, disgust, and sadness. Sadness recognizes 9 images properly and 5 images are in misclassification with fear, disgust, and happiness. Surprise detects 7 images positively and a large number of images are in a mismatch with different expressions.

The recognition matrix of D-T signature is shown in Table 6.34. Anger recognizes 21 images correctly. Disgust recognizes 20 images properly with no misclassification. Fear identifies 9 images positively and 5 images are in misclassification with anger and disgust. Happiness detects 12 images rightly and 2 images are in a mismatch with anger. Sadness recognizes 10 images accurately and 2 images are in misclassification with disgust. Surprise recognizes 14 images accurately.

Table 6.35 indicates the recognition of expressions of the distance, texture, and D-T signatures on the JAFFE dataset using CNN. The distance signature achieves an overall recognition rate of 86.6% with the highest recognition rate of 100% for anger and the lowest recognition rate of 71.4% for sadness. The texture signature gets an

Table 6.34 The confusion matrix of D-T signature on JAFFE database using CNN

	Anger	Disgust	Fear	Happiness	Sadness	Surprise
Anger	21	0	0	0	0	0
Disgust	0	20	0	0	0	0
Fear	4	1	9	0	0	0
Happiness	2	0	0	12	0	0
Sadness	0	2	0	2	10	0
Surprise	0	0	0	0	0	14

Table 6.35 Testing performance on JAFFE database using CNN

	Anger	Disgust	Fear	Happiness	Sadness	Surprise	Avg.
Distance signature	100	95.9	92.9	78.6	71.4	71.4	86.6
Texture signature	71.4	75	92.9	57.1	64.3	50	69.1
D-T signature	100	100	64.3	85.7	71.4	100	88.7

average recognition rate of 69.1% with the highest recognition rate of 92.9% for fear and the lowest recognition rate of 50% for sadness. D-T signature obtains an overall recognition rate of 88.7% with the highest recognition rate of 100% for anger and the lowest recognition rate of 64.3% for fear. From these results, we observe that the D-T signature achieved a better recognition rate over the other signatures.

The performance of recalls of distance signature is produced as anger $= 1.00$, disgust $= 0.95$, fear $= 0.92$, happiness $= 0.78$, sadness $= 0.71$, and surprise $= 0.71$ and F-measures are achieved as anger $= 0.91$, disgust $= 0.86$, fear $= 0.92$, happiness $= 0.88$, sadness $= 0.74$, and surprise $= 0.83$. The performance of recall and F-measure is mentioned as (Recall: anger $= 0.71$, disgust $= 0.75$, fear $= 0.92$, happiness $= 0.57$, sadness $= 0.64$, and surprise $= 0.50$ and F-measure: anger $= 0.76$, disgust $= 0.68$, fear $= 0.78$, happiness $= 0.66$, sadness $= 0.56$, and surprise $= 0.63$) for texture signature. The performance of recall and F-measure is indicated as (Recall: anger $= 1.00$, disgust $= 1.00$, fear $= 0.64$, happiness $= 0.85$, sadness $= 0.71$, and surprise $= 1.00$ and F-measure: anger $= 0.87$, disgust $= 0.93$, fear $= 0.78$, happiness $= 0.85$, sadness $= 0.83$, and surprise $= 1.00$) for D-T signature.

6.4.3 *Experiment on MMI Database*

MMI dataset is more demanding than the other datasets. A total of 493 expressions are used to label the expressed emotions. A total of 313 expressions are used to conduct the training and 180 expressions are used to perform the testing. There are many heterogeneous expressions in this dataset. This dataset has also many spontaneous expressions. Few expressed images wear many accessories such as headcloth, mustache, and glasses.

Table 6.36 The MLP-based recognition matrix of distance signature on MMI

	Anger	Disgust	Fear	Happiness	Sadness	Surprise
Anger	39	0	0	0	1	0
Disgust	0	29	1	6	3	0
Fear	0	0	17	0	5	3
Happiness	0	0	0	24	0	0
Sadness	1	0	1	0	26	2
Surprise	0	0	1	0	4	17

Table 6.37 The NARX-based recognition matrix of distance signature on MMI

	Anger	Disgust	Fear	Happiness	Sadness	Surprise
Anger	39	1	0	0	0	0
Disgust	0	38	0	0	0	1
Fear	0	0	24	1	0	0
Happiness	1	0	0	23	0	0
Sadness	0	0	8	0	21	1
Surprise	0	0	0	0	0	22

The MLP-Based Recognition Matrix of Distance Signature

Table 6.36 produces the recognition of distance signature using MLP on MMI. Anger classifies 39 images properly and 1 image is misidentified with sadness. Disgust identifies 29 images properly and 10 images are in a mismatch as anger and fear, happiness, and sadness. Fear recognizes 17 images properly and 8 images are in misclassification with sadness and surprise. Happiness recognizes 24 images accurately. Sadness indicates 26 images properly and 4 images are in a mismatch with anger, fear, and surprise. Surprise detects 17 images rightly and 5 images are misclassified with sadness and fear.

The NARX-Based Recognition Matrix of Distance Signature

The classification of distance signature using NARX is mentioned in Table 6.37. Anger identifies 39 images accurately and 1 image is misidentified with disgust. Disgust recognizes 38 images perfectly and 1 image is confused surprise. Fear recognizes 24 images properly and 1 image is misidentified with happiness. Happiness identifies 23 images accurately and 1 image is mismatched with anger. Sadness identifies 21 images properly and 9 images are misidentified with fear and surprise. Surprise classifies 22 images accurately.

The RBF-Based Recognition Matrix of Distance Signature

The classification of distance signature using RBF is indicated in Table 6.38. Anger identifies 36 images accurately and 4 images are mismatched with sadness. Disgust recognizes 39 images perfectly. Fear recognizes 19 images properly and 6 images are

Table 6.38 The RBF-base recognition matrix of distance signature on MMI

	Anger	Disgust	Fear	Happiness	Sadness	Surprise
Anger	36	0	0	0	4	0
Disgust	0	39	0	0	0	0
Fear	0	0	19	0	6	0
Happiness	0	0	0	16	8	0
Sadness	0	0	0	0	30	0
Surprise	0	1	0	0	4	17

Table 6.39 The MLP-based recognition matrix of texture signature on MMI

	Anger	Disgust	Fear	Happiness	Sadness	Surprise
Anger	34	0	0	6	0	0
Disgust	0	38	0	1	0	0
Fear	0	3	14	6	1	1
Happiness	0	0	0	24	0	0
Sadness	0	0	1	0	29	0
Surprise	0	0	1	4	0	17

misidentified with sadness. Happiness identifies 16 images accurately and 8 images are misclassified with sadness. Sadness identifies 30 images properly. Surprise classifies 17 images rightly and 5 images are misidentified with disgust and sadness.

The MLP-Based Recognition Matrix of Texture Signature

The recognition matrix of texture signature using MLP is shown in Table 6.39. Anger recognizes 34 images accurately and 6 images are misidentified with happiness. Disgust identifies 38 images perfectly and 1 image is misclassified with happiness. Fear recognizes 14 images properly and 11 images are misclassified with all expressions except anger. Happiness classifies 24 images correctly. The sadness classifies 29 images accurately and 1 image is in a mismatch with fear. Surprise expression identifies 17 images rightly and 5 images are in a mismatch with fear and happiness.

The NARX-Based Recognition Matrix of Texture Signature

The recognition matrix of texture signature using NARX is shown in Table 6.40. Anger recognizes 35 images properly and 5 images are misidentified with disgust and fear. Disgust detects 37 images perfectly and 2 images are in misclassification with fear. Fear recognizes 20 images positively and 5 images are in a mismatch with disgust, sadness, and surprise. Happiness detects 22 images properly and 2 images are misidentified with sadness and surprise. The sadness recognizes 29 images positively and 1 image is mismatched with fear. Surprise identifies 22 images accurately.

The RBF-Based Recognition Matrix of Texture Signature

The RBF-based recognition matrix of texture signature is shown in Table 6.41. Anger recognizes 40 images accurately and 4 images are misidentified with sadness. Disgust identifies 34 images properly and 5 images are misidentified with anger. Fear recognizes 16 images perfectly and 9 images are in a mismatch with anger. Happiness detects 16 images positively and 8 images are misidentified with anger. The sadness identifies 23 images rightly and 7 images are mismatched with anger and sadness. Surprise expression identifies 18 images positively and 2 images are in a mismatch with fear and happiness.

The MLP-Based Recognition Matrix of D-T Signature

The MLP-based recognition matrix of D-T signature is shown in Table 6.42. Anger recognizes 31 images accurately and 9 images are misidentified with disgust, fear, and sadness. Disgust detects 38 images properly and 1 image is confused with happiness. Fear recognizes 23 images positively and 2 images are misidentified with sadness. Happiness recognizes 21 images perfectly and 3 images are misidentified with sadness. The sadness recognizes 27 images properly and 3 images are mismatched with fear. Surprise expression identifies 19 images accurately.

The NARX-Based Recognition Matrix of D-T Signature

The confusion matrix of the D-T signature using NARX is shown in Table 6.43. Anger recognizes 39 images accurately and 1 image is mismatched with disgust. Disgust

Table 6.40   The NARX-based recognition matrix of texture signature on MMI

	Anger	Disgust	Fear	Happiness	Sadness	Surprise
Anger	35	2	3	0	0	0
Disgust	0	37	2	0	0	0
Fear	0	2	20	0	2	1
Happiness	0	0	0	22	1	1
Sadness	0	0	1	0	29	0
Surprise	0	0	0	0	0	22

Table 6.41   The RBF-based recognition matrix of texture signature on MMI

	Anger	Disgust	Fear	Happiness	Sadness	Surprise
Anger	40	0	0	0	4	0
Disgust	5	34	0	0	0	0
Fear	9	0	16	0	0	0
Happiness	8	0	0	16	0	0
Sadness	1	0	6	0	23	0
Surprise	2	0	1	1	0	18

Table 6.42 The MLP-based recognition matrix of D-T signature on MMI

	Anger	Disgust	Fear	Happiness	Sadness	Surprise
Anger	31	1	7	0	1	0
Disgust	0	38	0	1	0	0
Fear	0	0	23	0	2	0
Happiness	0	0	0	21	3	0
Sadness	0	0	3	0	27	0
Surprise	1	0	0	2	0	19

Table 6.43 The NARX-based recognition matrix of D-T signature on MMI

	Anger	Disgust	Fear	Happiness	Sadness	Surprise
A	39	1	0	0	0	0
D	0	37	2	0	0	0
F	0	0	22	2	1	0
H	0	0	0	22	2	0
S	0	0	0	0	28	2
G	0	0	0	0	0	22

classifies 37 images correctly and 2 images are in misclassification with fear. Fear recognizes 22 images positively and 3 images are confused as happiness and sadness. Happiness detects 22 images rightly and 2 images are misclassified with sadness. The sadness identifies 28 images positively and 2 images are in misclassification with surprise. Surprise identifies 22 images accurately.

The RBF-Based Recognition Matrix of D-T Signature

The classification matrix of D-T signature using RBF is indicated in Table 6.44. Anger recognizes 39 images accurately and 1 image is misidentified with fear. Disgust classifies 37 images perfectly and 2 images are misidentified as fear. Fear recognizes 22 images positively and 3 images are misidentified with happiness and sadness. Happiness detects 22 images rightly and 2 images are misclassified as fear, sadness, and surprise. The sadness recognizes 29 images properly and 1 image is mismatched with sadness. Surprise expression identifies 22 images accurately.

Recognition Rate on MMI Database of Distance, Texture, and D-T Signatures Using MLP, NARX, and RBF

Table 6.45 produces the recognition of distance signature through the performing of MLP, RBF, NARX networks. The overall classification rate of distance signature is mentioned in Table 6.45. The overall recognition rate of 83.9% is achieved by MLP with the highest recognition rate of 100% for happiness and the lowest recognition rate of 68% for fear. The distance signature runs 380 iterations in 18 s to minimize MSE in MLP training. The overall recognition rate of 92.8% is got using NARX

Table 6.44 The RBF-based recognition matrix of D-T signature on MMI

	Anger	Disgust	Fear	Happiness	Sadness	Surprise
Anger	39	0	1	0	0	0
Disgust	0	34	1	0	0	0
Fear	0	0	25	0	0	0
Happiness	0	0	3	15	3	3
Sadness	0	0	0	1	29	0
Surprise	0	0	1	0	0	21

Table 6.45 Recognition rate on MMI with the state-of-the-art approaches

	Anger	Disgust	Fear	Happiness	Sadness	Surprise	Avg.
Distance signature on MLP	97.5	74.4	68	100	86.7	77.3	83.9
Distance signature on NARX	97.5	97.4	96	95.8	70	100	92.8
Distance signature on RBF	90	100	76	66.7	100	77.3	85
Texture signature on MLP	85	97.4	56	100	96.7	77.3	85.4
Texture signature on NARX	87.5	94.9	80	91.7	96.7	100	91.8
Texture signature on RBF	100	87.2	64	66.7	76.7	81.8	79.4
D-T signature on MLP	77.5	97.4	92	87.5	90	86.4	88.5
D-T signature on NARX	100	97.4	92	83.3	93.3	100	94.3
D-T signature on RBF	97.5	71.8	88	95.8	96.7	95.5	90.9
[20]	80.1	78.2	81.3	83.2	77.1	81	80.1
[7]	65.6	72.5	72.5	88.2	71.1	93.8	77.4

with the highest recognition rate of 100% for surprise and the lowest recognition rate of 70% for sadness. The distance signature runs 381 iterations in 20 s to minimize MSE in NARX. In this way, RBF has obtained an average identification rate of 85% with the highest recognition rate of 100% for sadness and the lowest recognition rate of 76% for fear. The distance signature runs 385 iterations in 21 s to minimize MSE in RBF. From these results, we conclude that the distance signature performed promising recognition rate of emotions in NARX.

The overall recognition of texture signature is shown in Table 6.45 through the experimenting of MLP, RBF, NARX networks. An overall recognition rate of 85.4% is obtained by MLP with the highest recognition rate of 100% for happiness and the lowest recognition rate of 56% for fear. The texture signature runs 375 iterations in 17 s to minimize MSE in MLP. The overall recognition rate of 91.8% is achieved by NARX with the highest recognition rate of 100% for surprise and the lowest recognition rate of 80% for fear. The texture signature runs 375 iterations in 18 s to minimize MSE in NARX. In this way, RBF has got an overall recognition rate of 79.4% with the highest recognition rate of 100% for anger and the lowest recognition rate of 64% for fear. The texture signature runs 385 iterations in 19 s to minimize MSE in RBF. It is showed that the NARX classifier performed better.

The joined D-T signature is indicated in Table 6.45 through the performing of MLP, RBF, NARX networks. An average combined D-T signature of 88.5% is obtained by MLP with the highest recognition rate of 97.4% for disgust and the lowest recognition rate of 77.5% for anger. The joined D-T signature runs 445 iterations in 25 s to minimize MSE in MLP. An overall recognition rate of 94.3% is achieved by NARX with the highest recognition rate of 100% for surprise and the lowest recognition rate of 83.3% for happiness. The joined D-T signature runs 439 iterations in 24 s to minimize MSE in NARX. The RBF has obtained an overall recognition rate of 90.9% with the highest recognition rate of 97.5% for anger and the lowest recognition rate of 71.8% for disgust. The joined D-T signature runs 465 iterations in 25 s to minimize MSE in RBF. Now we show that the joined D-T signature achieved a promising recognition rate of emotions in NARX.

F-measure and Recall on MMI Database of Distance, Texture, and D-T Signatures Using MLP, RBF, and NARX

Table 6.46 presents the recall and F-measure of distance signature using MLP, RBF, and NARX. The performance of f-measure and recall of texture signature is shown in Table 6.47. In the same way, the corresponding performance of F-measure and recall of the D-T signature is presented in Table 6.48. From these Tables we observe

Table 6.46 The performance of distance signature on MMI dataset

	Distance					
	MLP		NARX		RBF	
	Recall	F-measure	Recall	F-measure	Recall	F-measure
Anger	0.97	0.97	0.97	0.97	0.90	0.94
Disgust	0.74	0.85	0.97	0.97	1	0.98
Fear	0.68	0.75	0.96	0.84	0.76	0.86
Happiness	1	0.88	0.95	0.95	0.66	0.80
Sadness	0.86	0.75	0.70	0.82	1	0.73
Surprise	0.77	0.77	0.95	0.98	0.77	0.87

Table 6.47 The performance of texture signature on MMI dataset

	Texture					
	MLP		NARX		RBF	
	Recall	F-measure	Recall	F-measure	Recall	F-measure
Anger	0.85	0.91	0.90	0.93	1	0.76
Disgust	0.97	0.95	0.94	0.92	0.87	0.93
Fear	0.56	0.68	0.92	0.93	0.64	0.66
Happiness	1	0.73	0.91	0.89	0.66	0.78
Sadness	0.96	0.96	0.93	0.93	0.76	0.86
Surprise	0.77	0.85	1	0.97	0.81	0.90

Table 6.48 The performance of D-T signature on MMI dataset

	D-T					
	MLP		NARX		RBF	
	Recall	F-measure	Recall	F-measure	Recall	F-measure
Anger	0.77	0.86	0.97	0.98	0.97	0.98
Disgust	0.97	0.97	0.94	0.96	0.87	0.93
Fear	0.92	0.79	0.89	0.96	1	0.89
Happiness	0.87	0.87	0.91	0.91	0.54	0.68
Sadness	0.90	0.85	0.93	0.91	0.96	0.90
Surprise	0.86	0.92	1	0.95	0.95	0.84

Table 6.49 The recognition matrix of distance signature on MMI dataset using CNN

	Anger	Disgust	Fear	Happiness	Sadness	Surprise
Anger	24	5	4	0	3	4
Disgust	6	23	2	1	6	1
Fear	4	1	15	0	5	0
Happiness	5	2	2	6	6	3
Sadness	2	3	4	0	18	3
Surprise	2	4	1	2	3	10

that the individual signature yields a promising classification rate of emotions but when we examine joined D-T signature which yields a fantastic classification rate of emotions.

6.4.3.1 Experimental Result of CNN on MMI Database

The distance, texture, and D-T signatures of the MMI dataset are examined to measure the accuracy of emotion classification through CNN. The recognition matrix of distance signature is shown in Table 6.49. Anger identifies 24 images perfectly and 16 images are misclassified with all expressions except happiness. The disgust recognizes 23 images properly and 16 images are misclassified with remaining expressions. Fear identifies 15 images accurately and 10 images are confused with remaining expressions except for happiness. Happiness indicates 6 images correctly and the maximum number of images are misidentified with remaining expressions. Sadness recognizes 18 images properly and 12 images are misclassified with anger, disgust, and fear. Surprise recognizes 10 images perfectly and the same number of images are misclassified with remaining expressions.

The recognition matrix of texture signature is shown in Table 6.50. Anger classifies 21 images properly and 19 images are in a mismatch with remaining expressions. Disgust detects 17 images positively and 22 images are misclassified with remain-

Table 6.50 The recognition matrix of texture signature on MMI dataset using CNN

	Anger	Disgust	Fear	Happiness	Sadness	Surprise
Anger	21	4	3	3	5	4
Disgust	9	17	1	2	4	6
Fear	3	5	8	2	4	3
Happiness	3	3	0	11	4	3
Sadness	2	6	2	1	18	1
Surprise	1	2	2	3	2	12

Table 6.51 The recognition matrix of D-T signature on MMI dataset using CNN

	Anger	Disgust	Fear	Happiness	Sadness	Surprise
Anger	24	5	4	0	3	4
Disgust	6	23	2	1	6	1
Fear	4	1	15	0	5	0
Happiness	5	2	2	6	6	3
Sadness	2	3	4	0	18	3
Surprise	2	4	1	2	3	10

ing expressions. Fear identifies 8 images accurately and 17 images are mismatched with remaining expressions. Happiness identifies 8 images perfectly and 4 images are in misclassification with anger, sadness, and disgust. Sadness recognizes 11 images properly and 13 images are misidentified with all expressions except fear. Surprise identifies 12 images correctly and a large number of images are confused with remaining expressions.

The confusion matrix of the D-T signature is shown in Table 6.51. Anger recognizes 24 images positively and 16 images are in misclassification with fear, disgust, surprise, and sadness. Disgust recognizes 23 images properly and 16 images are misclassified with remaining expressions. Fear identifies 15 images accurately and 10 images are misclassified with anger, disgust, and sadness. Happiness detects 6 images correctly and the maximum number of images are misclassified with remaining expressions. Sadness recognizes 18 images properly and 12 images are misidentified with anger, disgust, fear, and surprise. Surprise detects 10 images positively.

The overall recognition of the distance, texture, and D-T signatures on the MMI dataset through CNN is mentioned in Table 6.52. Distance signature gets an overall recognition rate of 48.3% with the highest recognition rate of 60% for anger, fear, and sadness and the lowest recognition rate of 25% for happiness. Texture signature recognizes 21 images as anger and 19 images are in misclassification with other expressions. The texture signature acquires an average recognition rate of 48% with the highest recognition rate of 60% for sadness and the lowest recognition rate of 32% for fear. The D-T signature gets an average recognition rate of 56.1% with the highest recognition rate of 80% for anger and the lowest recognition rate of 20%

Table 6.52 Testing performance on MMI database using CNN

	Anger	Disgust	Fear	Happiness	Sadness	Surprise	Avg.
Distance signature	60	59	60	25	60	45.3	48.3
Texture signature	52.5	43.6	32	45.8	60	54.5	000
D-T signature	80	59	20	29.2	50	86.4	56.1

for fear. From the above experimentation, we show that the D-T signature presents a fantastic classification rate of emotions.

The recalls are produced as anger $= 0.60$, fear $= 0.60$, disgust $= 0.58$, happiness $= 0.25$, surprise $= 0.45$, and sadness $= 0.60$ and F-measures are produced as anger $= 0.57$, fear $= 0.56$, disgust $= 0.59$, sadness $= 0.50$, happiness $= 0.36$, and surprise $= 0.46$ of distance signature. The recall and F-measure are produced as (Recall: anger $= 0.52$, fear $= 0.32$, disgust $= 0.43$, sadness $= 0.60$, happiness $= 0.45$, and surprise $= 0.54$ and F-measure: anger $= 0.53$, fear $= 0.39$, disgust $= 0.44$, sadness $= 0.53$, happiness $= 0.47$, and surprise $= 0.47$) of texture signature. The recall and F-measure are indicated as (Recall: anger $= 0.80$, disgust $= 0.58$, fear $= 0.20$, sadness $= 0.50$, happiness $= 0.29$, and surprise $= 0.86$ and F-measure: anger $= 0.62$, disgust $= 0.63$, fear $= 0.27$, Sadness $= 0.58$, happiness $= 0.40$, and surprise $= 0.59$) of D-T signature.

6.4.4   Experimental Result on MUG Dataset

MUG [17] dataset is examined to measure the classification rate of emotion recognition. In this experiment, a total of 297 images are used for training and the remaining 141 images are used for testing.

The MLP-Based Recognition Matrix of Distance Signature

The recognition of distance signature using MLP is shown in Table 6.53. Anger identifies 19 images accurately. Disgust classifies 31 images correctly. Fear recognizes 11 images properly and 3 images are misidentified with happiness and disgust. Happiness classifies 83 images accurately and 1 image is confused with fear. Sadness identifies 20 images positively and 2 images are misidentified with surprise. Surprise recognizes 26 images accurately.

The NARX-Based Recognition Matrix of Distance Signature

The recognition of distance signature using NARX is shown in Table 6.54. Anger identifies 18 images accurately and 1 image is misidentified with disgust. Disgust identifies 30 images perfectly and 1 image is confused with fear. Fear recognizes 13 images positively and 1 image is misidentified with happiness. Happiness recognizes 29 images accurately and 1 image is misclassified with sadness. Sadness identifies 19 images rightly and 2 images are in a mismatch with surprise. Surprise identifies 26 images accurately.

Table 6.53 The confusion matrix of distance signature on MUG database using MLP

	Anger	Disgust	Fear	Happiness	Sadness	Surprise
Anger	19	0	0	0	0	0
Disgust	0	31	0	0	0	0
Fear	0	1	11	2	0	0
Happiness	0	0	1	29	0	0
Sadness	0	0	0	0	20	2
Surprise	0	0	0	0	0	26

Table 6.54 The NARX-based recognition matrix of distance signature on MUG dataset

	Anger	Disgust	Fear	Happiness	Sadness	Surprise
Anger	18	1	0	0	0	0
Disgust	0	30	1	0	0	0
Fear	0	0	13	1	0	0
Happiness	0	0	0	29	1	0
Sadness	0	0	0	0	19	2
Surprise	0	0	0	0	0	26

Table 6.55 The RBF-based recognition matrix of distance signature on MUG dataset

	Anger	Disgust	Fear	Happiness	Sadness	Surprise
Anger	19	0	0	0	0	0
Disgust	0	31	0	0	0	0
Fear	0	0	13	1	0	0
Happiness	0	2	0	28	0	0
Sadness	0	0	0	0	21	0
Surprise	0	0	0	0	0	26

The Recognition Matrix of Distance Signature Through RBF

The classification of distance signature using RBF is indicated in Table 6.55. Anger identifies 19 images accurately. Disgust classifies 31 images correctly. Fear recognizes 13 images positively and 1 image is misidentified with happiness. Happiness classifies 28 images positively and 2 images are in a mismatch with disgust. Sadness identifies 21 images accurately. Surprise classifies 26 images properly.

The Recognition Matrix of Texture Signature Through MLP

The recognition matrix of texture signature using MLP is shown in Table 6.56. Anger recognizes 15 images positively and 4 images are misidentified with sadness. Disgust identifies 31 images accurately. Fear recognizes 10 images perfectly and 4 images are confused with happiness and sadness. Happiness recognizes 28 images perfectly and

Table 6.56 The MLP-based recognition matrix of texture signature on MUG dataset

	Anger	Disgust	Fear	Happiness	Sadness	Surprise
Anger	15	0	0	0	4	0
Disgust	0	31	0	0	0	0
Fear	0	0	10	2	2	0
Happiness	0	0	0	28	0	2
Sadness	0	0	0	0	21	0
Surprise	0	0	0	0	1	25

Table 6.57 The NARX-based recognition matrix of texture signature on MUG dataset

	Anger	Disgust	Fear	Happiness	Sadness	Surprise
Anger	17	1	0	0	0	1
Disgust	0	29	1	1	0	0
Fear	0	0	14	0	0	0
Happiness	0	0	0	28	2	0
Sadness	0	0	0	0	20	1
Surprise	0	0	0	0	0	26

2 images are misidentified with surprise. The sadness identifies 21 images correctly. Surprise classifies 25 images accurately and 1 image is confused with sadness.

The Recognition Matrix of Texture Signature Through NARX

The classification matrix of texture signature through NARX is shown in Table 6.57. Anger recognizes 17 images accurately and 2 images are mismatched with surprise and disgust. Disgust detects 29 images properly and 1 image is misidentified with fear. Fear recognizes 14 images accurately. Happiness detects 28 images positively and 2 images are in a mismatch with sadness. The sadness recognizes 20 images perfectly and 1 image is mismatched with disgust. Surprise identifies 26 images accurately.

The Recognition Matrix of Texture Signature Through RBF

The recognition matrix of texture signature using RBF is shown in Table 6.58. Anger recognizes 18 images accurately and 1 image is mismatched with sadness. Disgust identifies 30 images properly and 1 image is in misclassification with fear. Fear recognizes 11 images properly and 2 images are misidentified with anger. Happiness detects 28 images properly and 2 images are misidentified with anger and sadness. The sadness identifies 21 images accurately. Surprise classifies 25 images accurately and 1 image is confused with disgust.

The Recognition Matrix of D-T Signature Through MLP

The classification matrix of D-T signature through MLP is shown in Table 6.59. Anger recognizes 19 images accurately. Disgust classifies 30 images positively and

Table 6.58 The RBF-based recognition matrix of texture signature on MUG dataset

	Anger	Disgust	Fear	Happiness	Sadness	Surprise
Anger	18	0	0	0	1	0
Disgust	0	30	1	0	0	0
Fear	2	0	11	0	1	0
Happiness	1	0	0	28	1	0
Sadness	0	0	0	0	21	0
Surprise	0	1	0	0	0	25

Table 6.59 The MLP-based recognition matrix of D-T signature on MUG dataset

	Anger	Disgust	Fear	Happiness	Sadness	Surprise
Anger	19	0	0	0	0	0
Disgust	0	30	1	0	0	0
Fear	0	0	14	0	0	0
Happiness	0	0	1	29	0	0
Sadness	0	0	0	0	21	0
Surprise	0	0	0	0	0	26

Table 6.60 The recognition matrix of D-T signature on MUG dataset through NARX

	Anger	Disgust	Fear	Happiness	Sadness	Surprise
Anger	18	1	0	0	0	0
Disgsut	0	30	1	0	0	0
Fear	0	0	12	2	0	0
Happiness	0	0	0	28	2	0
Sadness	0	0	0	0	19	2
Surprise	0	0	0	0	0	26

1 image is in a mismatch with fear. Fear recognizes 14 images properly. Happiness classifies 29 images rightly and 1 image is in misclassification with fear. The sadness classifies 21 images correctly. Surprise identifies 26 images accurately.

The Recognition Matrix of D-T Signature Through NARX

The classification matrix of D-T signature through NARX is shown in Table 6.60. Anger recognizes 18 images accurately and 1 image is misidentified with disgust. Disgust classifies 30 images positively and 1 image is confused with fear. Fear recognizes 12 images rightly and 2 images are misidentified with fear. Happiness identifies 28 images properly and 2 images are misclassified with sadness. Sadness recognizes 19 images perfectly and 2 images are a mismatch with surprise. Surprise expression identifies 26 images accurately.

The Recognition Matrix of D-T Signature Through RBF

The recognition matrix of D-T signature through RBF is shown in Table 6.61. Anger recognizes 19 images accurately. Disgust classifies 31 images correctly. Fear recognizes 14 images properly. Happiness classifies 19 images perfectly and 1 image is confused with fear. The sadness classifies 21 images correctly. Surprise identifies 26 images accurately.

In Table 6.62, the recognition matrix indicates the classification of different expressions of distance signature through MLP, RBF, and NARX. MLP detects accurately for anger, disgust, and sadness expressions but fear is misidentified with disgust. An overall recognition rate of 95.1% is achieved by MLP with the highest recognition rate of 100% for anger and the lowest recognition rate of 78.6% for fear. The distance signature completes 390 iterations in 20 s to minimize MSE through MLP. An overall recognition rate of 95.2% is got by NARX with the highest recognition rate of 100% for surprise and the lowest recognition rate of 90.5% for sadness. The distance signature completes 375 iterations in 19 s to minimize MSE through NARX. In this way, RBF has gained an overall recognition rate of 97.7% with the highest recognition rate of 100% for sadness and the lowest recognition rate of 92.9% for fear. The distance signature completes iterations in 22 s to minimize MSE through RBF. It is noticed that the distance signature using RBF achieves a fantastic classification rate of emotions.

Table 6.61 The recognition matrix of D-T signature on MUG dataset through RBF

	Anger	Disgust	Fear	Happiness	Sadness	Surprise
Anger	19	0	0	0	0	0
Disgust	0	31	0	0	0	0
Fear	0	0	14	0	0	0
Happiness	0	0	1	29	0	0
Sadness	0	0	0	0	21	0
Surprise	0	0	0	0	0	26

Table 6.62 Recognition rate on MUG dataset with various state-of-the-art approaches

	Anger	Disgust	Fear	Happiness	Sadness	Surprise	Avg.
Distance signature on MLP	100	100	78.6	96.7	95.2	100	95.1
Distance signature on NARX	94.7	96.8	92.9	96.7	90.5	100	95.2
Distance signature on RBF	100	100	92.9	93.3	100	100	97.7
Texture signature on MLP	78.9	100	71.4	93.3	100	96.2	92.2
Texture signature on NARX	89.5	93.5	100	93.3	95.2	100	95
Texture signature on RBF	94.7	96.8	78.6	93.3	100	96.2	94.3
D-T signature on MLP	100	96.8	100	96.7	100	100	98.6
D-T signature on NARX	94.7	96.8	100	93.3	90.5	100	95.9
D-T signature on RBF	100	100	100	96.7	100	100	99.3

The expression recognition of the texture signature of various networks is indicated in Table 6.62. The overall classification of texture signature is mentioned in Table 6.62. An overall recognition rate of 92.9% is got by MLP with the highest in Table 6.62 of 100% for disgust and the lowest recognition rate of 71.4% for fear. The texture signature takes 380 iterations in 18 s to minimize MSE through MLP. The overall recognition rate of 95% is got by NARX with the highest recognition rate of 100% for fear and the lowest recognition rate of 89.5% for anger. The NARX-based texture signature takes 390 iterations in 20 s to converge to the MSE. In the same way, RBF has got an average recognition rate of 94.3% with the highest recognition rate of 100% for sadness and the lowest recognition rate of 78.6% for fear. The RBF-based texture signature completes 395 iterations in 21 s to converge to the MSE. The NARX-based classifier yields a better result than others.

The classification of facial expression of joined D-T signature is indicated in Table 6.62 by three MLP, RBF, and NARX networks. An overall recognition rate of 98.6% is achieved by MLP with the highest recognition rate of 100% for anger, sadness, fear, and surprise and the lowest recognition rate of 96.8% for disgust. The joined D-T signature runs 485 iterations in 21 s to minimize MSE through MLP. The overall recognition rate of 95.9% is gained by NARX with the highest recognition rate of 100% for surprise and the lowest recognition rate of 90.5% for sadness. The joined D-T signature runs 480 iterations in 25 s to minimize MSE through NARX. RBF has got an overall recognition rate of 99.3% with the highest recognition rate of 100% for five expressions and the lowest recognition rate of 96.7% for happiness. The joined D-T signature runs 492 iterations in 28 s to minimize MSE through RBF. The joined D-T signature achieved a fantastic recognition rate compare to distance and texture signature.

Recall and F-measure on JAFFE Database of Distance, Texture, and D-T Signatures Using MLP, NARX, and RBF

Table 6.63 indicates the performance of F-measure and recall of distance signature through MLP, RBF, and NARX. The performance of f-measure and recall of texture signature is shown in Table 6.64. In the same way, the corresponding f-measure and

Table 6.63 The performance of distance signature on MUG dataset

| | Distance | | | | | |
| | MLP | | NARX | | RBF | |
	Recall	F-measure	Recall	F-measure	Recall	F-measure
Anger	1	1	0.94	0.97	1	1
Disgust	1	0.98	0.96	0.96	1	0.96
Fear	0.78	0.84	0.92	0.92	0.92	0.96
Happiness	0.96	0.95	0.96	0.96	0.93	0.94
Sadness	0.95	0.97	0.90	0.92	1	1
Surprise	1	0.98	1	0.96	1	1

Table 6.64 The performance of texture signature on MUG dataset

| | Texture | | | | | |
| | MLP | | NARX | | RBF | |
	Recall	F-measure	Recall	F-measure	Recall	F-measure
Anger	0.78	0.88	0.89	0.94	0.94	0.90
Disgsut	1	1	0.93	0.95	0.96	0.96
Fear	0.71	0.83	1	0.96	0.78	0.84
Happiness	0.93	0.93	0.93	0.94	0.93	0.96
Sadness	1	0.85	0.95	0.93	1	0.93
Surprise	0.96	0.94	1	0.96	0.96	0.98

Table 6.65 The performance of D-T signature on MUG dataset

| | D-T | | | | | |
| | MLP | | NARX | | RBF | |
	Recall	F-measure	Recall	F-measure	Recall	F-measure
Anger	1	1	0.94	0.97	1	1
Disgust	0.96	0.98	0.96	0.96	1	1
Fear	1	0.93	0.85	0.88	1	0.96
Happiness	0.96	98	0.93	0.93	0.96	0.98
Sadness	1	1	0.90	0.90	1	1
Surprise	1	1	1	0.96	1	1

recall of D-T signature are mentioned in Table 6.65. From this table we examine that the individual signature produces encouraging recognition rate of expressions but when we consider combined D-T signature yields encouraging classification rate of emotions.

6.4.4.1   Experimental Result of CNN on MUG Database

The distance, texture, and D-T signatures of the MMI dataset are considered to examine the classification rate of emotions through CNN. The recognition matrix of distance signature is shown in Table 6.66. Anger identifies 17 images positively and 2 images are in misclassification with disgust and fear. The disgust recognizes 25 images properly and 6 images are in a mismatch with anger and happiness. Fear detects 3 images positively and the maximum number of images are confused with all expressions. Happiness indicates 25 images perfectly and 5 images are misidentified with surprise and disgust. Sadness recognizes 9 images properly and 12 images are confused with all expressions. Surprise identifies 24 images properly and 2 images are in a mismatch with disgust and sadness.

Table 6.66 The recognition matrix of distance signature on MUG dataset through CNN

	Anger	Disgust	Fear	Happiness	Sadness	Surprise
Anger	17	1	1	0	0	0
Disgust	1	25	0	5	0	0
Fear	1	1	3	4	2	3
Happiness	0	4	0	25	0	1
Sadness	4	3	1	1	9	3
Surprise	0	1	0	0	1	24

Table 6.67 The recognition matrix of texture signature on MUG dataset through CNN

	Anger	Disgust	Fear	Happiness	Sadness	Surprise
Anger	10	2	1	4	0	2
Disgust	1	24	0	3	1	2
Fear	0	4	4	1	1	4
Happiness	1	0	10	12	1	5
Sadness	2	6	0	1	5	7
Surprise	0	3	3	3	1	16

The recognition matrix of texture signature is shown in Table 6.67. Anger identifies 10 images positively and 9 images are mismatched with all expressions except sadness. Disgust identifies 24 images rightly and 7 images are misclassified with anger, happiness, sadness, and surprise. Fear recognizes 4 images accurately and 1 image is in misclassification with surprise. Happiness identifies 8 images positively and 10 images are in a mismatch with anger. Sadness recognizes 5 images properly and a huge number of images are confused with all expressions except fear. Surprise identifies 16 images correctly and a large number of images are mismatched with the remaining expressions except anger.

The recognition matrix of D-T signature is shown in Table 6.68. Anger recognizes 16 images properly and 2 images are in misclassification with surprise and happiness. Disgust detects 13 images positively and a large number of images are mismatched with remaining positively except fear. Fear identifies 5 images accurately and 9 images are misclassified with remaining expressions. Happiness identifies 22 images accurately and 8 images are in a mismatch with disgust, anger, fear, and surprise. Sadness recognizes 10 images rightly and 11 images are misclassified with all expressions except fear. Surprise identifies 21 images positively and 5 images are misidentified with anger, happiness, and sadness.

The overall classification of the distance, texture, and D-T signatures is indicated in Table 6.69 on MMI for CNN. Distance signature gains an average recognition rate of 61.7% with the highest recognition rate of 80.8% for surprise and the lowest recognition rate of 35.7% for fear. The texture signature obtains an average recognition rate of 50.4% with the highest recognition rate of 77.4% for disgust and the lowest

Table 6.68 The recognition matrix of D-T signature on MUG dataset through CNN

	Anger	Disgust	Fear	Happiness	Sadness	Surprise
Anger	16	1	0	1	0	1
Disgust	1	13	0	15	1	1
Fear	1	0	5	2	3	3
Happiness	1	2	4	22	0	1
Sadness	1	2	0	4	10	4
Surprise	1	0	0	3	1	21

Table 6.69 Performance comparison on MUG datasets using CNN

	Anger	Disgust	Fear	Happiness	Sadness	Surprise	Avg.
Distance signature	84.2	41.9	35.7	73.3	47.6	80.8	61.7
Texture signature	52.6	77.4	28.6	40	23.8	61.5	50.4
D-T signature	89.5	80.6	21.4	83.3	42.9	92.3	73

recognition rate of 23.8% for surprise. The D-T signature gets an overall recognition rate of 73% with the highest recognition rate of 92.3% for surprise and the lowest recognition rate of 21.4% for fear. The D-T signature gains fantastic results.

The recalls are indicated as disgust $= 0.80$, anger $= 0.89$, happiness $= 0.83$, sadness $= 0.42$, fear $= 0.21$, and surprise $= 0.92$ and F-measures are mentioned as disgust $= 0.75$, anger $= 0.80$, happiness $= 0.76$, sadness $= 0.54$, fear $= 0.31$, and surprise $= 0.84$ of distance signature. The recall and F-measure are mentioned as (Recall: disgust $= 0.77$, anger $= 0.52$, happiness $= 0.40$, sadness $= 0.23$, fear $= 0.28$, and surprise $= 0.61$ and F-measure: disgust $= 0.60$, anger $= 0.60$, happiness $= 0.44$, sadness $= 0.33$, fear $= 0.34$, and surprise $= 0.51$) of texture signature. The recall and F-measure are indicated as (Recall: disgust $= 0.41$, anger $= 0.84$, happiness $= 0.73$, sadness $= 0.47$, fear $= 0.35$, and surprise $= 0.80$ and F-measure: disgust $= 0.53$, anger $= 0.80$, happiness $= 0.57$, sadness $= 0.55$, fear $= 0.43$, and surprise $= 0.73$) of D-T signature.

6.5 Discussion

The recognition rate on the CK+ dataset indicates that the evaluated distance, texture, and D-T techniques yield encouraging classification of expressions using three different MLP, RBF, and NARX networks. Though still there is also misclassification of emotion recognition. Table 6.70 indicates the overall recognition rate of six

Table 6.70 Performance comparison on benchmark datasets with various state-of-the-art

	Database	Anger	Disgust	Fear	Happiness	Sadness	Surprise	Avg.
Distance signature on MLP	CK+	98.6	100	97.3	95.2	91.5	92.8	95.9
Distance signature on NARX	CK+	98.6	98.1	97.7	98.8	97.2	100	98.4
Distance signature on RBF	CK+	100	98.1	100	100	94.4	100	98.7
Texture signature on MLP	CK+	88.9	96.3	81.4	85.7	97.2	89.9	89.9
Texture signature on NARX	CK+	98.6	98.1	97.7	98.8	98.6	100	98.6
Texture signature on RBF	CK+	98.6	90.7	83.7	100	95.8	100	94.8
D-T signature on MLP	CK+	98.6	100	97.7	94	98.6	98.6	97.9
D-T signature on NARX	CK+	98.6	96.3	97.7	98.8	98.6	100	98.3
D-T signature on RBF	CK+	100	100	100	100	93	98.6	98.6
[18]	CK+	87.8	93.3	94.3	94.2	96.4	98.4	94.1
[19]	CK+	87.1	90.2	92	98.1	91.4	100	93.1
[20]	CK+	87	91.5	90.9	96.9	84.5	91.2	90.3
[7]	CK+	71.3	95.3	81.1	95.4	88.2	98.2	88.2
Distance signature on MLP	JAFFE	100	100	78.6	100	85.7	100	94.1
Distance signature on NARX	JAFFE	95.2	100	85.7	85.7	100	100	93.2
Distance signature on RBF	JAFFE	100	100	78.6	100	100	100	96.4
Texture signature on MLP	JAFFE	100	75	92.9	100	92.9	100	93.5
Texture signature on NARX	JAFFE	85.7	90	85.7	92.9	85.7	100	90
Texture signature on RBF	JAFFE	100	95	100	85.7	92.9	92.9	94.4
D-T signature on MLP	JAFFE	100	100	100	100	71.4	100	95.2
D-T signature on NARX	JAFFE	95.2	95	85.7	92.9	85.7	100	92.4
D-T signature on RBF	JAFFE	100	100	100	100	85.7	100	97.6
[18]	JAFFE	100	86.2	93.7	96.7	77.4	96.6	91.7
[19]	JAFFE	96.6	90	93.7	93.5	93.5	90	92.8
[20]	JAFFE	89.3	90.7	91.1	92.6	90.2	92.3	91.1
Distance signature on MLP	MMI	97.5	74.4	68	100	86.7	77.3	83.9
Distance signature on NARX	MMI	97.5	97.4	96	95.8	70	100	92.8
Distance signature on RBF	MMI	90	100	76	66.7	100	77.3	85
Texture signature on MLP	MMI	85	97.4	56	100	96.7	77.3	85.4
Texture signature on NARX	MMI	87.5	94.9	80	91.7	96.7	100	91.8
Texture signature on RBF	MMI	100	87.2	64	66.7	76.7	81.8	79.4
D-T signature on MLP	MMI	77.5	97.4	92	87.5	90	86.4	88.5
D-T signature on NARX	MMI	100	97.4	92	83.3	93.3	100	94.3
D-T signature on RBF	MMI	97.5	71.8	88	95.8	96.7	95.5	90.9
[20]	MMI	80.1	78.2	81.3	83.2	77.1	81	80.1
[7]	MMI	65.6	72.5	72.5	88.2	71.1	93.8	77.4
Distance signature on MLP	MUG	100	100	78.6	96.7	95.2	100	95.1
Distance signature on NARX	MUG	94.7	96.8	92.9	96.7	90.5	100	95.2
Distance signature on RBF	MUG	100	100	92.9	93.3	100	100	97.7

(continued)

Table 6.70 (continued)

	Database	Anger	Disgust	Fear	Happiness	Sadness	Surprise	Avg.
Texture signature on MLP	MUG	78.9	100	71.4	93.3	100	96.2	92.2
Texture signature on NARX	MUG	89.5	93.5	100	93.3	95.2	100	95
Texture signature on RBF	MUG	94.7	96.8	78.6	93.3	100	96.2	94.3
D-T signature on MLP	MUG	100	96.8	100	96.7	100	100	98.6
D-T signature on NARX	MUG	94.7	96.8	100	93.3	90.5	100	95.9
D-T signature on RBF	MUG	100	100	100	96.7	100	100	99.3

Table 6.71 Performance comparison on benchmark datasets with CNN

	Database	Anger	Disgust	Fear	Happiness	Sadness	Surprise	Avg.
Distance signature	CK+	80.6	72.2	88.4	92.9	71.8	82.6	81.7
Texture signature	CK+	66.7	77.8	25.6	75	54.9	71	64.1
D-T signature	CK+	91.7	88.9	88.4	91.7	87.3	94.2	90.6
Distance signature	JAFFE	100	95.9	92.9	78.6	71.4	71.4	86.6
Texture signature	JAFFE	71.4	75	92.9	57.1	64.3	50	69.1
D-T signature	JAFFE	100	100	64.3	85.7	71.4	100	88.7
Distance signature	MMI	60	59	60	25	60	45.3	48.3
Texture signature	MMI	52.5	43.6	32	45.8	60	54.5	000
D-T signature	MMI	80	59	20	29.2	50	86.4	56.1
Distance signature	MUG	84.2	41.9	35.7	73.3	47.6	80.8	61.7
Texture signature	MUG	52.6	77.4	28.6	40	23.8	61.5	50.4
D-T signature	MUG	89.5	80.6	21.4	83.3	42.9	92.3	73

basic expressions. The D-T signature is gained encouraging recognition rate than the individual distance signature and texture signature. The RBF is achieved better approximation of result compared to MLP and NARX. Table 6.70 is used to compare the system performance on CK+. It is shown that the sadness is classified accurately through RBF and NARX.

The recognition rate on the JAFFE dataset indicates that the experimented distance, texture, and D-T techniques yield encouraging classification of expressions through different MLP, RBF, and NARX networks. Table 6.28 mentions the average recognition rate of six basic expressions. Though still there is also misclassification of expression recognition. The D-T signature yields promising results than the individual distance and texture signature. RBF performs better approximation result than the MLP and NARX. Table 6.70 is used to measure the system performance. It is shown that the fear gains poor recognition rate of expressions for each distance, texture, and combined D-T signature using MLP, RBF, and NARX.

A similar outcome occurred when experimenting with the MMI dataset. The classification rate on the MMI dataset indicates that the evaluated distance, texture, and D-T techniques yield encouraging classification of expression using three different

MLP, RBF, and NARX networks. Table 6.70 is used to measure the system performance on MMI dataset. Though still there is also misclassification of expressions recognition. It is shown that the recognition rate of D-T signature gains encouraging results compared to distance and texture signatures.

The classification rate on the MUG dataset indicates that the evaluated distance, texture, and D-T techniques yield encouraging classification of expressions using three different MLP, RBF, and NARX networks. Table 6.70 is used to measure the system performance on MUG dataset. Though still there is also misclassification of expression recognition. It is shown that the recognition rate of the D-T signature gains encouraging results.

The system performance of the expressions on four benchmark datasets (CK+, MMI, JAFE, and MUG) indicates that the examined classical networks perform encouraging accuracy compared to CNN on each distance, texture, and D-T approaches. Table 6.71 indicates the overall classification rate of emotions. Here we used some pre-processing approaches to detect the prominent feature set such as distance, texture, and D-T signature features set. The size of the individual signature (distance and texture) is a 9-dimensional vector space as a feature set. The combined D-T signature has an 18-dimensional vector space as a feature set. CNN yields a poor classification rate of expression for the less size of input feature.

6.5.1 Performance Measure with State of the Art

The proposed Distance signature, Texture signature, and D-T signature approaches are also measured with others literature [7, 18–24] for comparison of expressions. The comparison task with the other literature is very difficult due to a lack of knowledge of data of experimentation. The D-T signature achieves 100%, 100%, 93%, 100%, 98.6%, and 100%, respectively, for anger, disgust, sadness, fear, surprise, and happiness on CK+ dataset using RBF. It performed encouraging classification rate of emotions compared to [18]. Table 6.72 shows summarized outcomes with other literature. From the above experimentation, it is observed that the joined D-T signature achieved 98.7% overall recognition rate of emotions on CK+. It is also mentioned that proposed procedures achieved encouraging classification rate of emotions compared to the literature in [18, 23]. The joined D-T signature is shown encouraging recognition rate of expression on all datasets.

We evaluate experiments on the JAFFE dataset for comparison with other literature. The experimented Distance signature, Texture signature, and D-T signature approaches are measured with the literature [7, 18, 20] for comparison of expressions on JAFFE dataset. D-T signature is (Table 6.70) achieved 100%, 100%, 100%, 100%, 85.7%, and 100%, respectively, for anger, disgust, fear, happiness, sadness, and surprise on JAFFE dataset using RBF. It performs encouraging classification rate of emotions compared to [18]. Table 6.72 shows the summarized results with other state-of-the-art methods. The D-T signature achieved 97.6% of the overall recognition rate on JAFFE which is fantastic compared to literature in [18]. The

Table 6.72 Performance comparison on publicly available databases with different state-of-the-art methods

	CK+	JAFFE	MMI	MUG
Proposed D-T signature using RBF	98.5	97.9	90.0	99.3
Proposed D-T signature using NARX	98.5	92.6	94.9	95.9
Proposed D-T signature using MLP	97.7	95.9	88.4	98.6
Proposed distance signature using RBF	98.7	96.9	87.2	97.7
Proposed distance signature using NARX	98.5	94.7	92.7	95.2
Proposed distance signature using MLP	95.7	94.8	84.4	95.1
Proposed texture signature using RBF	95.9	94.8	81.7	94.3
Proposed texture signature using NARX	98.7	89.5	91.5	95
Proposed texture signature using MLP	90.1	92.8	85.4	92.2
[21]	95.1	–	–	–
[18]	94.1	91.8	–	–
[19]	93.1	92.9	–	–
[20]	90.4	95.0	80.1	–
[7]	88.2	–	71.49	–
[22]	88.2	–	71.5	–
[23]	96.6	–	–	–
[24]	90.9	–	–	–

joined D-T signature is shown encouraging the recognition rate of emotion on all datasets.

The experimented Distance signature, Texture signature, and D-T signature approaches are measured with other literature [7, 20, 22] for comparison of expressions on MMI dataset. The D-T signature (Table 6.70) achieved 97.5%, 71.8%, 88%, 95.8%, 96.7%, and 95.5%, respectively, for anger, disgust, fear, happiness, sadness, and surprise on MMI dataset using RBF. It performs encouraging recognition rate of expressions compared to [20]. Table 6.72 shows summarized outcomes with other literature. D-T signature achieved 80.1% of the average recognition rate of expressions on MMI dataset which is convincing compared to literature in [20]. The joined D-T signature is shown encouraging the classification rate of emotions on all datasets.

6.6 Sum-up Discussion

This chapter highlights the issue of expressed emotion recognition by using individual distance signature and texture signature and also joined the D-T signature. It also measures the classification rate of six basic emotions using different RBF, NARX, MLP, and CNN networks separately. The effectiveness of the proposed approaches is measured by the recognition rate of expressions and also compares to state-of-the-art methods. The evaluated results also establish the significant improvements in recognition rate due to the incorporation of distance signature, texture signature, and joined D-T signature. Individual signature (Distance and texture) yields an encouraging classification rate of emotions compared to other literature. It is also examined that the joined D-T signature achieves a more promising recognition rate of expressions compared to other literature. We will examine it into big data context including video in future work.

In the next chapter, we consider shape and texture signatures to form a shape-texture (S-T) signature to classify the expressions from human face images using neural networks such as MLP and DBN. We already introduced facial expression recognition using individual distance, shape, and texture signature features in Chaps. Chaps. 2, 3, and 4. After introducing the individual feature, we consider combined Distance-Shape (D-S) and Distance-Texture (D-T) signatures for recognizing the expressions from benchmark datasets. The S-T signature is evaluated on benchmark datasets to measure the system performances. It is also considered to measure the comparison with respect to individual distance, shape, and texture signatures and also combined D-S and D-T signature features.

References

1. T.F. Cootes, G.J. Edwards, C.J. Taylor, et al., Active appearance models. IEEE Trans. Pattern Anal. Mach. Intell. **23**(6), 681–685 (2001)
2. T. Ojala, M. Pietikäinen, D. Harwood, A comparative study of texture measures with classification based on featured distributions. Pattern Recognit. **29**(1), 51–59 (1996)
3. C. Shan, S. Gong, P.W. McOwan, Facial expression recognition based on local binary patterns: a comprehensive study. Image Vis. Comput. **27**(6), 803–816 (2009)
4. G. Tzimiropoulos, M. Pantic, Optimization problems for fast aam fitting in-the-wild, in *Proceedings of the IEEE International Conference on Computer Vision* (2013), pp. 593–600
5. Y. Tong, Y. Wang, Z. Zhu, Q. Ji, Robust facial feature tracking under varying face pose and facial expression. Pattern Recognit. **40**(11), 3195–3208 (2007)
6. X. Zhu, D. Ramanan, Face detection, pose estimation, and landmark localization in the wild, in *2012 IEEE Conference on Computer Vision and Pattern Recognition (CVPR)* (IEEE, 2012), pp. 2879–2886
7. L. Zhong, Q. Liu, P. Yang, J. Huang, D.N. Metaxas, Learning multiscale active facial patches for expression analysis. IEEE Trans. Cybern. **45**(8), 1499–1510 (2015)
8. A. Barman, P. Dutta, Facial expression recognition using distance and texture signature relevant features. Appl. Soft Comput. **77**, 88–105 (2019)
9. D. Chakrabarti, D. Dutta, Facial expression recognition using eigenspaces. Procedia Technol. **10**, 755–761 (2013)
10. M. Rosenblum, Y. Yacoob, L.S. Davis, Human expression recognition from motion using a radial basis function network architecture. IEEE Trans. Neural Netw. **7**(5), 1121–1138 (1996)
11. H. Jaeger, *Tutorial on Training Recurrent Neural Networks, Covering BPPT, RTRL, EKF and the "Echo State Network" Approach*, vol. 5 (GMD-Forschungszentrum Informationstechnik, 2002)
12. T. Lin, B.G. Horne, P. Tino, C.L. Giles, Learning long-term dependencies in narx recurrent neural networks. IEEE Trans. Neural Netw. **7**(6), 1329–1338 (1996)
13. R. Pascanu, T. Mikolov, Y. Bengio, On the difficulty of training recurrent neural networks. ICML **3**(28), 1310–1318 (2013)

14. P. Lucey, J.F. Cohn, T. Kanade, J. Saragih, Z. Ambadar, I. Matthews, The extended cohn-kanade dataset (ck+): a complete dataset for action unit and emotion-specified expression, in *Computer Society Conference on Computer Vision and Pattern Recognition-Workshops* (IEEE, 2010), pp. 94–101

15. M.F. Valstar, M. Pantic, Induced disgust, happiness and surprise: an addition to the mmi facial expression database, in *Proceedings of International Conference on Language Resources and Evaluation, Workshop on EMOTION* (Malta, May 2010), pp. 65–70

16. M. Lyons, S. Akamatsu, M. Kamachi, J. Gyoba, Coding facial expressions with gabor wavelets, in *Proceedings of Third IEEE International Conference on Automatic Face and Gesture Recognition, 1998* (IEEE, 1998), pp. 200–205

17. N. Aifanti, C. Papachristou, A. Delopoulos, The mug facial expression database, in *Proceedings of 11th International Workshop on Image Analysis for Facial Expression Database* (Desenzano, Italy, April 2010), pp. 12–14

18. SL Happy and Aurobinda Routray, Automatic facial expression recognition using features of salient facial patches. IEEE Trans. Affect. Comput. **6**(1), 1–12 (2015)

19. L. Zhang, D. Tjondronegoro, Facial expression recognition using facial movement features. IEEE Trans. Affect. Comput. **2**(4), 219–229 (2011)

20. A. Poursaberi, H.A. Noubari, M. Gavrilova, S.N. Yanushkevich, Gauss–laguerre wavelet textural feature fusion with geometrical information for facial expression identification. EURASIP J. Image Video Process. (1), 1–13 (2012)

21. I. Kotsia, I. Pitas, Facial expression recognition in image sequences using geometric deformation features and support vector machines. IEEE Trans. Image Process. **16**(1), 172–187 (2007)

22. L. Zhong, Q. Liu, P. Yang, B. Liu, J. Huang, D.N. Metaxas, Learning active facial patches for expression analysis, in *2012 IEEE Conference on Computer Vision and Pattern Recognition (CVPR)* (IEEE, 2012), pp. 2562–2569

23. H. Boughrara, M. Chtourou, C.B. Amar, L. Chen, Facial expression recognition based on a mlp neural network using constructive training algorithm. Multimed. Tools Appl. **75**(2), 709–731 (2016)

24. A.T. Lopes, E. de Aguiar, T. Oliveira-Santos, A facial expression recognition system using convolutional networks, in *2015 28th SIBGRAPI Conference on Graphics, Patterns and Images (SIBGRAPI)* (IEEE, 2015), pp. 273–280

Chapter 7
Human Emotion Recognition Using Combination of Shape-Texture Signature Feature

7.1 Introduction

In the previous Chaps. 2, 3, and 4 consist of feature descriptors individually distance signature, shape signature, and texture signature and Chaps. 5 and 6 are considered as combined descriptors such as distance and shape (D-S) and distance and texture (D-T). In course of Shape-Texture (S-T) signature respective stability indices and statistical measures supplement the signature features with a view to enhance the performance task of facial expression classification. Incorporation of these supplementary features is duly justified through extensive study and analysis of results obtained thereon.

While appreciating the usefulness of individual signature features in a marginal sense, the question coming up next is whether the joint contribution of the signature descriptors discussed in the previous chapters is in a portion to offer even more impressive performance. When we consider the join contribution of the feature, they gave promising recognition rates of facial expressions. For that reason again shape and texture features are joined together to measure the system accuracy of expression recognition. Accordingly, in this chapter, we use prominent attributes such as shape signature, texture signature, stability indices, and statistical measures viz. moment, kurtosis etc. These attributes are used as input to MLP and DBN for the classification of expressions in a supervised manner. The regions viz. eyebrows, eyes, jaw, and mouth have the prominent characteristic to identify the expressions from one emotion to another emotion. The appearance model is used to detect the landmark points from human face images. Most important landmarks are marked on the nose, mouth, eyes, and eyebrows regions. We consider three landmarks on the nose, four landmarks on the mouth, three landmarks on the eyebrow, and four landmarks on each eye. These most noticeable landmarks form a grid and the corresponding triangles are identified within the grid. Shape signature is extracted from triangles and texture signature is obtained from active facial patches. The relative stability indices are obtained from the shape and texture signatures and these attributes have an important role to

© Springer Nature Singapore Pte Ltd. 2020
P. Dutta and A. Barman, *Human Emotion Recognition from Face Images*,
Cognitive Intelligence and Robotics,
https://doi.org/10.1007/978-981-15-3883-4_7

identify the expressions. Statistical analyses such as moment, kurtosis, skewness etc. are computed from the normalized shape and texture signature duo. The merging of all these attributes for a particular signature is used as input of MLP and DBN for recognition of emotions. We mention that the combination of Shape-Texture (S-T) signature duo performs an overwhelming identification rate of expression over the individual signature.

In this chapter we consider the following terms:

1. Grid formation: Appearance model is applied on face image to detect the land-marks. Most noticeable landmarks are marked on the nose, mouth, eyes, and eyebrows regions. These important landmarks form a grid.
2. Now possible triangles are found within the grid and it also helps to extract shape signature.
3. Active facial patches are extracted from the mouth, eyebrows, eyes, and nose regions to deploy a texture region.
4. Shape signature is determined from the triangles of the grid and texture signature is calculated from the identified texture region. A Shape-Texture (S-T) signature duo is formed after joining the individual signature for the classification of emotions.
5. Stability indices are determined from individual and joined S-T signatures.
6. Statistical parameters such as moment, kurtosis, skewness, and entropy are deter-mined for the proficiency of features set.

Organization of This Chapter

This chapter is organized in six parts. In the first part, consisting of Sect. 7.1, we discuss about introduction of the individual signature of human emotion recognition. The second part of the Sect. 7.2 explores the overview of emotion recognition of shape, texture, and joined Shape-Texture (S-T) features.

The third part of this chapter, consisting of Sect. 7.3 shows the discussion on grid formation and triangle identification. In this part, we also discuss a shape signature. We also discuss a texture region formation and correspondingly local binary pattern are extracted. Why stability index plays an important role for recognizing the expres-sions. Statistical analyses such as moment, kurtosis, range, skewness, and entropy are deployed to form a formidable feature set.

In the next part, consisting of Sect. 7.4 shows the training of MLP and DBN. This part also discusses classification of emotions into different categories.

The Sect. 7.5 discusses the experiment and result analysis on four benchmark databases.

The chapter concludes with a conclusion in Sect. 7.6.

7.2   Overview of Proposed Facial Expression Recognition

The proposed facial expression recognition of shape signature and texture signature is indicated in Fig. 7.1. The AAM [1, 2] is considered to get the landmark points from face images. Most noticeable landmarks are marked on eyebrows, eyes, mouth,

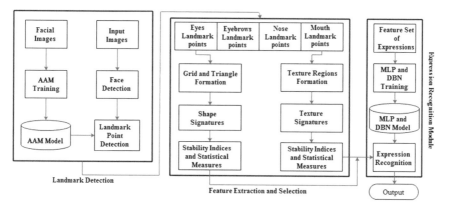

Fig. 7.1 Proposed methodology of emotion recognition using individual signature and combined S-T signature duo

and nose regions to get prominent features. These noticeable landmarks form a grid on a face image and corresponding facial patches are extracted from the identified landmarks. For the central geometric location of a human face, the nose region landmarks are marked as reference points to constitute triangles with other landmarks for any facial expression. The triangles are found within a grid and any such formed triangle has a distinct shape signature as per Eq. 3.12. It is observed that the shape signature of a specific triangle is sensitive to the facial expression under consideration. The formation of texture signature is constituted with the help of Local Binary Pattern (LBP). The stability indices are computed from both individual and combined S-T signatures. The statistical parameters viz. skewness, range, kurtosis, moment etc are determined from both normalized shape and texture signature and combined S-T signature for the proficiency of the feature set. These attributes are fed as input to MLP and DBN to recognize the emotions.

7.3   Formation of Grid and Triangle

The AAM fitting model is used to extract the landmark points on the facial image. The procedure of the AAM is discussed in the second chapter of Sect. 2.2.1 to detect the landmark points on the face image. The most noticeable landmarks are marked on mouth, nose, eyebrows, and eye regions due to their differentiation of expressions. The detailed discussion of the salient landmark points is also available in the second chapter of Sect. 2.2.2. These prominent landmarks are used to form triangles from the grid. The triangle formation discussion is elaborated in the third chapter of Sect. 3.2.2. The possibles triangles of the various facial expressions are indicated in Fig. 7.2.

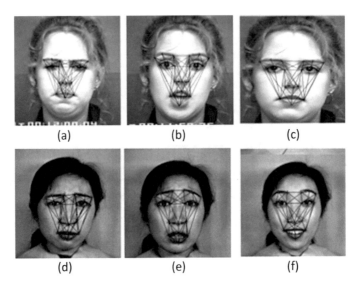

Fig. 7.2 Formation of grid and triangles on CK+ and JAFFE datasets

7.3.1 Formation of Texture Region

Prominent facial patches are extracted from a face dataset due to their elicitation of noticeable active patches. These noticeable patches are marked at the nose corner, mouth corner, and eye corner regions to get active facial patches from a particular face dataset. We already showed that the texture regions play a crucial role to recognize the expressions from different datasets. This discussion is available in the fourth chapter of Sect. 4.2.2. The numbering active facial patches are indicated in Fig. 7.3. The prominent patches are joined to form a texture region on a particular face dataset.

7.3.2 Shape Signature and Texture Signature

The individual shape and texture signature play an important role in recognizing facial expressions. Now we combine this individual signature to form a signature duo as Shape-Texture (S-T) to recognize the expressions and also measures the performance of D-T signature. The individual shape signature and texture signature are explained in the third and fourth chapters. The normalized shape signature is computed using Eq. 3.12. In the same way, normalized texture signature is computed using Eq. 4.3. This individual signature is combined together to get a S-T signature for recognizing the expressions.

Fig. 7.3 Position of facial
patches

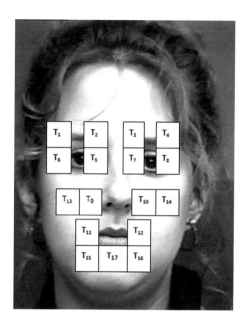

7.3.3 Stability Index of Shape and Texture Signature Features

The stability index is mentioned as a formidable attribute to identify the expressions. Higher-order signatures are computed to get the stability indices for each signature. The individual stability index plays a crucial role in recognizing expressions. Now a merged S-T signature duo is used to find the stability index for measuring the performance of emotions. The definition of the stability indices of shape and texture signatures is elaborated in the third and fourth chapters. These discussions are also available in Sects. 3.3.2 and 4.3.1.

7.3.4 Statistical Analysis of Shape and Texture Signature Features

In the previous third and fourth chapters, we observed that the statistical measures play a crucial role to recognize the expressions for individual shape and texture signature features. A huge number of features yields promising recognition rate of expression than the fewer attributes. For that reason, the statistical analyses such as moment, range, skewness, entropy, and kurtosis are supplemented as attributes set from each signature (shape and texture) to improve the efficiency of emotion identification.

7.3.5   Combined S-T Signature Duo

We compute the shape signature using Eq. 3.12 and texture signature using Eq. 4.3. Now corresponding stability indices are obtained from each signature (shape and texture). We also compute statistical parameters viz. moment, skewness, range, entropy, and kurtosis from the individual signature. Now we combine both shape and texture signatures for getting combined Shape-Texture (S-T) signature duo [3] for recognizing the expressions from the face image.

7.4   Feature Classification

Individual shape and texture signature features are represented as 9-dimensional elements in a vector space. The combined shape and texture (S-T) signature is represented as an 18-dimensional element of vector space for a particular face image. A min–max process is used for normalizing a feature vector. These features feed as input to MLP [4] and DBN [5] for classifying the emotions based on the minimum errors [6]. The proposed training algorithm of individual signature (Shape and Texture) and combined S-T signature duo are indicated in Algorithm 7.1.

7.4.1   The Training Procedure of MLP

The training procedure of MLP is completed by decreasing the Mean Square Error (MSE) [6] $e_k = 1/2 \sum (t_k - y_k)^2$ for different expressions. The term t_k and y_k represent target and expected outcome. The index of the $k =$ is 6 for MLP. The training procedure of MLP consists of four steps: weight initialization Feed-forward, Error backpropagation, and updation of weights and biases. In the first step, small random values are assigned as weight initialization. Input neuron x_i $(i = 1, \ldots, n)$, where n indicates number of the input information and sends this information to all hidden neurons z_j $(j = 8)$. We represent the biases and weights as v_o & w_o. Each hidden neuron calculates the output using a tan$h$ activation function and again it transmits z_j information to each output neuron. The last neurons compute the output responses through a linear function. The output neurons compute the associated errors as the difference between y_k and t_k. Depending on these errors, a δ_k $(k = 1, \ldots, m)$ factor is measured at output neuron y_k and send back to all the previous neurons. Here, m represents the output responses and it is set as $m = 6$. In the same way, the factor δ_j $(j = 1, \ldots, p)$ is computed to all hidden neurons as z_j, here p is set as 8 for all hidden units. In the last stage, biases and weights are modified through a δ factor. The terms ζ and η represent as threshold and learning rate. The process is terminated when it satisfies the condition $e_k \leq \zeta$. Now at the time of testing, six basic emotions are identified after getting the maximum value of the output neurons.

Algorithm 7.1 Proposed emotion recognition training algorithm of shape and texture signature features

---

Input: A $m \times n$ face image of emotion.
1: Appearance model is used to identify the landmarks on a face image.
2: Noticeable landmarks are marked on mouth, eyebrows, nose, and eyes regions.
3: Grid is formed with identified landmarks and triangles within the grid.
4: Texture feature is calculated from the texture region.
5: Compute the normalized shape and texture signature features.
6: Compute the stability indices for both signatures (shape and texture) and also find the moment, skewness, kurtosis, and entropy.
7: merge all these features for the formation of prominent feature set individually and jointly.
8: MLP and DBN are used to recognize the emotions into six basic categories.
Output: Recognized emotions.

7.4.2 Training Procedure of Deep Belief Network

The training procedure of DBN [5] consists of two stages: a pre-training in the first stage and fine-tuning in the second stage. The pre-training step follows the process of Restricted Boltzmann Machine (RBM) [7]. The RBM decreases the local optimum error using supervised learning mode. The noticeable point of DBN is its proficiency for collecting prominent attributes as input feature set. The RBM level is modified by the support of the previous level. After computing, the weight matrices of the first stage are used as an input signal of the second level and it continues the same procedure until the last level found. This procedure is repeated during the training of RBM. At the time of training, the input feature is decreased level by level and hence, the selected attributes at the hidden neurons of the last level can be identified as a vector of an attribute for the current level. The Contrastive Divergence (CD) [8] modifies the weight matrices level by level. The architecture of the DBN has three hidden levels with the different numbers of neurons at various levels such as 9/18 for input level, 8/16 for first hidden level, 6/12 for second hidden level, 4/8 for third hidden level, and 6 for output level. The greedy training procedure is used for weights initialization. When the first RBM weights are trained, 1st hidden level (h_1) remains fixed. The 2nd RBM weights are updated during training with the previous fixed hidden level. The previous RBM weights are used to train the 3rd RBM. The RBM procedure includes few crucial stages. First of all, a bias vector H for the hidden layer, a bias vector P for the visible layer, a weight matrix T all are set to zero in the initialization stage.

$$h_1(x) = \begin{cases} 1, & \text{if } f(H + P_1 T^T) > \gamma; \\ 0, & \text{otherwise} \end{cases} \qquad (7.1)$$

$$P_{rec} = \begin{cases} 1, & \text{if } f(P + h_1 T^> \gamma; \\ 0, & \text{otherwise} \end{cases} \qquad (7.2)$$

$$h_{\text{rec}} = f(H + P_{\text{rec}} T^T) \tag{7.3}$$

Next, the binary state of the hidden layer h_1 is computed and later on it is useful for reconstruction of binary state for the visible layer p_{rec} using Eq. 7.2. Then, the hidden layer h_{rec} is computed using p_{rec} where

$$f(t) = 1/(1 + \exp(-t)) \tag{7.4}$$

The threshold (γ) is adjusted with the weights to compute the output through sigmoid activation in the network and the difference of the weight is computed as

$$\Delta T = (h_1 p_1 / B) - (h_{\text{rec}} . P_{\text{rec}}) / B \tag{7.5}$$

where B represents the batch size. At last, the current weight becomes a summation of the previous level weights. These procedures are continued for all batches. When RBM is terminated, a classical back propagation mechanism is used for fine-tuning of parameters.

7.5 Experiment and Result

The classification rate of shape signature and texture signature are measured individually and in combination with Cohn-Kanade (CK+) [9], JAFFE [10], MMI [11], MUG [12], and Wild [13, 14] datasets. Prominent features of each signature (shape and texture) are mentioned as 9-dimensional vector space elements. MLP and DBN have been considered to recognize the emotions. The evaluated results are compared with the different state-of-the-art procedures for the effectiveness of the proposed system.

We also compute the false rejection rate (FRR), false acceptance rate (FAR), and error rate (ERR) of each dataset to measure the system performance. False acceptance rate (FAR): it is the probability that the system incorrectly matches with images stored with the input image database. False rejection rate (FRR): it is the ratio of a number of correct persons rejected in the database to the total number of persons in the database.

7.5.1 Experimental Result on CK+ Dataset

The CK+ dataset has a hundred university students and they are aged within 18–30 years. This dataset consists of 15% of African–American, 65% of female, and 3% of Asian or Latino faces. The MLP and DBN are used to recognize the expressions. To validate the classification rate, the dataset has been divided into two parts. One

Table 7.1 The MLP-based recognition matrix of Shape signature on CK+ dataset

	Anger	Disgust	Fear	Happiness	Sadness	Surprise
Anger	70	2	0	0	0	0
Disgust	0	50	4	0	0	0
Fear	0	0	41	2	0	0
Happiness	0	0	0	82	2	0
Sadness	1	0	0	1	69	0
Surprise	0	0	0	0	0	69

Table 7.2 The performance of Shape signature on CK+ dataset through MLP

	FAR	FRR	ERR
Anger	0.003	0.027	0.007
Disgust	0.005	0.074	0.015
Fear	0.011	0.046	0.015
Happiness	0.009	0.023	0.012
Sadness	0.006	0.023	0.010
Surprise	0	0	0

is training (782 images or samples) and the remaining one is testing (393 images or samples) set for measuring the recognition rate of facial expressions.

7.5.1.1 Results Analysis of Shape, Texture, and S-T Signature Features on CK+ Dataset

The shape, texture, and S-T signature features use a total of 393 images to test the recognition rate of facial expressions. The images are divided as 71 for anger, 54 for disgust, 44 for fear, 71 for sadness, 84 for happiness, and 69 for surprise.

Shape signature: Table 7.1 indicates the classification rate of shape signature using MLP. Anger identifies 70 images perfectly and 2 images are misidentified with disgust. Disgust recognizes 50 images positively and 4 images are in confusion with fear. Fear identifies 41 images properly and 2 images are misclassified as happiness. Happiness recognizes 82 images perfectly and 2 images are misidentified as sadness. Sadness recognizes 69 images properly and 1 image is misidentified as happiness. Surprise identifies 69 images properly.

The parameter of FAR, FRR, and ERR are also considered to measure the system performance of shape signature using MLP. Table 7.2 shows the evaluated results of FAR, FRR, and ERR. The FAR represents the higher recognition rate of facial expressions. The disgust yields FRR as 0.005. The disgust produces 0.015 as ERR. It also indicates that the system has the highest recognition rate of expressions.

Table 7.3 The MLP-based recognition matrix of Texture signature on CK+ dataset

	Anger	Disgust	Fear	Happiness	Sadness	Surprise
Anger	68	2	1	0	0	1
Disgust	0	47	2	0	0	5
Fear	0	10	31	1	0	1
Happiness	1	0	0	80	0	3
Sadness	1	0	0	2	67	1
Surprise	0	0	0	0	0	69

Table 7.4 The performance of Texture signature on CK+ dataset through MLP

	FAR	FRR	ERR
Anger	0.006	0.055	0.015
Disgust	0.035	0.129	0.048
Fear	0.008	0.279	0.038
Happiness	0.009	0.047	0.017
Sadness	0	0.056	0.010
Surprise	0.034	0	0.028

Table 7.3 indicates the proper classification of expressions with misclassification. **Texture signature** recognizes 68 images properly as anger and 4 images are misidentified with fear, disgust, and surprise. Disgust recognizes 47 images properly and 7 images are in misclassification with fear and surprise. Fear indicates 31 images perfectly and 2 images are misclassified with happiness and surprise. Happiness recognizes 80 images properly and 4 images are misidentified with surprise and anger. Sadness identifies 67 images positively and 2 images are in a mismatch with anger and surprise. Surprise classifies 69 accurately.

The parameter of FAR, FRR, and ERR are also considered to measure the system performance of texture signature using MLP. The evaluated results of FAR, FRR, and ERR are shown in Table 7.4. The FAR value of anger is 0.006 that means it produces a 6/1000 false accept rate. The anger produces FRR as 0.055. The lowest ERR is 0.010 for sadness.

S-T signature represents the recognition rate of emotion in Table 7.5. Anger identifies 70 images positively and 2 images are in a mismatch as disgust. Disgust identifies 51 images positively and 3 images are in misclassification with fear and happiness. Fear recognizes 41 images properly and 2 images are confused with happiness. Happiness identifies 82 images rightly and 2 images are in misclassification as sadness. Sadness detects 69 images accurately and 2 images are misclassified with happiness and anger. Surprise identifies 69 images accurately.

The FAR, FRR, and ERR are considered to evaluate the system performances of shape signature using NARX. Table 7.6 shows the evaluated results of FAR, FRR,

Table 7.5 The MLP-based recognition matrix of S-T signature on CK+ dataset

	Anger	Disgust	Fear	Happiness	Sadness	Surprise
Anger	70	2	0	0	0	0
Disgust	0	51	1	2	0	0
Fear	0	0	41	2	0	0
Happiness	0	0	0	82	2	0
Sadness	1	0	0	1	69	0
Surprise	0	0	0	0	0	69

Table 7.6 The performance of S-T signature on CK+ dataset through MLP

	FAR	FRR	ERR
Anger	0.003	0.027	0.007
Disgust	0.005	0.055	0.012
Fear	0.002	0.046	0.007
Happiness	0.016	0.023	0.017
Sadness	0.006	0.028	0.010
Surprise	0	0	0

Fig. 7.4 FAR of CK+ using MLP

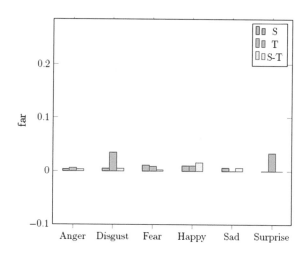

and ERR. The FAR value of fear is 0.002 that means it produces a 2/1000 false accept rate. The anger produces FRR as 0.027.

The comparison of the FAR for shape, texture, and S-T signature features through MLP on CK+ is shown in Fig. 7.4. The FAR graph analysis of shape signature yields a poor recognition rate in happiness. FAR graph analysis of texture signature shows a less promising performance than the shape signature. From this graph analysis, we

Fig. 7.5 FRR of CK+ using
MLP

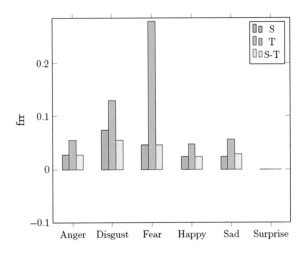

Fig. 7.5 FRR of CK+ using
MLP

Fig. 7.6 ERR of CK+ using
MLP

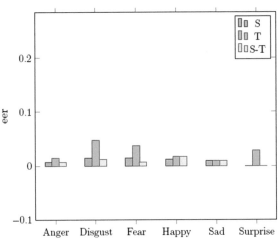

also conclude that the joined D-S signature yields a promising recognition rate of
individual expressions.

The comparison of the FRR for shape, texture and S-T signature features through
MLP on CK+ is shown in Fig. 7.5. The FRR graph analysis of shape signature yields
a poor recognition rate in sadness. The FRR graph analysis of the texture signature
feature performs a poor classification rate of emotions. It is also shown that the joined
D-S signature indicates a promising identification rate of individual expressions.

The comparison of the ERR for shape, texture, and S-T signatures through MLP
on CK+ is shown in Fig. 7.6. The ERR graph analysis of shape signature yields a
poor recognition rate in sadness. The ERR graph analysis of texture signature shows
a less promising performance than the shape signature. From this graph analysis, it

Table 7.7 The DBN-based recognition matrix of shape signature on CK+ dataset

	Anger	Disgust	Fear	Happiness	Sadness	Surprise
Anger	70	2	0	0	0	0
Disgust	0	50	4	0	0	0
Fear	0	0	41	2	0	0
Happiness	0	0	0	82	2	0
Sadness	1	0	0	1	69	0
Surprise	0	0	0	0	0	69

Table 7.8 The performance of Shape signature on CK+ dataset through DBN

	FAR	FRR	ERR
Anger	0.003	0.027	0.007
Disgust	0.005	0.074	0.015
Fear	0.011	0.046	0.015
Happiness	0.009	0.023	0.012
Sadness	0.006	0.028	0.010
Surprise	0	0	0

is also showed that the combined D-S signature yields a promising recognition rate of individual expressions.

Results Analysis of Shape, Texture, and S-T Signature Features on CK+ Dataset Through DBN

The overall classification of the shape signature through DBN is presented in Table 7.7. **Shape signature** recognizes 70 samples as anger rightly and 2 samples are in misclassification with disgust. The disgust identifies 50 samples correctly and 4 samples are misidentified as fear. Fear recognizes 41 samples perfectly and 2 samples are misidentified with happiness. Happiness indicates 82 images as correct classification and 2 images in misidentified with sadness. Sadness identifies 69 samples properly and 2 samples are in misclassification with happiness and anger. Surprise identifies the proper classification.

The FAR, FRR, and ERR parameters are used to measure the system performance of shape signature. The FAR, FRR, and ERR of the shape signature through DBN on CK+ dataset is tabulated in Table 7.8. The FAR value of anger is 0.003 which means it produces a 3/1000 as a false accept rate. The anger produces FRR as 0.027.

Texture signature presents the proper recognition of expressions with misclassification in Table 7.9. Here we observe that anger recognizes 66 images perfectly and 6 images are in confusion with fear and disgust. It is also identified that surprise expression yields excellent classification and 4 samples are misidentified with

Table 7.9 The DBN-based recognition matrix of Texture signature on CK+ dataset

	Anger	Disgust	Fear	Happiness	Sadness	Surprise
Anger	66	4	2	0	0	0
Disgust	0	50	1	1	2	0
Fear	0	1	41	0	1	0
Happiness	0	0	0	80	1	3
Sadness	0	1	0	2	66	2
Surprise	1	0	0	0	0	68

Table 7.10 The performance of Texture signature on CK+ dataset through DBN

	FAR	FRR	ERR
Anger	0.003	0.083	0.017
Disgust	0.017	0.074	0.025
Fear	0.008	0.046	0.012
Happiness	0.009	0.047	0.017
Sadness	0.012	0.070	0.022
Surprise	0.015	0.014	0.015

anger, happiness, and sadness. Fear indicates 41 images as correct classification and 2 samples are misclassified with disgust and sadness. Happiness detects 80 images properly and 4 images are misclassified with sadness and surprise. Sadness classifies 66 images positively and 5 samples are misidentified with disgust, happiness, and surprise. Surprise recognizes 69 images perfectly but only 1 image is misclassified with anger.

The FAR, FRR, and ERR parameters are used to measure the system performance of texture signature. The FAR, FRR, and ERR of texture signature using DBN for CK+ database are presented in Table 7.10. The FAR value of anger is 0.003 that means it produces a 3/1000 as false accept rate. The anger produces FRR as 0.083. The lowest ERR is 0.12 for fear.

S-T signature indicates the proper identification of expressions with misclassification in Table 7.11. Anger identifies 70 images correctly and 2 samples are misidentified as disgust. Disgust recognizes 53 samples properly and 1 image is misclassified as fear. Fear indicates 41 samples properly and 2 images are confused with happiness. Happiness identifies 84 samples properly and 1 image is in confusion with anger. Sadness recognizes 69 samples properly and 2 images are in a mismatch with happiness and anger. Surprise indicates correct identification.

The recognition rate of facial expression is also computed in parameters of the FAR, FRR, and ERR. The FAR, FRR, and ERR of the S-T signature using DBN for CK+ dataset is mentioned in Table 7.12. The FAR value of anger is 0.003 that means it produces a 3/1000 as false accept rate. The anger produces FRR as 0.027.

Table 7.11 The recognition matrix of S-T signature on CK+ dataset through DBN

	Anger	Disgust	Fear	Happiness	Sadness	Surprise
Anger	70	2	0	0	0	0
Disgust	0	53	1	0	0	0
Fear	0	0	41	2	0	0
Happiness	1	0	0	84	0	0
Sadness	1	0	0	1	69	0
Surprise	0	0	0	0	0	69

Table 7.12 The performance of S-T signature on CK+ dataset through DBN

	FAR	FRR	ERR
Anger	0.003	0.027	0.007
Disgust	0.005	0.018	0.007
Fear	0.002	0.046	0.007
Happiness	0.009	0	0.007
Sadness	0	0.028	0.005
Surprise	0	0	0

Fig. 7.7 FAR of CK+ using DBN

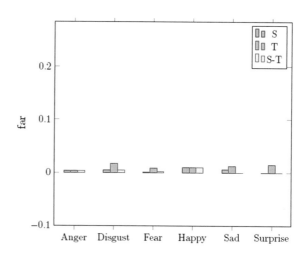

The comparison of the FAR for shape, texture, and S-T signature features through MLP on CK+ is shown in Fig. 7.7. The FAR graph analysis of shape signature yields poor recognition rate in happiness. FAR graph analysis of texture signature shows a less promising performance than the shape signature. From this graph analysis, we also conclude that the joined D-S signature feature yields promising identification rate of individual expressions.

Fig. 7.8 FRR of CK+ using DBN

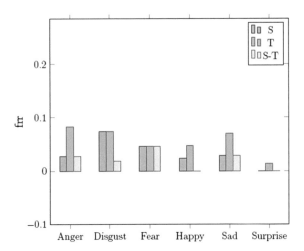

Fig. 7.9 ERR of CK+ using DBN

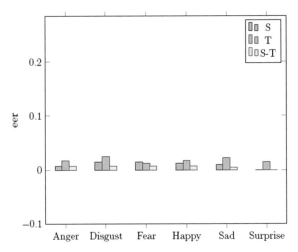

The comparison of the FRR for shape, texture, and S-T signature features through DBN on CK+ is shown in Fig. 7.8. The FRR graph analysis of shape signature yields a poor recognition rate in sadness. The FRR graph analysis of texture signature shows poor detection rate of emotions. It is also shown that the joined D-S signature indicates a promising detection rate of individual emotions.

The comparison of the ERR for shape, texture, and S-T signature features using DBN on CK+ is shown in Fig. 7.9. The ERR graph analysis of shape signature yields poor recognition rate in sadness. The ERR graph analysis of texture signature shows a less promising performance than the shape signature. From this graph analysis, it is also shown that the joined D-S signature yields a promising detection rate of individual emotions.

7.5.2 Discussion

In Table 7.3, fear indicates most difficult emotion in correct classification for texture
signature through MLP. It is noticed that shape and S-T signature features yield excellent recognition rate of expression whereas texture signature yields a less promising
identification rate of emotion for fear.

It presents that the disgust shows an indispensable detection rate of emotion for the
S-T signature feature through DBN. The disgust is misidentified with fear in a shape
signature feature. It shows that the disgust and fear emotions share common regions
of triangles during feature extraction of shape features. In this way, the disgust is
misidentified with fear, happiness, and sadness in the texture feature set. It indicates
that they extract common facial patches from the texture feature set.

7.5.3 Comparison of Results with State of the Art

The suggested Shape signature, Texture signature, and joined S-T signature procedures are measured with evaluated results of state-of-the-art methods [15–22].
We evaluate our investigation on the CK+ dataset of three different attributes
through MLP and DBN for comparison with other literature. Table 7.13 shows the
results of our proposed method with state-of-the-art methods. Our different proposed
approaches are compared with other approaches [21, 22] for comparison. From the
above observations, we notice that our suggested methods yield promising identification rate of emotion than the other approaches [21, 22]. We get an overall accuracy
of shape feature through DBN as 97.1% on CK+ dataset which is more promising
than [16] presented in Table 7.13. Shape, texture, and S-T signature features yield an
overwhelming recognition rate of expressions on CK+ using both MLP and DBN. It
is also noticed that the DBN-based emotion recognition yields a promising detection
rate. Table 7.13 indicates the average accuracy of six basic emotions from which it
indicates that joined S-T signature performs promising detection rate of emotion.

7.5.4 Experimental Result on JAFFE Dataset

The JAFFE [10] dataset consists of a total of 213 gray level images of ten Japanese
females. Six basic expressions include sadness, anger, disgust, fear, surprise, and
happiness. To measure the identification rate of emotion, the dataset has been divided
into two parts. One is training (116 images or samples) and the second one is a testing
set (97 images or samples).

Table 7.13 Performance analysis on CK+ dataset with the state-of-the-art methods

	Anger	Disgust	Fear	Happiness	Sadness	Surprise	
Shape (MLP)	97.2	92.6	95.3	97.6	97.2	100	96.6
Texture (MLP)	94.4	87	72.1	95.2	94.4	100	90.5
S-T (MLP)	97.2	94.4	95.3	97.6	97.2	100	96.9
Shape (DBN)	97.2	92.6	95.3	100	97.2	100	97.1
Texture (DBN)	91.7	92.6	95.3	95.2	93	98.6	94.4
S-T (DBN)	97.2	98.1	95.3	100	97.2	100	98
[15]	98.5	99	98.5	99.4	99.1	99	98.9
[16]	85.1	97.7	85.3	98.5	79.7	98.8	91
[18]	87.8	94.3	93.3	94.2	96.4	98.4	94.1
[20]	87.1	90.2	92	98.7	91.4	100	93.1
[19]	88.2	94.9	92.2	97.8	87.8	92.1	92.2
[17]	71.9	95.3	81.1	95.4	88	98.2	88.1
[21]	92.5	95	–	97.5	97.5	97.5	96
[22]	97.5	96.6	96	100	96.6	100	97.7

Table 7.14 The MLP-based recognition matrix of Shape signature on JAFFE dataset

	Anger	Disgust	Fear	Happiness	Sadness	Surprise
Anger	21	0	0	0	0	0
Disgust	0	18	0	0	0	2
Fear	2	1	11	0	0	0
Happiness	0	0	0	14	0	0
Sadness	0	0	2	0	12	0
Surprise	0	0	0	0	0	14

7.5.4.1 Results Analysis on JAFFE Dataset Through MLP

A total of 97 samples are used to measure the system accuracy of six basic expressions. These images are decomposed as 20 for disgust, 21 for anger, 14 for fear, 14 for sadness, 14 for surprise, and 14 for happiness.

Table 7.14 indicates correct classification of expressions of shape signature using MLP with misclassification. **Shape signature**: anger identifies 21 samples accurately. Disgust recognizes 18 samples perfectly and 2 samples are in a mismatch as a surprise. Fear identifies 11 samples perfectly and 3 samples are misidentified

Table 7.15 The performance of Shape signature on JAFFE dataset through MLP

	FAR	FRR	ERR
Anger	0.026	0	0.020
Disgust	0.013	0.100	0.030
Fear	0.024	0.214	0.051
Happiness	0	0	0
Sadness	0	0.142	0.020
Surprise	0.024	0	0.020

Table 7.16 The MLP-based recognition matrix of Texture signature on JAFFE dataset

	Anger	Disgust	Fear	Happiness	Sadness	Surprise
Anger	18	0	0	0	3	0
Disgust	0	20	0	0	0	0
Fear	2	1	11	0	0	0
Happiness	0	0	0	12	2	0
Sadness	0	0	0	0	14	0
Surprise	0	0	0	0	0	14

with disgust and anger. The happiness and surprise recognize 14 samples perfectly. Sadness detects 12 samples properly and 2 samples are in misclassification with fear. Surprise indicates 14 images properly in classification.

The expression recognition accuracy of suggested approach is measured in terms of FAR, FRR, and ERR. The FAR, FRR, and ERR of shape signature through MLP on JAFFE dataset are tabulated in Table 7.15. The FAR value of disgust is 0.013 which means it produces a 13/1000 as a false accept rate. The disgust produces FRR as 0.010.

The **texture signature** presents the proper classification of expression with misclassification in Table 7.16. Anger identifies 18 images perfectly and 3 samples are in confusion with sadness. Disgust detects 20 samples positively. Fear recognizes 11 samples properly and 3 samples are misidentified with disgust and anger. Happiness identifies 12 images perfectly and 2 samples are in misclassification with sadness. Sadness and surprise recognize the expressions accurately.

The FAR, FRR, and ERR are also used to measure the expression recognition accuracy of the proposed method. The values of FAR, ERR, and FRR of texture feature through MLP on JAFFE dataset are tabulated in Table 7.17. The FAR value of anger is 0.026 that means it produces a 26/1000 as false accept rate. The disgust produces FRR as 0.142.

The **S-T signature** indicates the correct recognition of expressions with misclassification in Table 7.18. Anger recognizes 21 images accurately. Disgust also identifies 20 images properly. Fear indicates 13 images positively and 1 sample is misidentified with anger. Happiness identifies 14 images properly. Sadness classi-

Table 7.17 The performance of Texture signature on JAFFE dataset through MLP

	FAR	FRR	ERR
Anger	0.026	0.142	0.051
Disgust	0.013	0	0.010
Fear	0	0.214	0.030
Happiness	0	0.014	0.020
Sadness	0.060	0	0.051
Surprise	0	0	0

Table 7.18 The MLP-based recognition matrix of S-T signature on JAFFE dataset

	Anger	Disgust	Fear	Happiness	Sadness	Surprise
Anger	21	0	0	0	0	0
Disgust	0	20	0	0	0	0
Fear	1	0	13	0	0	0
Happiness	0	0	0	14	0	0
Sadness	0	0	2	0	12	0
Surprise	0	0	0	0	1	13

Table 7.19 The performance of S-T signature on JAFFE dataset through MLP

	FAR	FRR	ERR
Anger	0.013	0	0.010
Disgust	0	0	0
Fear	0.024	0.071	0.030
Happiness	0	0	0
Sadness	0.012	0.142	0.030
Surprise	0	0.071	0.010

fies 12 images rightly and 2 samples are misclassified as fear. Surprise indicates 13 samples positively and 1 sample is in confusion with sadness.

The FAR, FRR, and ERR of S-T signature through MLP on JAFFE dataset are tabulated in Table 7.19. The FAR value of fear is 0.024 that means it produces a 24/1000 as false accept rate. The disgust produces FRR as 0.071.

The performance of the FAR for shape, texture, and S-T signature features through MLP on the JAFFE dataset is shown in Fig. 7.10. The FAR graph analysis of shape signature yields poor recognition rate in happiness and sadness. the FAR graph analysis of texture signature shows a less promising recognition rate in fear, happiness, and surprise. From this graph analysis, we also conclude that the joined S-T signature yields a promising detection rate in fear.

Fig. 7.10 FAR of JAFFE using MLP

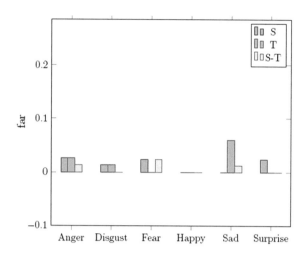

Fig. 7.11 FRR of JAFFE using MLP

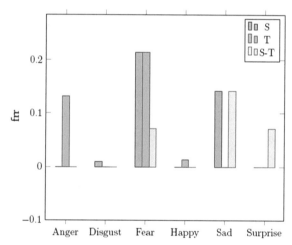

The comparison of the FRR for shape, texture, and S-T signature features through MLP on the JAFFE dataset is shown in Fig. 7.11. The FRR graph analysis of shape signature yields a poor recognition rate in anger, happiness, and surprise expressions. The FRR graph analysis of texture features shows a poor detection rate of emotion in disgust, sadness, and surprise expressions. It is also showed that the joined S-T signature indicates a promising identification rate in surprise.

The comparison of the ERR for shape, texture, and S-T signatures using MLP on the JAFFE dataset is shown in Fig. 7.12. The ERR graph analysis of shape signature yields a poor recognition rate in happiness. The ERR graph analysis of texture signature shows a less promising performance than the shape signature. From this graph analysis, it is also shown that the joined S-T feature yields a higher detection rate in fear and sadness.

Fig. 7.12 ERR of JAFFE
using MLP

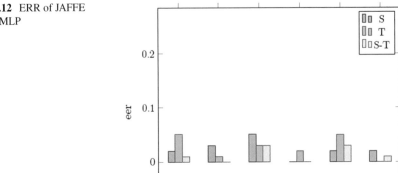

Table 7.20 The DBN-based recognition matrix of Shape signature on JAFFE dataset

	Anger	Disgust	Fear	Happiness	Sadness	Surprise
Anger	21	0	0	0	0	0
Disgust	0	20	0	0	0	0
Fear	1	0	12	0	0	1
Happiness	0	0	0	14	0	0
Sadness	0	0	0	0	13	1
Surprise	0	0	1	0	0	13

Results Evaluation on JAFFE Database Using DBN

The DBN is also used to measure the system performance of emotion through shape, texture, and S-T signature features.

Table 7.20 indicates the classification of expression recognition of shape signature through DBN. **Shape signature** produces proper detection in disgust, anger, and happiness. Fear identifies 12 samples perfectly and 2 samples are in misclassification with anger and surprise. Sadness classifies 13 samples positively and 1 sample is misclassified with Surprise. Sadness identifies 13 samples rightly and 1 sample is in confusion with fear.

The expression recognition accuracy of the proposed method is computed in terms of FAR, FRR, and ERR. The FAR, FRR, and ERR of shape signature through DBN on the JAFFE dataset are tabulated in Table 7.21. The FAR value of fear is 0.012 that means it produces a 12/1000 as false accept rate. The FRR of fear is produced as 0.142.

Texture signature produces the correct recognition of expressions with misclassification in Table 7.22. Anger and disgust recognize the images accurately. Fear

Table 7.21 performance of Shape signature on JAFFE dataset through DBN

	FAR	FRR	ERR
Anger	0.013	0	0.010
Disgust	0	0	0
Fear	0.012	0.142	0.030
Happiness	0	0	0
Sadness	0	0.071	0.010
Surprise	0.024	0.071	0.030

Table 7.22 The DBN-based recognition matrix of Texture signature on JAFFE dataset

	Anger	Disgust	Fear	Happiness	Sadness	Surprise
Anger	21	0	0	0	0	0
Disgust	0	20	0	0	0	0
Fear	2	1	11	0	0	0
Happiness	2	0	0	12	0	0
Sadness	0	0	0	0	14	0
Surprise	0	0	0	0	0	14

Table 7.23 The performance of Texture signature on JAFFE dataset through DBN

	FAR	FRR	ERR
Anger	0.052	0	0.041
Disgust	0.013	0	0.010
Fear	0	0.214	0.030
Happiness	0	0.142	0.020
Sadness	0	0	0
Surprise	0	0	0

identifies 11 samples properly and 3 samples are misidentified with fear and anger. Happiness identifies 12 images accurately and 2 samples are in misclassification with anger. Sadness and surprise detect the samples correctly.

The FAR, FRR, and ERR are also used to measure expression recognition accuracy of the proposed method. The FAR, FRR, and ERR of texture signature through DBN on the JAFFE dataset are tabulated in Table 7.23. The FAR value of anger is 0.052 that means it produces a 52/1000 as false accept rate. The fear produces FRR as 0.214.

S-T signature indicates the proper recognition of emotion with wrong classification in Table 7.24. Anger and disgust identify the images accurately. Fear recognizes 13 samples positively and 1 sample is misidentified with fear. Happiness, Sadness, and surprise identify the images accurately.

Table 7.24 The DBN-based recognition matrix of S-T signature on JAFFE dataset

	Anger	Disgust	Fear	Happiness	Sadness	Surprise
Anger	21	0	0	0	0	0
Disgust	0	20	0	0	0	0
Fear	1	0	13	0	0	0
Happiness	0	0	0	14	0	0
Sadness	0	0	0	0	14	0
Surprise	0	0	0	0	0	14

Table 7.25 The performance of S-T signature on JAFFE dataset through DBN

	FAR	FRR	ERR
Anger	0.005	0	0.010
Disgust	0	0	0
Fear	0.012	0.071	0.010
Happiness	0	0	0
Sadness	0	0	0
Surprise	0	0	0

Fig. 7.13 FAR of JAFFE using DBN

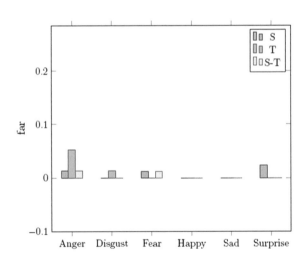

The FAR, FRR, and ERR are also tabulated to show the performance of the proposed method. The FAR, ERR, & FRR of S-T signature using DBN for the JAFFE database are tabulated in Table 7.25. The FAR value of fear is 0.012 that means it produces a 12/1000 as false accept rate. The disgust produces FRR as 0.071.

The performance of the FAR for shape, texture, and S-T signature features through DBN on the JAFFE dataset is shown in Fig. 7.13. The FAR graph analysis of shape signature yields poor recognition rate in disgust, happiness, and sadness. The FAR

Fig. 7.14 FRR of JAFFE using DBN

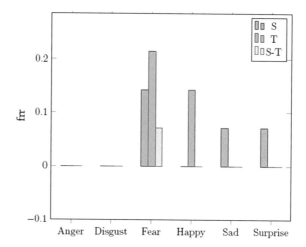

Fig. 7.15 ERR of JAFFE using DBN

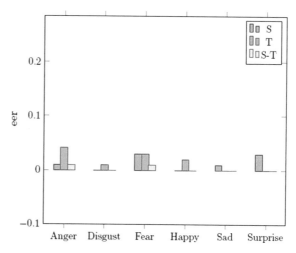

graph analysis of texture signature shows a less promising recognition rate in fear, happiness, and surprise. From this graph analysis, we also notice that the joined D-S feature yields a promising detection rate in anger.

The comparison of the FRR for shape, texture, and S-T signature feature through DBN on the JAFFE dataset is shown in Fig. 7.14. The FRR graph analysis of shape signature yields a poor recognition rate in fear expression. The FRR graph analysis of texture signature performs a poor recognition rate of expressions in fear and happiness expressions. It is also shown that the joined D-S feature indicates a promising classification rate in anger, disgust, and surprise expressions.

The comparison of the ERR for shape, texture, and S-T signature features through MLP on JAFFE dataset is shown in Fig. 7.15. The ERR graph analysis of the shape signature yields a poor recognition rate in surprise. The ERR graph analysis of texture

Table 7.26 Performance analysis on JAFFE Database with state-of-the-art

	Anger	Disgust	Fear	Happiness	Sadness	Surprise	
Shape (MLP)	100	90	78.6	100	85.7	100	92.4
Texture (MLP)	85.7	100	78.6	85.7	100	100	91.6
S-T (MLP)	100	100	92.9	100	85.7	92.9	95.2
Shape (DBN)	100	100	85.7	100	92.9	92.9	95.2
Texture (DBN)	100	100	78.6	85.7	100	100	94
S-T (DBN)	100	100	92.9	100	100	100	98.8
[18]	100	86.2	93.7	96.7	77.4	96.6	91.7
[19]	89.3	90.1	91.1	92.6	90.2	92.3	90.9

signature shows a less promising performance than the shape signature. From this graph analysis, it is also shown that the joined D-S feature yields a higher detection rate than the individual shape and texture signature features.

7.5.4.2 Discussion

The Tables 7.14, 7.15, and 7.16 indicate that fear yield less promising recognition rate of expression for shape and texture signature features through MLP. The S-T signature produces a promising identification rate of emotion in case of fear.

We also observe that the fear is a challenging expression for considering texture signature through DBN. It occurs for producing common facial patches with anger and disgust.

7.5.4.3 Compare Analysis with Different State of the Art

The suggested Shape, Texture, and S-T signature features are measured with the experimental results in other literature [18, 19]. We validate our experiments on the JAFFE dataset for a comparison task with the other literature. Table 7.26 indicates the summary of the experimental results of emotion through MLP and DBN. We get an average accuracy of shape signature through MLP as 92.4% on JAFFE dataset which is much more better than in [18]. The joined S-T (MLP and DBN) signature yield a promising emotion recognition accuracy of facial expression on the JAFFE dataset.

Table 7.27 The MLP-based recognition matrix of Shape signature on MMI dataset

	Anger	Disgust	Fear	Happiness	Sadness	Surprise
Anger	39	0	0	1	0	0
Disgust	4	35	0	0	3	0
Fear	1	0	18	3	0	3
Happiness	2	0	0	18	0	4
Sadness	7	0	0	0	22	1
Surprise	0	0	0	3	1	17

7.5.5 Experiment on MMI Database

The MMI dataset consists of research members and students aged between 19 and 62 years. This dataset is more challenging than the others. It includes posed, as well as spontaneous emotions for expressed behavior. To measure the emotion identification rate of this dataset training and testing (179 images or samples) mechanisms are performed.

7.5.5.1 Results Analysis on MMI Dataset

The MMI dataset is also used to test the performances of facial expression recognition. The recognition matrix presents the classification of emotion for shape signature through MLP in Table 7.27. **Shape signature** recognizes 39 samples properly as anger and 1 sample is in misclassification with happiness. Disgust identifies 35 samples positively and 7 samples are in misclassification with happiness and anger. Fear recognizes 18 images perfectly and 6 images are misidentified with anger and happiness. Happiness indicates 18 images correctly and 6 samples are in confusion with anger and surprise. Sadness recognizes 22 samples accurately and 8 samples are in a mismatch with anger and surprise. Surprise classifies 17 samples positively and 4 samples are misclassified with happiness and sadness.

The expression recognition accuracy of the suggested approach is measured in terms of FAR, FRR, and ERR. The FAR, FRR, and ERR of shape signature through MLP on the MMI dataset are tabulated in Table 7.28. The anger produces the FAR as 0.100. The anger also generates the value of 0.025 as FRR. The lowest FAR, FRR, and ERR values also represent the highest recognition rate of facial expressions.

Texture signature presents proper identification of emotion with misclassification in Table 7.29. Anger identifies 34 images perfectly and 6 images are misidentified with disgust, happiness, and sadness. Disgust recognizes 33 samples positively and 6 samples are misidentified with happiness, sadness, and surprise. Fear indicates 17 images accurately and 8 samples are in confusion with anger, happiness, and surprise. Happiness indicates 12 images as correct recognition and same number of samples are misidentified with disgust, sadness, and surprise. Sadness recognizes 27 images

Table 7.28 The performance of Shape signature on MMI dataset through MLP

	FAR	FRR	ERR
Anger	0.100	0.025	0.083
Disgust	0	0.102	0.022
Fear	0	0.280	0.039
Happiness	0.045	0.250	0.072
Sadness	0.006	0.266	0.050
Surprise	0.050	0.190	0.067

Table 7.29 The MLP-based recognition matrix of Texture signature on MMI dataset

	Anger	Disgust	Fear	Happiness	Sadness	Surprise
Anger	34	1	0	2	3	0
Disgust	0	33	0	3	1	2
Fear	1	0	17	4	0	3
Happiness	0	3	0	12	3	6
Sadness	0	1	0	0	27	2
Surprise	0	0	0	2	0	19

Table 7.30 The performance of Texture signature on MMI dataset through MLP

	FAR	FRR	ERR
Anger	0.007	0.150	0.039
Disgust	0.035	0.153	0.061
Fear	0	0.320	0.044
Happiness	0.071	0.500	0.128
Sadness	0.047	0.100	0.055
Surprise	0.082	0.095	0.083

accurately and 3 samples are in misclassification with surprise and disgust. Surprise recognizes 19 samples accurately and 2 images are misclassified with happiness.

The FAR, FRR, and ERR are considered to evaluate the system performances of texture signature through MLP. Table 7.30 shows the evaluated results of FAR, FRR, and ERR. The anger produces the FAR as 0.007. The anger also generates a value 0.150 as FRR. The lowest FAR, FRR, and ERR values also represent the highest recognition rate of facial expressions.

Table **S-T signature** indicates the correct recognition of emotion with misclassification in Table 7.31. Anger recognizes 39 images properly and 1 sample is in mismatch with surprise. Disgust identifies 36 samples positively and 3 images are misidentified with sadness. Fear recognizes correctly 18 images and 7 images are misidentified with all expressions except disgust. Happiness indicates 17 images as

Table 7.31 MLP-based recognition matrix of S-T signature on MMI dataset

	Anger	Disgust	Fear	Happiness	Sadness	Surprise
Anger	39	0	0	0	0	1
Disgust	0	36	0	0	3	0
Fear	1	0	18	2	1	3
Happiness	3	1	0	17	2	1
Sadness	0	0	0	0	26	4
Surprise	0	0	0	0	4	17

Table 7.32 The performance of S-T signature on MMI dataset through MLP

	FAR	FRR	ERR
Anger	0.028	0.025	0.027
Disgust	0.007	0.076	0.022
Fear	0	0.280	0.039
Happiness	0.012	0.291	0.050
Sadness	0.067	0.133	0.078
Surprise	0.057	0.190	0.072

correct classification and remaining are confused with all expressions except fear. Sadness recognizes 26 images properly and 4 images are misclassified with surprise. Surprise identifies 17 images properly and 4 images are misclassification with sadness.

The expression recognition accuracy of the suggested approach is measured in terms of FAR, FRR, and ERR. The FAR, FRR, and ERR of S-T signature through MLP on the MMI dataset are tabulated in Table 7.32. The anger produces the FAR as 0.028. The anger also generates a value 0.028 as FRR. The ERR value of anger is 0.025. The ERR value of S-T signature using MLP is 0.027. The lowest FAR, FRR, and ERR values also represent the highest recognition rate of facial expressions.

The performance of the FAR for shape, texture, and S-T signature features through MLP on the MUG dataset is shown in Fig. 7.16. The FAR graph analysis of shape signature yields a poor recognition rate in surprise. The FAR graph analysis of texture signature shows the less promising recognition rate in surprise. From this graph analysis, we also indicate that the joined D-S feature yields promising identification rate in anger.

The comparison of the FRR for shape, texture, and S-T signature features through MLP on MUG dataset is shown in Fig. 7.17. The FRR graph analysis of shape signature yields a poor recognition rate in fear expression. The FRR graph analysis of texture features shows a poor identification rate of emotion in anger, disgust, fear, and happiness. It is also showed that the combined D-S signature indicates a promising recognition rate in anger, disgust, and surprise expressions.

Fig. 7.16 FAR of MMI
using MLP

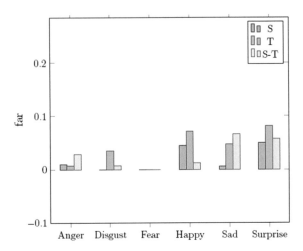

Fig. 7.17 FRR of MMI
using MLP

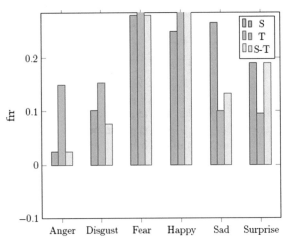

The comparison of the ERR for shape, texture, and S-T signature features through MLP on the MMI dataset is shown in Fig. 7.18. The ERR graph analysis of shape signature yields a poor recognition rate in anger and surprise. The ERR graph analysis of texture features shows a less promising performance than the shape signature. From this graph analysis, it is also showed that the joined D-S feature yields a higher identification rate than the shape and texture signatures.

Results Evaluation on MMI Database Using DBN

The recognition of emotion of shape signature through DBN is shown in Table 7.33. Anger classifies 37 images properly and 3 samples are in confusion with happiness and surprise. Disgust identifies 36 samples correctly and 3 samples are in a mismatch

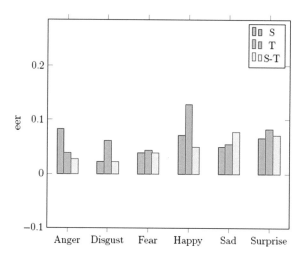

Fig. 7.18 ERR of MMI using MLP

Table 7.33 The DBN-based recognition matrix of Shape signature on MMI dataset

	Anger	Disgust	Fear	Happiness	Sadness	Surprise
Anger	37	0	0	2	0	1
Disgust	0	36	0	2	0	1
Fear	1	0	18	2	1	3
Happiness	0	0	0	21	1	2
Sadness	0	0	0	0	28	2
Surprise	0	0	0	1	0	20

Table 7.34 The performance of Shape signature on MMI dataset through DBN

	FAR	FRR	ERR
Anger	0.007	0.075	0.022
Disgust	0	0.076	0.016
Fear	0	0.280	0.039
Happiness	0.045	0.125	0.055
Sadness	0.013	0.066	0.022
Surprise	0.057	0.047	0.055

with happiness and surprise. Fear classifies 18 samples positively and many more samples are in confusion with other expressions. In the same way happiness, sadness, and surprise give a promising classification of expressions.

The expression recognition accuracy of suggested approach is measured in terms of FAR, FRR, and ERR. The FAR, FRR, and ERR of shape signature through DBN on MMI dataset are tabulated in Table 7.34. The anger produces the FAR as 0.007. The

Table 7.35 The DBN-based recognition matrix of Texture signature on MMI dataset

	Anger	Disgust	Fear	Happiness	Sadness	Surprise
Anger	39	0	0	0	1	0
Disgust	1	27	0	0	7	4
Fear	0	0	20	0	2	3
Happiness	0	0	0	19	5	0
Sadness	0	0	0	0	27	3
Surprise	0	0	0	0	1	20

Table 7.36 The FAR, FRR, and ERR of Texture signature on MMI Database using DBN

	FAR	FRR	ERR
Anger	0.007	0.025	0.011
Disgust	0	0.307	0.067
Fear	0	0.200	0.027
Happiness	0	0.208	0.027
Sadness	0.107	0.100	0.106
Surprise	0.063	0.047	0.061

anger also generates the value of 0.075 as FRR. The ERR value of shape signature using DBN is 0.022. The lowest FAR, FRR, and ERR values also represent the highest recognition rate of facial expressions.

Texture signature presents identification rate of emotion in Table 7.35. Anger recognizes 39 samples rightly and 1 sample is in confusion with sadness. Disgust classifies 27 samples positively and 12 samples are in misclassification with anger, sadness, and surprise. Fear identifies 20 images properly and 5 images are misidentified with sadness and surprise. Happiness indicates 19 images properly and 5 images are misidentified with sadness. Sadness identifies 27 samples properly and 3 samples are misclassified with surprise. Surprise recognizes 20 images accurately and 1 image is misclassified with sadness.

The FAR, FRR, and ERR of texture signature through DBN on the MMI dataset are presented in Table 7.36. The anger produces the FAR as 0.007. The anger also generates the value of 0.007 as FRR. The ERR value of anger is 0.025. The ERR value of the S-T signature using MLP is 0.011. The lowest FAR, FRR, and ERR values also represent the highest recognition rate of facial expressions.

The S-T signature indicates the recognition of expressions in Table 7.37. Anger recognizes 39 samples rightly and 1 sample is misidentified with surprise. Disgust identifies 37 samples positively and 1 image is confused with anger. Fear recognizes 21 images accurately and 4 images are misidentified with anger. Happiness indicates 21 images perfectly and 3 samples are in misclassification with sadness. Sadness identifies 30 samples accurately. Surprise classifies 19 images accurately and 2 images are misidentified with anger.

Table 7.37 The DBN-based recognition matrix of S-T signature on MMI dataset

	Anger	Disgust	Fear	Happiness	Sadness	Surprise
Anger	39	0	0	0	0	1
Disgust	1	37	0	0	0	0
Fear	4	0	21	0	0	0
Happiness	0	0	0	21	3	0
Sadness	0	0	0	0	30	0
Surprise	2	0	0	0	0	19

Table 7.38 The performance of S-T signature on MMI dataset through DBN

	FAR	FRR	ERR
Anger	0.050	0.025	0.044
Disgust	0	0.051	0.011
Fear	0	0.160	0.022
Happiness	0	0.125	0.016
Sadness	0.026	0	0.022
Surprise	0.006	0.095	0.016

Fig. 7.19 FAR of MMI using DBN

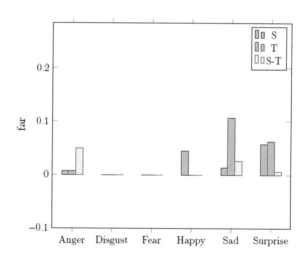

The FAR, FRR, and ERR of S-T signature through DBN on the MMI dataset are indicated in Table 7.38. The anger produces the FAR as 0.050. The anger also generates a value of 0.025 as FRR. The ERR value of anger is 0.025. The ERR value of the S-T signature using MLP is 0.044. The lowest FAR, FRR, and ERR values also represent the highest identification rate of emotion.

The performance of the FAR for shape, texture, and S-T signature features through MLP on the MMI dataset is shown in Fig. 7.19. The FAR graph analysis of shape

Fig. 7.20 FRR of MMI
using DBN

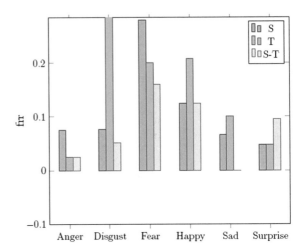

Fig. 7.21 ERR of MMI
through DBN

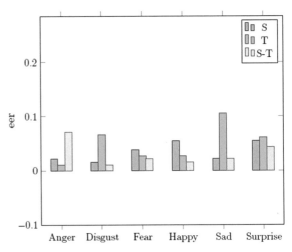

signature yields a poor recognition rate in surprise. The FAR graph analysis of texture
signature shows the less promising recognition rate in surprise. From this graph
analysis, we also mention that the joined D-S feature yields a promising identification
rate in anger expression.

The comparison of the FRR for shape, texture, and S-T signature features through
MLP on the MMI dataset is shown in Fig. 7.20. The FRR graph analysis of shape
signature yields a poor recognition rate in fear expression. The FRR graph analysis of
texture signature presents a poor identification rate of emotion in disgust and happiness. It is also showed that the joined D-S feature indicates a promising identification
rate in sadness.

The comparison of the ERR for shape, texture, and S-T signature features through
MLP on the MMI dataset is shown in Fig. 7.21. The ERR graph analysis of shape

signature yields a poor recognition rate in anger and fear. The ERR graph analysis of texture signature shows a less promising performance than the shape signature. From this graph analysis, it is also shown that the joined D-S feature yields a higher identification rate than the shape and texture signature features.

7.5.5.2 Discussion

We observe that anger, disgust, sadness, and surprise expressions give promising recognition rates but whereas fear and happiness give better performance than the texture signature. On the other hand, fear yields less promising recognition rate of expressions for shape, texture, and S-T signatures. When shape, texture, and S-T signature features are used for classification, fear expression is in misclassification with surprise and happiness. It indicates that they extract the same triangles and active patches during feature extraction. It is also observed that the joined S-T feature yields an indispensable identification rate of emotion.

7.5.5.3 Performance Comparison with State of the Art

The suggested Shape, Texture, and S-T signature features are measured with the results evaluated in literature [15, 17, 19, 22]. We conduct our experiments on the MMI dataset for comparison tasks with other literature. Table 7.39 shows the summary results of our proposed method with state-of-the-art methods. The overall average classification rate of S-T signature through MLP is 83.4% on the MMI dataset. The shape, texture, and S-T signature features are also yielding indispensable performance in emotion recognition on the MMI dataset through MLP and DBN. The emotion recognition through DBN achieves an overwhelming identification rate.

7.5.6 Experimental Result on MUG Dataset

MUG [12] dataset is also considered to measure the identification rate of emotion. The dataset has 86 subjects with Caucasian origin aged between 20 and 35 years. It has 51 males and 35 females without or with a beard. To evaluate the system identification rate of emotion of the suggested approaches, we divided a total of 420 images as training (279 images or samples) and testing (141 images or samples) set.

7.5.6.1 Results Analysis on MUG Dataset

The suggested approach selects a total of 141 samples to measure the identification rate of emotion. The recognition matrix of shape signature through MLP is shown in

Table 7.39 Result analysis on MMI dataset with the state-of-the-art approaches

	Anger	Disgust	Fear	Happiness	Sadness	Surprise	Avg.
Shape (MLP)	97.5	89.7	72	75	73.3	81	81.4
Texture (MLP)	85	84.6	68	70.8	90	90.5	81.9
S-T (MLP)	97.5	92.3	72	70.8	86.7	81	83.4
Shape (DBN)	92.5	92.3	72	87.5	93.3	95.2	88.8
Texture (DBN)	97.5	69.2	80	79.2	90	95.2	85.1
S-T (DBN)	97.5	94.9	84	87.5	100	95	93.1
[15]	96.2	96.5	97.7	98.5	97.5	98.7	97.5
[19]	80.1	78.2	81.3	83.2	77.1	81	80.1
[17]	50.2	79.8	67.1	82.9	60.2	88.5	71.4
[22]	70	70	80	85	73.3	85	77.2

Table 7.40 The MLP-based recognition matrix of Shape signature on MUG dataset

	Anger	Disgust	Fear	Happiness	Sadness	Surprise
Anger	18	0	0	0	0	1
Disgust	0	30	0	1	0	0
Fear	0	1	12	1	0	0
Happiness	0	0	0	30	0	0
Sadness	0	0	0	0	21	0
Surprise	0	0	1	0	0	25

Table 7.40. It is mentioned that happiness, sadness, and disgust identify the accurate classification of emotion. Fear identifies 12 images properly and 2 samples are in misclassification with happiness and disgust. Surprise recognizes 25 samples properly and 1 sample is in a mismatch with fear.

The emotion recognition accuracy of the suggested approach is measured in terms of the FAR, FRR, and ERR. The FAR, FRR, and ERR of shape signature through MLP on the MUG dataset are presented in Table 7.41. The FAR value of disgust is 0.009 that means it produces a 9/1000 as a false accept rate. The FRR of the disgust is 0.071. The value of ERR of corresponding expressions is shown in the mentioned table. The lowest FRR means it produces the highest recognition rate in expressions.

Table 7.41 The performance of shape signature on MUG dataset through MLP

	FAR	FRR	ERR
Anger	0	0.052	0.007
Disgust	0.009	0.032	0.012
Fear	0.007	0.142	0.021
Happiness	0.018	0	0.014
Sadness	0	0	0
Surprise	0.008	0.038	0.014

Table 7.42 The MLP-based recognition matrix of Texture signature on MUG dataset

	Anger	Disgust	Fear	Happiness	Sadness	Surprise
Anger	18	0	0	0	0	1
Disgust	0	30	1	0	0	0
Fear	0	0	10	1	1	2
Happiness	0	0	0	30	0	0
Sadness	0	0	2	0	19	0
Surprise	0	0	0	0	0	26

Table 7.43 The performance of Texture signature on MUG dataset through MLP

	FAR	FRR	ERR
Anger	0	0.052	0.007
Disgust	0	0.032	0.007
Fear	0.023	0.285	0.049
Happiness	0.009	0	0.007
Sadness	0.008	0.095	0.021
Surprise	0.026	0	0.021

The **texture** signature indicates the correct recognition of expressions with misclassification in Table 7.42. Anger classifies 18 images properly and 1 image is misidentified with surprise. Disgust identifies 30 samples rightly and 1 sample is in confusion with fear. Fear recognizes 10 samples perfectly and 4 samples are in misclassification with happiness, sadness, and surprise. Happiness indicates 30 images accurately. Sadness determines 19 samples positively and 2 samples are in a mismatch with fear. Surprise recognizes 26 images accurately.

The emotion recognition accuracy of suggested approach is measured in terms of the FAR, FRR, and ERR. The FAR, FRR, and ERR of texture signature through MLP on the MUG dataset are presented in Tables 7.43. The FAR value of fear is 0.023 that means it produces a 23/1000 as false accept rate. The fear produces the FRR as

Table 7.44 The MLP-based recognition matrix of S-T signature on MUG dataset

	Anger	Disgust	Fear	Happiness	Sadness	Surprise
Anger	18	0	0	0	0	1
Disgust	0	31	0	0	0	0
Fear	0	0	12	2	0	0
Happiness	0	0	0	30	0	0
Sadness	0	0	0	0	21	0
Surprise	0	0	0	0	0	26

Table 7.45 The performance of S-T signature on MUG dataset through MLP

	FAR	FRR	ERR
Anger	0	0.052	0.007
Disgust	0	0	0
Fear	0	0.142	0.014
Happiness	0.009	0	0.007
Sadness	0.016	0	0.014
Surprise	0	0	0

0.285. The value of ERR of corresponding expressions is shown in the mentioned table. The lowest FRR means it produces the highest recognition rate in expression.

The **S-T** signature indicates the correct recognition of expressions with misclassification in Table 7.44. Anger identifies 18 samples positively and 1 sample is in confusion with surprise. Disgust determines 31 images accurately. Fear recognizes 12 samples rightly and 2 samples are misidentified with happiness. Happiness classifies 30 images accurately. Sadness and surprise recognize the expressions properly.

The emotion recognition accuracy of the suggested approach is measured in terms of the FAR, FRR, and ERR. The FAR, FRR, and ERR of S-T signature through MLP on the MUG dataset are presented in Table 7.45. The FAR value of sadness is 0.016 that means it produces a 16/1000 as a false accept rate. The anger produces the FRR as 0.052. The value of the ERR of corresponding expressions is shown in the mentioned table. The lowest FRR means it produces the highest recognition rate in expressions.

The performance of the FAR for shape, texture, and S-T signature features through MLP on the MUG dataset is shown in Fig. 7.22. The FAR graph analysis of shape signature yields a poor recognition rate in surprise. The FAR graph analysis of texture signature shows the less promising recognition rate in surprise. From this graph analysis, we also mention that the joined D-S feature yields a promising recognition rate in anger expression.

The comparison of the FRR for shape, texture, and S-T signature features through MLP on the MUG dataset is shown in Fig. 7.23. The FRR graph analysis of shape signature yields a poor recognition rate in surprise expression. The FRR graph analysis

Fig. 7.22 FAR of MUG using MLP

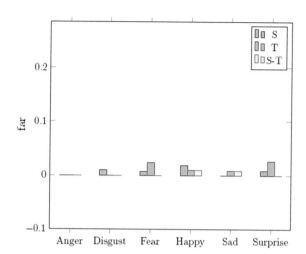

Fig. 7.23 FRR of MUG using MLP

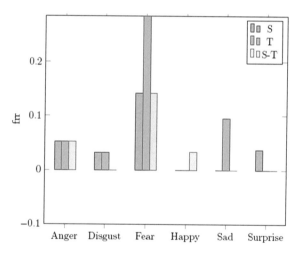

of texture signature presents a poor identification rate of emotion in fear, happiness, and surprise. It is also shown that the joined D-S feature indicates a promising recognition rate in sadness and surprise.

The comparison of the ERR for shape, texture, and S-T signature feature through MLP on the MUG dataset is shown in Fig. 7.24. The ERR graph analysis of shape signature yields a poor recognition rate in anger and fear. The ERR graph analysis of texture signature shows a less promising performance than the shape signature. From this graph analysis, it is also shown that the joined D-S feature yields a higher recognition rate than the shape and texture signatures.

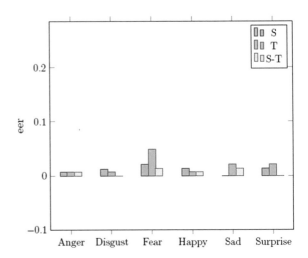

Fig. 7.24 ERR of MUG using MLP

Table 7.46 The DBN-based recognition matrix of Shape signature on MUG dataset

	Anger	Disgust	Fear	Happiness	Sadness	Surprise
Anger	18	0	0	0	0	1
Disgust	0	31	0	0	0	0
Fear	0	0	12	1	1	0
Happiness	0	0	0	29	0	1
Sadness	0	0	0	0	21	0
Surprise	0	0	0	0	0	26

Results Evaluation on MUG Database Using DBN

The **shape** signature through DBN presets proper identification of emotion in Table 7.46. Here we observe that the disgust, sadness, and surprise indicate the accurate classification. Anger recognizes 18 images properly and 1 image is misidentified with surprise. Fear determines 12 samples properly and 2 samples are in confusion with happiness and sadness. Happiness identifies 29 images accurately and 1 image is misidentified with surprise.

The emotion recognition accuracy of the suggested approach is measured in terms of the FAR, FRR, and ERR. The FAR, FRR, and ERR of shape signature through DBN on MUG dataset are presented in Table 7.46. The FAR value of happiness is 0.009 that means it produces a 9/1000 as a false accept rate. The happiness produces the FRR as 0.033. The value of ERR of corresponding expressions is shown in the mentioned table. The lowest FRR means it produces the highest recognition rate in expressions.

Texture signature produces the recognition of expressions of texture signature feature using DBN in Table 7.48. Anger classifies 18 images perfectly and 1 image is

Table 7.47   The performance of Shape signature on MUG dataset through DBN

	FAR	FRR	ERR
Anger	0	0.052	0.007
Disgust	0	0	0
Fear	0	0.142	0.014
Happiness	0.009	0.033	0.014
Sadness	0.008	0	0.007
Surprise	0.017	0	0.014

Table 7.48   The DBN-based recognition matrix of Texture signature on MUG dataset

	Anger	Disgust	Fear	Happiness	Sadness	Surprise
Anger	18	0	0	0	1	0
Disgust	0	28	0	0	3	0
Fear	0	0	13	1	0	0
Happiness	0	0	0	30	0	0
Sadness	0	0	0	0	21	0
Surprise	0	1	0	0	0	25

Table 7.49   The performance of Texture signature on MUG dataset through DBN

	FAR	FRR	ERR
Anger	0	0.052	0.007
Disgust	0.009	0.096	0.028
Fear	0	0.071	0.007
Happiness	0.009	0	0.007
Sadness	0.033	0	0.028
Surprise	0	0.038	0.007

misidentified with sadness. Disgust recognizes 28 images properly and 3 images are misidentified with sadness. Fear identifies 13 images accurately and 1 sample is in confusion with happiness. The happiness, sadness, and surprise recognize accurately.

The emotion recognition accuracy of the suggested approach is measured in terms of the FAR, FRR, and ERR. The FAR, FRR, and ERR of texture signature through DBN on the MUG dataset are presented in Table 7.49. The FAR value of disgust is 0.009 that means it produces a 9/1000 as a false accept rate. The disgust produces the FRR as 0.096. The value of ERR of corresponding expressions is shown in the mentioned table. The lowest FRR means it produces the highest recognition rate in expressions.

Table 7.50 The DBN-based recognition matrix of S-T signature on MUG dataset

	Anger	Disgust	Fear	Happiness	Sadness	Surprise
Anger	18	0	0	0	1	0
Disgust	0	31	0	0	0	0
Fear	0	0	14	0	0	0
Happiness	0	0	0	30	0	0
Sadness	0	0	0	0	21	0
Surprise	0	0	0	0	0	26

Table 7.51 The performance of S-T signature on MUG dataset through DBN

	FAR	FRR	ERR
Anger	0	0.052	0.007
Disgust	0	0	0
Fear	0	0	0
Happiness	0	0	0
Sadness	0	0	0
Surprise	0.008	0	0.007

S-T signature indicates the recognition of emotion of the S-T signature feature through DBN in Table 7.50. Anger classifies 18 samples positively and 1 sample is misidentified with sadness. The accurate classifications occur in disgust, fear, happiness, sadness, and surprise.

The emotion recognition accuracy of suggested approach is measured in terms of the FAR, FRR, and ERR. The FAR, FRR, and ERR of S-T signature through DBN on the MUG dataset are presented in Table 7.51. The anger produces the FRR as 0.052. The value of ERR of corresponding expressions is shown in mentioned table. The lowest FRR means it produces the highest recognition rate in expressions.

The performance of the FAR for shape, texture, and S-T signature features through DBN on the MUG dataset is shown in Fig. 7.25. The FAR graph analysis of shape signature yields a poor recognition rate in surprise. The FAR graph analysis of texture signature shows the less promising recognition rate in sadness. From this graph analysis, we also present that the joined D-S feature yields a promising identification rate in anger expression.

The comparison of the FRR for shape, texture, and S-T signature features through DBN on the MUG dataset is shown in Fig. 7.26. The FRR graph analysis of shape signature yields a poor recognition rate in fear expression. The FRR graph analysis of texture signature indicates the poor identification rate of emotion in anger, disgust, and surprise. It is also shown that the joined D-S feature indicates a promising identification rate in sadness and surprise.

The comparison of the ERR for shape, texture, and S-T signature features through DBN on the MUG dataset is shown in Fig. 7.27. The ERR graph analysis of shape

Fig. 7.25 FAR of MUG using DBN

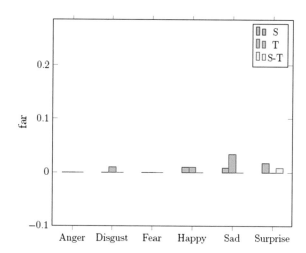

Fig. 7.26 FRR of MUG using DBN

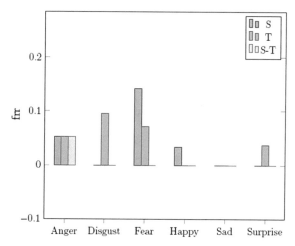

signature yields a poor recognition rate in anger and surprise. The ERR graph analysis of texture signature shows a less promising performance than the shape signature. From this graph analysis, it is also shown that the joined D-S signature yields a higher recognition rate of emotion than the shape and texture signatures.

7.5.6.2 Discussion

It is noticed that when we consider shape, texture, and S-T signature features for identification of emotion, fear shows most misclassification in emotion through MLP. The fear is in misclassification with disgust, surprise, and happiness due to sharing common triangles and active patches at feature extraction.

Fig. 7.27 ERR of MUG
using DBN

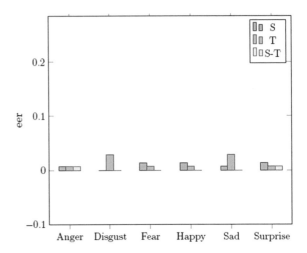

We also observe that the identification of fear is more challenging for shape and texture signature features through DBN. The fear produces an indispensable identification rate of emotion when we consider joined signature (S-T) feature.

7.5.6.3 Performance Comparison with State of the Art Methods

The suggested Shape, Texture, and S-T signature approaches are measured with the evaluated results in literature [22, 23]. We evaluate our experiments on the MUG dataset for comparison tasks with other literature. Table 7.52 shows a summary result of our suggested method with state-of-the-art. We get an average identification rate of S-T signature through DBN as 99.1% on the MUG dataset which is much more effective than the obtained result in [22, 23]. Shape, texture, and S-T signature features produce excellent identification rate of emotion on the MUG dataset through MLP and DBN. Moreover, DBN-based emotion identification yields a overwhelming classification rate of emotion.

7.5.7 Experiment on Wild Database

A real Wild [13, 14] dataset is considered to measure the system identification rate of emotion. Previously used datasets are made in laboratory regulated environment to variate different facial expressions. However, in our daily life activities posed expressions are expressed in different ways of the same person. For that reason, spontaneous expressions are really challenging in the field of facial expression recognition and also it is a challenging dataset for capturing spontaneous emotions to the research community. Now researchers are engaged to build a facial expression recognition

Table 7.52 Performance analysis on MUG dataset with state-of-the-art

	Anger	Disgust	Fear	Happiness	Sadness	Surprise	Avg.
Shape (MLP)	94.7	96.8	85.7	100	100	96.2	95.5
Texture (MLP)	94.7	96.8	71.4	100	90.5	100	92.2
S-T (MLP)	94.7	90.3	92.9	100	100	96.2	95.6
Shape (DBN)	94.7	100	85.7	96.7	100	100	96.1
Texture (DBN)	94.7	90.3	92.9	100	100	96.2	95.6
S-T (DBN)	94.7	100	100	100	100	100	99.1
[22]	100	100	85	100	90	98	95.5
[23]	94.6	99.8	93.8	85.8	87.4	64.6	87.6

Table 7.53 The MLP-base recognition matrix of Shape signature on Wild dataset

	Anger	Happiness	Sadness	Surprise
Anger	15	10	0	0
Happiness	3	67	4	0
Sadness	3	9	5	1
Surprise	1	5	1	12

system from the real-time dataset (wild). In this dataset, we only study four emotions such as happiness, anger, surprise, and sadness to measure the system performance of expression recognition compared to other datasets.

Result Evaluation on Wild Dataset Using MLP

Shape signature: The recognition matrix of shape through MLP is shown in Table 7.53. Anger determines 15 images properly and 10 images are misclassified as happiness. Happiness identifies 67 samples properly and 7 samples are in misclassification with anger and sadness. Sadness recognizes 5 images accurately and the maximum number of images are confused with all expressions. Surprise indicates 12 samples positively and 7 samples are misidentified with anger, happiness, and sadness.

The performance of suggested approach is computed as FRR, FAR, and ERR. The FAR, FRR, and ERR of shape signature through MLP on the Wild dataset are indicated in Table 7.54. The FAR value of anger is 0.069 that means it produces a 69/1000 as a false accept rate. The anger produces FRR as 0.275. The lowest ERR is 0.044 for surprise.

Table 7.54 The performance of shape signature on Wild dataset through MLP

	FAR	FRR	ERR
Anger	0.063	0.400	0.125
Happiness	0.0387	0.094	0.227
Sadness	0.042	0.722	0.132
Surprise	0.008	0.368	0.058

Table 7.55 The MLP-base recognition matrix of Texture signature on Wild dataset

	Anger	Happiness	Sadness	Surprise
Anger	12	12	1	0
Happiness	4	62	3	5
Sadness	1	10	6	1
Surprise	0	4	0	15

Table 7.56 The MLP-based performance of Texture signature on Wild dataset

	FAR	FRR	ERR
Anger	0.045	0.052	0.132
Happiness	0.419	0.162	0.279
Sadness	0.033	0.667	0.117
Surprise	0.051	0.210	0.073

The recognition matrix of the Texture feature on the Wild dataset through MLP is shown in Table 7.55. Anger recognizes 12 samples positively and 13 samples are in misclassification with happiness and sadness. Happiness recognizes 62 images properly and 12 samples are in a mismatch with anger, sadness, and surprise. Sadness identifies only 6 images properly and 12 images are misidentified with all expressions. Surprise indicates 15 images perfectly and 4 images are misidentified with happiness.

The accuracy of suggested approach is measured by FRR, FAR, and ERR. The FAR, FRR, and ERR of texture signature using MLP for Wild dataset are mentioned in Table 7.56. The FAR value of anger is 0.045 that means it produces a 45/1000 as a false accept rate. The anger produces FRR as 0.052. The lowest ERR is 0.073 for surprise.

The recognition matrix of S-T feature on Wild dataset through MLP is shown in Table 7.57. Anger determines 21 images properly and 4 images are in misclassification with happiness, surprise, and sadness. Happiness recognizes 66 samples properly and 8 samples are misidentified with anger, sadness, and surprise. Sadness indicates 7 images perfectly and 11 samples are misclassified with anger and sadness. Surprise detects 18 samples accurately and 1 sample is in mismatch with happiness.

The accuracy of suggested approach is measured by FAR, FRR, and ERR. The FAR, FRR, and ERR of S-T signature through MLP on Wild dataset are mentioned

Table 7.57 The MLP-base recognition matrix of S-T signature on Wild dataset

	Anger	Happiness	Sadness	Surprise
Anger	21	2	1	1
Happiness	2	66	2	4
Sadness	2	9	7	0
Surprise	0	1	0	18

Table 7.58 The performance of S-T signature on Wild dataset through MLP

	FAR	FRR	ERR
Anger	0.069	0.275	0.111
Happiness	0.324	0.195	0.256
Sadness	0.049	0.758	0.187
Surprise	0.042	0.052	0.044

Table 7.59 The DBN-base recognition matrix of shape signature on Wild dataset

	Anger	Happiness	Sadness	Surprise
Anger	14	8	2	1
Happiness	2	63	6	3
Sadness	2	5	11	0
Surprise	0	5	0	14

in Table 7.58. The FAR value of anger is 0.069 that means it produces a 69/1000 as false accept rate. The anger produces FRR as 0.275. The lowest ERR is 0.044 for surprise.

Result Evaluation on Wild Dataset Using DBN

Shape signature: The recognition matrix of shape feature through DBN is presented in Table 7.59. Anger determines 14 samples positively and 11 samples are in a mismatch with happiness, sadness, and surprise. Happiness identifies 63 images properly and 11 samples are misclassified with anger, sadness, and surprise. Sadness recognizes 11 images perfectly and 7 samples are in confusion with happiness and anger. Surprise indicates 14 samples rightly and 5 samples are misidentified with happiness.

The performance of suggested approach is measured by FAR, FRR, and ERR. The FAR, FRR, and ERR of shape signature through DBN on Wild dataset are indicated in Table 7.60. The FAR value of anger is 0.036 that means it produces a 36/1000 as false accept rate. The anger produces FRR as 0.440. The lowest ERR is 0.066 for surprise.

The recognition matrix of the texture signature on the Wild dataset using DBN is shown in Table 7.61. Anger recognizes 15 images properly and 10 samples are misclassified with happiness and surprise. Happiness detects 68 samples properly

Table 7.60 The performance of shape signature on Wild dataset through DBN

	FAR	FRR	ERR
Anger	0.036	0.440	0.110
Happiness	0.290	0.148	0.213
Sadness	0.067	0.388	0.110
Surprise	0.0342	0.263	0.066

Table 7.61 The DBN-base recognition matrix of Texture signature on Wild dataset

	Anger	Happiness	Sadness	Surprise
Anger	15	9	0	1
Happiness	4	68	0	2
Sadness	2	7	5	4
Surprise	0	4	0	15

Table 7.62 The performance of Texture signature on Wild dataset through DBN

	FAR	FRR	ERR
Anger	0.054	0.400	0.117
Happiness	0.322	0.081	0.191
Sadness	0.722	0.095	0.025
Surprise	0.059	0.210	0.080

and 6 samples are misclassified with surprise and anger. Sadness classifies only 5 images properly and 13 images are misidentified with all expressions. Surprise indicates 15 samples positively and 4 samples are misidentified with happiness.

The accuracy of the suggested approach is measured by FAR, FRR, and ERR. The FAR, FRR, and ERR of texture signature through DBN on Wild dataset are mentioned in Table 7.62. The FAR value of anger is 0.054 that means it produces a 54/1000 as a false accept rate. The anger produces FRR as 0.400. The lowest ERR is 0.025 for sadness.

The recognition matrix of the S-T signature on the Wild dataset through DBN is shown in Table 7.63. Anger determines 18 images perfectly and 7 images are misidentified with happiness, sadness, and surprise. Happiness recognizes 68 images properly and 6 samples are misidentified with anger, sadness, and surprise. Sadness indicates 11 images properly and 7 samples are in confusion with happiness and anger. Surprise detects 16 samples accurately and 3 images are misclassified with happiness.

The accuracy of suggested approach is measured by FAR, FRR, and ERR. The FAR, FRR, and ERR of S-T signature through DBN on Wild dataset are mentioned in Table 7.64. The FAR value of anger is 0.036 that means it produces a 36/1000 as

Table 7.63 The DBN-base recognition matrix of S-T signature on Wild dataset

	Anger	Happiness	Sadness	Surprise
Anger	18	4	2	1
Happiness	3	68	1	2
Sadness	1	6	11	0
Surprise	0	3	0	16

Table 7.64 The performance of S-T signature on Wild dataset through DBN

	FAR	FRR	ERR
Anger	0.036	0.280	0.080
Happiness	0.209	0.081	0.139
Sadness	0.025	0.338	0.073
Surprise	0.025	0.157	0.044

false accept rate. The anger produces FRR as 0.280. The lowest ERR is 0.044 for surprise.

7.5.7.1 Discussion

We select a total of 136 samples to evaluate the system classification rate of the suggested approach. They are divided as training (70% samples) and testing (30% samples) to measure the system performance. The overall identification rate of shape signature is acquired as 72.8% through MLP and 75% through DBN. The average recognition rate of texture signature is achieved as 69.9% through MLP and 75.7% through DBN. The joined S-T feature is achieved as 82.4% overall identification rate of four emotions through MLP and 83.1% through DBN.

The authors [24] experimented on the World Wild Web and acquired an overall accuracy as 58.8% for six basic emotions. In [25], authors evaluated on AffectNet and achieved an overall accuracy as 60.7% of different emotions. The identification of the suggested approach is measured by FAR, ERR, and FRR. The FAR, FRR, and ERR of shape, texture, and S-T signature features through MLP and DBN on Wild dataset are above mentioned. The analysis of FAR, FRR, and ERR on various datasets is shown in Figs. 7.28, 7.29, 7.30, 7.31, 7.32, 7.33, 7.34, 7.35 and 7.36 through MLP and DBN.

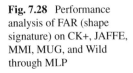
Fig. 7.28 Performance
analysis of FAR (shape
signature) on CK+, JAFFE,
MMI, MUG, and Wild
through MLP

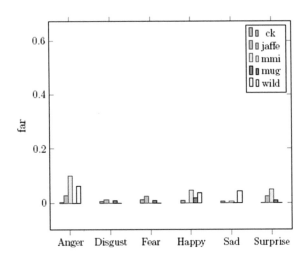

7.6   Performance Analysis of FAR, FRR, and ERR on CK+, JAFFE, MMI, MUG and Wild Datasets

We consider CK+, JAFFE, MMI, MUG, and Wild benchmark databases to measure
the identification rate of emotion for shape, texture, and S-T signature features.
The values of far of shape signature using MLP have been computed to show the
comparison of different expressions.

The performance analysis of FAR for shape signature using MLP is shown in
Fig. 7.28 on different benchmark databases. The highest recognition occurs in surprise on the CK+ dataset. The JAFFE dataset shows the promising recognition of
expression in sadness. The MMI shows the highest recognition rate in disgust. The
MUG dataset yields a promising classification rate in anger. The Wild dataset indicates the promising recognition rate in surprise.

The performance analysis of FRR for shape signature using MLP is shown in
Fig. 7.29 on different benchmark databases. The lowest FRR means indicates the
highest classification rate of expressions. The disgust shows the highest misclassification on CK+. The JAFFE dataset shows the promising recognition of expression in
anger. The MMI shows the highest misclassification in happiness. The MUG dataset
yields a poor classification rate in fear. The Wild dataset shows the poor classification
in anger.

The comparison analysis of ERR for shape signature through MLP is shown in
Fig. 7.30 on different benchmark databases. The lowest ERR indicates the highest
recognition rate in expressions. The highest misclassification occurs in disgust on
the CK+ dataset. The JAFFE dataset shows the poor recognition of expression in
fear. The MMI shows the lowest recognition rate in happiness. The MUG dataset
yields a promising classification rate in anger. The Wild dataset indicates the highest
misclassification in anger.

Fig. 7.29 Performance metrics of FRR (shape signature) on CK+, JAFFE, MMI, MUG, and Wild through MLP

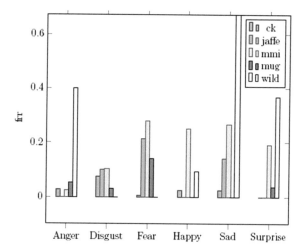

Fig. 7.30 Performance metrics of ERR (shape signature) on CK+, JAFFE, MMI, MUG, and Wild through MLP

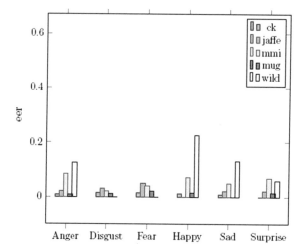

The performance analysis of FAR for texture signature using MLP is shown in Fig. 7.31 on different benchmark databases. The highest recognition occurs in sadness on the CK+ dataset. The JAFFE dataset shows the promising recognition of expressions in happiness, fear, and surprise. The MMI shows the highest recognition rate in fear. The MUG dataset yields a promising classification rate in anger. The Wild dataset indicates the promising recognition rate in sadness.

The performance analysis of FRR for texture signature using MLP is shown in Fig. 7.32 on different benchmark databases. The lowest FRR means, it indicates the highest classification rate of expressions. The fear shows the highest misclassification on CK+. The JAFFE dataset shows the promising recognition of expression in surprise. The MMI shows the highest misclassification in happiness. The MUG

Fig. 7.31 Performance
analysis of FAR (texture
signature) on CK+, JAFFE,
MMI, MUG, and Wild
through MLP

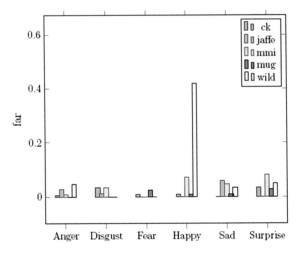

Fig. 7.32 Performance
metrics of FRR (texture
signature) on CK+, JAFFE,
MMI, MUG, and Wild
through MLP

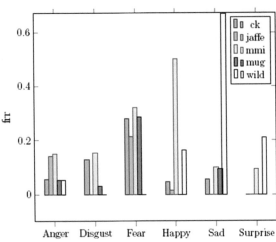

dataset yields a poor classification rate in fear. The Wild dataset shows the poor
classification in sadness.

The comparison analysis of ERR for texture signature using MLP is shown in
Fig. 7.33 on different benchmark databases. The lowest ERR indicates the highest
recognition rate in expressions. The highest misclassification occurs in fear on the
CK+ dataset. The JAFFE dataset shows the poor recognition of expression in fear.
The MMI shows the lowest recognition rate in fear. The MUG dataset yields a
promising classification rate in happiness. The Wild dataset indicates the highest
misclassification in sadness.

The performance analysis of FAR for the S-T signature using MLP is shown
in Fig. 7.34 on different benchmark databases. The highest recognition occurs in
surprise on the CK+ dataset. The JAFFE dataset shows the promising recognition

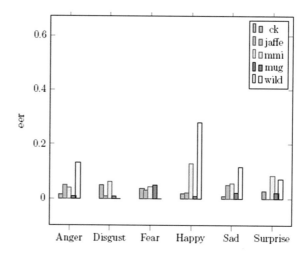

Fig. 7.33 Performance analysis of ERR (texture signature) on CK+, JAFFE, MMI, MUG, and Wild through MLP

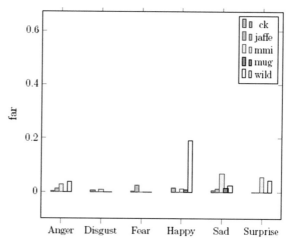

Fig. 7.34 Performance analysis of FAR (S-T signature) on CK+, JAFFE, MMI, MUG, and Wild through MLP

of expression in surprise. The MMI shows the highest recognition rate in fear. The MUG dataset yields a promising classification rate in surprise. The Wild dataset indicates the promising recognition rate in sadness.

The performance analysis of FRR for the S-T signature using MLP is shown in Fig. 7.35 on different benchmark databases. The lowest FRR means, it indicates the highest classification rate of expressions. The disgust shows the highest misclassification on CK+. The JAFFE dataset shows the promising recognition of expression in anger. The MMI shows the highest misclassification in fear. The MUG dataset yields poor classification rate in fear. The Wild dataset shows the poor classification in anger.

The comparison analysis of ERR for the S-T signature using MLP is shown in Fig. 7.36 on different benchmark databases. The lowest ERR indicates the highest

Fig. 7.35 Performance analysis of FRR (S-T signature) on CK+, JAFFE, MMI, MUG, and Wild through MLP

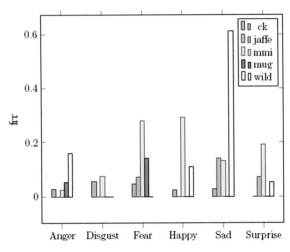

Fig. 7.36 Performance analysis of ERR (S-T signature) on CK+, JAFFE, MMI, MUG, and Wild through MLP

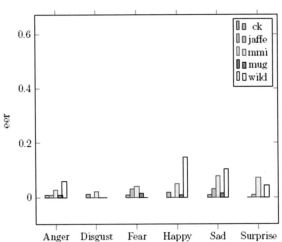

recognition rate in expressions. The highest misclassification occur in happiness on the CK+ dataset. The JAFFE dataset shows the poor recognition of expression in sadness. The MMI shows the lowest recognition rate in sadness The MUG dataset yields a promising classification rate in surprise. The Wild dataset indicates the highest misclassification in surprise.

Fig. 7.37 Performance
analysis of Shape (S),
Texture (T), and S-T features
on four benchmark databases
through MLP

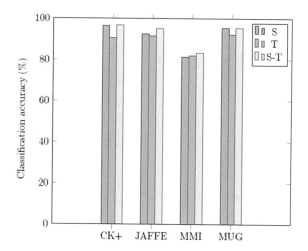

7.7   Comparison of Shape, Texture, and S-T Based Facial Expression Recognition

We evaluate the suggested methods on benchmark datasets through different networks for showing a comparison task of individual features. The comparison task of emotion identification of different features is presented in Figs. 7.37 and 7.38. The average recognition rate of shape, texture, and S-T signatures through MLP is presented as 96.6%, 90.5%, and 96.9% on CK+ dataset, 92.4%, 91.6%, and 95.2% on JAFFE dataset, 81.4%, 81.9%, and 83.4% on MMI dataset, and 95.5%, 92.2%, and 95.6%, respectively, on MUG dataset. The average recognition rate of shape, texture, and S-T signatures through DBN is presented as 97.1%, 94.4%, and 98% on CK+ dataset, 95.2%, 94%, and 98.8% on JAFFE dataset, 88.8%, 85.1%, and 93.1% on MMI dataset, and 96.1%, 95.6%, and 99.1%, respectively, on MUG dataset. From these observations, the combined S-T feature yields promising recognition rate expressions than the individual signature. It is also mentioned that the DBN-based emotion recognition yields excellent classification rate of expressions than MLP.

The identification rate of emotion on the MMI dataset is less as compared to JAFFE, CK+, and MUG datasets. MMI is a most challenging dataset for its spontaneous expressions. The S-T signature feature yields a promising recognition rate than the individual shape and texture signature features.

7.8   Conclusion

This chapter proposed a facial expression recognition using shape signature, texture signature, and joined S-T signature features through MLP and DBN. The effectiveness of the suggested methods is measured by the identification rate of emotion and

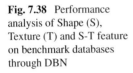
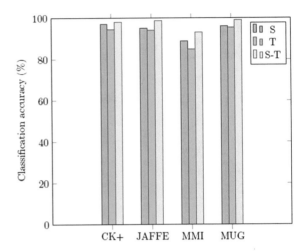

Fig. 7.38 Performance analysis of Shape (S), Texture (T) and S-T feature on benchmark databases through DBN

estimation of similarities with the state-of-the-art. The evaluated results also present an indispensable identification rate of emotion for considering an individual signature (shape & texture) and joined signature (S-T) features on expressed images. The joined S-T signature feature achieves an indispensable identification rate of emotion than the individual signature (shape and texture). Furthermore, our approaches perform quite an impressive identification rate of emotion when experimented on JAFFE, CK+, and MUG datasets. Our suggested approaches also yield even better identification rate of emotion than the state-of-the-art methods. Nowadays, It is a big challenge to the researchers who are engaged in emotion identification from the Wild dataset. The FAR, FRR, and ERR parameters are also used to validate the system performance on benchmark datasets and established an indispensable identification rate of emotion recognition.

In the last chapter, we consider distance, shape, and texture signatures to form a Distance-Shape-Texture (D-S-T) signature to classify the expressions from human face images using different neural networks such as MLP, NARX, and RBF. We already introduce the emotion recognition of individual signature (distance, shape, and texture) features. After introducing the individual feature, we consider joined Distance-Shape (D-S), Distance-Texture (D-T), and Shape-Texture (S-T) signature feature for recognizing the expressions from benchmark datasets. The D-S-T signature is evaluated to measure the system performances. It is also considered to measure the comparison with respect to individual distance, shape, and texture signatures and also combined D-S, D-T, and S-T features.

References

1. T.F. Cootes, G.J. Edwards, C.J. Taylor et al., Active appearance models. IEEE Trans. Pattern Anal. Mach. Intell. **23**(6), 681–685 (2001)
2. G. Tzimiropoulos, M. Pantic, Optimization problems for fast AAM fitting in-the-wild, in *Proceedings of the IEEE international conference on computer vision* (2013), pp. 593–600
3. A. Barman, P. Dutta, Influence of shape and texture features on facial expression recognition. IET Image Process. **13**(8), 1349–1363 (2019)
4. H. Boughrara, M. Chtourou, C.B. Amar, L. Chen, Facial expression recognition based on a mlp neural network using constructive training algorithm. Multimedia Tools Appl. **75**(2), 709–731 (2016)
5. J. Susskind, V. Mnih, G. Hinton et al., On deep generative models with applications to recognition, in *2011 IEEE Conference on Computer Vision and Pattern Recognition (CVPR)* (IEEE, 2011), pp. 2857–2864
6. D. Chakrabarti, D. Dutta, Facial expression recognition using eigenspaces. Procedia Technol. **10**, 755–761 (2013)
7. G. Hinton, A practical guide to training restricted boltzmann machines. Momentum **9**(1), 926 (2010)
8. M.A. Carreira-Perpinan, G.E. Hinton, On contrastive divergence learning, in *Aistats*, vol. 10 (2005), pp. 33–40
9. P. Lucey, J.F. Cohn, T. Kanade, J. Saragih, Z. Ambadar, I. Matthews, The extended Cohn-Kanade dataset (ck+): a complete dataset for action unit and emotion-specified expression, in *Computer Society Conference on Computer Vision and Pattern Recognition-Workshops* (IEEE, 2010), pp. 94–101
10. M. Lyons, S. Akamatsu, M. Kamachi, J. Gyoba, Coding facial expressions with Gabor wavelets, in *Proceedings of the Third IEEE International Conference on Automatic Face and Gesture Recognition* (IEEE, 1998), pp. 200–205
11. M.F. Valstar, M. Pantic, Induced disgust, happiness and surprise: an addition to the mmi facial expression database, in *Proceedings of International Conference on Language Resources and Evaluation, Workshop on EMOTION* (Malta, 2010), pp. 65–70
12. N. Aifanti, C. Papachristou, A. Delopoulos, The mug facial expression database, in *Proceedings of the 11th International Workshop on Image Analysis for Facial Expression Database* (Desenzano, Italy, 2010), pp. 12–14
13. C. Sagonas, E. Antonakos, G. Tzimiropoulos, S. Zafeiriou, M. Pantic, 300 faces in-the-wild challenge: database and results. Image Vis. Comput. **47**, 3–18 (2016)
14. C. Sagonas, G. Tzimiropoulos, S. Zafeiriou, M. Pantic, 300 faces in-the-wild challenge: the first facial landmark localization challenge, in *Proceedings of the IEEE International Conference on Computer Vision Workshops* (2013), pp. 397–403
15. A. Majumder, L. Behera, V.K. Subramanian, Automatic facial expression recognition system using deep network-based data fusion. IEEE Trans. Cybern. **48**(1), 103–114 (2018)
16. A.T. Lopes, E. de Aguiar, T. Oliveira-Santos, A facial expression recognition system using convolutional networks, in *2015 28th SIBGRAPI Conference on Graphics, Patterns and Images (SIBGRAPI)* (IEEE, 2015), pp. 273–280
17. L. Zhong, Q. Liu, P. Yang, J. Huang, D.N. Metaxas, Learning multiscale active facial patches for expression analysis. IEEE Trans. Cybern. **45**(8), 1499–1510 (2015)
18. S.L. Happy, A. Routray, Automatic facial expression recognition using features of salient facial patches. IEEE Trans. Affect. Comput. **6**(1), 1–12 (2015)
19. A. Poursaberi, H.A. Noubari, M. Gavrilova, S.N. Yanushkevich, Gauss–laguerre wavelet textural feature fusion with geometrical information for facial expression identification. EURASIP J. Image Video Process. **2012**(1), 1–13 (2012)
20. L. Zhang, D. Tjondronegoro, Facial expression recognition using facial movement features. IEEE Trans. Affect. Comput. **2**(4), 219–229 (2011)

21. M.Z. Uddin, M.M. Hassan, A. Almogren, A. Alamri, M. Alrubaian, G. Fortino, Facial expression recognition utilizing local direction-based robust features and deep belief network. IEEE Access **5**, 4525–4536 (2017)
22. D. Ghimire, J. Lee, Z.N. Li, S. Jeong, Recognition of facial expressions based on salient geometric features and support vector machines. Multimedia Tools Appl. **76**(6), 7921–7946 (2017)
23. Y. Lv, Z. Feng, C. Xu, Facial expression recognition via deep learning, in *2014 International Conference on Smart Computing (SMARTCOMP)* (IEEE, 2014), pp. 303–308
24. A. Mollahosseini, B. Hasani, M.J. Salvador, H. Abdollahi, D. Chan, M.H. Mahoor, Facial expression recognition from world wild web, in *Proceedings of the IEEE Conference on Computer Vision and Pattern Recognition Workshops* (2016), pp. 58–65
25. A. Mollahosseini, B. Hasani, M.H. Mahoor, Affectnet: a database for facial expression, valence, and arousal computing in the wild (2017). arXiv:1708.03985

Chapter 8
Human Emotion Recognition from Distance-Shape-Texture Signature Trio

8.1 Introduction

The previous Chaps. 2, 3, and 4 consist of feature descriptors individually distance signature, shape signature, and texture signature and Chaps. 5, 6, and 7 are considered as combined descriptors such as distance and shape (D-S), distance and texture (D-T), and shape and texture (S-T). In course of Distance-Shape-Texture (D-S-T) signature trio respective stability indices and statistical measures supplement the signature features with a view to enhance the performance task of facial expression classification. Incorporation of these supplementary features is duly justified through extensive study and analysis of results obtained thereon.

While appreciating the usefulness of individual signature features in a marginal sense, the question coming up next is whether the join contribution of the signature descriptors discussed in the previous chapters is in a portion to offer even more impressive performance. When we consider the joint contribution of the feature, they gave promising recognition rates of facial expressions. Now we combine all three individual signature to form a D-S-T signature trio for facial expression recognition and also measure the performances of expressions. Accordingly, in this chapter, the Distance-Shape-Texture signature trio is used to identify human facial expressions. The distance, shape, and texture signatures are considered individually to form a signature trio. The identification of proper landmark is a challenging issue in emotion recognition. Active Appearance Model (AAM) [1] is considered to identify the landmark points on a face. The few landmarks are extracted around the eye, nose, eyebrow, and mouth region to constitute a grid. A grid is used to find the relative distances and normalized to get a distance signature. The triangles are formed among the grid. A normalized shape signature is derived from triangles. The texture regions are extracted using salient landmark points and are subsequently the Local Binary Pattern (LBP) [2] is applied to detect the texture features. These features are normalized to get texture signature. These signature are combined to form a Distance-Shape-Texture signature trio for the recognition of facial. The respective stability indices are

© Springer Nature Singapore Pte Ltd. 2020
P. Dutta and A. Barman, *Human Emotion Recognition from Face Images*,
Cognitive Intelligence and Robotics,
https://doi.org/10.1007/978-981-15-3883-4_8

obtained from a Distance-Shape-Texture signature trio. The moment, range, entropy, kurtosis, and skewness are also calculated from a Distance-Shape-Texture signature trio. These features are used as input to NARX, MLP, and RBF for classification of emotions. The four benchmark datasets such as CK+, MMI, JAFFE, and MUG are evaluated to test the performance of emotion recognition.

Organization of This Chapter

This chapter is organized in eight parts. In the first part, consisting of Sect. 8.1, we introduce distance, shape, and texture signatures useful for human emotion recognition.

The second part of the chapter explores the proposed framework of emotion recognition of Distance-Shape-Texture (D-S-T) signatures trio from face images.

The third part of this chapter, consisting of Sect. 8.3 shows the discussion on the feature extraction mechanism. In this part, we also discuss the facial landmark and subsequent signatures.

In the next part, comprising Sect. 8.4 shows the formation of Distance-Shape-Texture signature trio.

The feature selection of Distance-Shape-Texture signature trio is described in Sect. 8.5.

The classification task is described in Sect. 8.6. This part also makes detailed discussion about the classification of emotions into different categories.

The penultimate part of the chapter discusses the experiment and result analysis on four benchmark databases.

The chapter sums up with a conclusion in Sect. 8.8.

8.2   Overview of the Proposed System

The schematic diagram is presented in Fig. 8.1 to show the proposed facial expression recognition. Active Appearance Model [3] is considered to extract the landmark points on a face. The eyes, eyebrows, nose, and mouth regions of a facial image are discriminative regions to identify the expressions from one face to another face. These points are considered in a way such that three points on each eyebrow, three points on the nose, four points on the mouth, and four points on each eye. The detected landmark points form a grid and also try to compute the distances to get a normalized distance signature. Now triangles are identified from the grid node and corresponding normalized shape signature is calculated. Detected landmarks are also applied to a face image to form texture regions. These regions are considered to extract the texture signature using the Local Binary Pattern (LBP). Now individual normalized distance, shape and texture signature are combined to form a Distance-Shape-Texture signature trio. Stability indices of the Distance-Shape-Texture signature trio are determined from a higher-order signature of each distance, shape, and texture signature. Statistical parameters such as moments, range, kurtosis, skewness, and entropy are derived from each Distance-Shape-Texture signature trio to supplement the feature set. The salient features are used as input MLP, NARX, and RBF networks to classify the

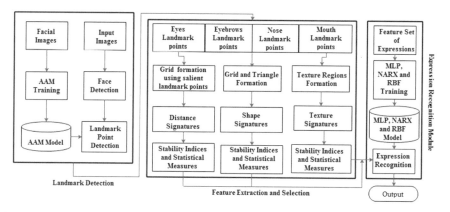

Fig. 8.1 Proposed block diagram of Distance-Shape-Texture signature trio

different expressions such as anger, fear, sadness, happiness, disgust, and surprise separately.

8.3 Facial Landmark Detection

Proper landmark detection of facial expressions is a vital task in emotion recognition. Few facial landmarks deserve an important role due to their variation of expressions from one face to another one. There are many methods to extract the landmark points on the face images. In this chapter we consider an Active Appearance Model (AAM) to extract the landmark points. The landmark detection procedure of the AAM is discussed in the second chapter of Sect. 2.2.1.

8.3.1 Grid Formation

The landmark points [4] play a vital role in the displacement of the facial components. In this context, the salient landmark points are marked around the nose, mouth, eyebrows, and eye regions due to their deformations of facial expression. The grid formation procedure is mentioned in the second chapter of Sect. 2.2.2. However, the four points are marked on each eye, three points on each eyebrow, four points on the mouth, and three points on the nose. These selected landmarks are linked to form a grid [5–9].

8.4 Formation of Distance-Shape-Texture Signature Trio for Feature Extraction

The distance, shape, and texture signature features play a crucial role to recognize the expressions from different face databases. After considering the individual feature for recognizing the expressions, we consider the combined features (Distance-Shape, Shape-Texture, and Distance-Texture) for recognizing the expressions. The individual and combined features experimented on four benchmark databases and validated its superior performances. We use distance, shape, and texture signatures individually to form a Distance-Shape-Texture (DST) signature trio for facial expression recognition. This signature trio is not directly fed as an input of different neural networks to identify the expressions. The stability index is computed from the DST trio as a vital feature to identify the expressions of different people. The statistical measures of skewness, kurtosis, range, moment, and entropy are computed from DST trio to get a prominent feature.

8.4.1 Stability Index of Distance-Shape-Texture Signature Trio

The stability index is a formidable feature in facial expression recognition. The individual stability index plays a crucial role in recognizing expressions. The discussion of stability indices of distance, shape, and texture features are available in the second, third, and fourth chapters. Now we combine the stability indices as Distance-Shape, Distance-Texture, and Shape-Texture signatures to test the system performance of expressions. The definition of the stability indices of distance and texture signatures is elaborated in second, third, and fourth chapters. These discussions are also available in Sects. 2.3.2 and 4.3.1. We already defined the definition of distance, shape, and texture signatures using Eqs. 2.4, 3.12, 4.3. Higher-order signatures are computed from normalized distance, shape and texture signatures. These higher-order signatures are considered to calculate a stability index of the D-S-T signature trio.

8.4.2 Range, Moment, Skewness, Kurtosis, and Entropy from Distance-Shape-Texture Signature Trio

The promising facial expression recognition is done by the involvement of more number of features. The statistical parameters such as moments, skewness, and entropy are used to extract the number of features set from normalized signatures.

The involvement of more appropriate features yields promising facial expression classification. For this reason, the statistical features such as range, moments, skewness, kurtosis, and entropy are computed from both normalized distance and texture signatures. The detailed discussion of the statistical measures is available in the second chapter of Sect. 2.3.3. These statistical measures play an important role to recognize the expression for individual distance and texture signature. These statistical measures are combined from an individual distance and texture signature to form a combined feature for recognizing the expressions.

8.5 Feature Selection of Distance-Shape-Texture Signature Trio

Each higher-order signatures are defined to compute the stability indices as per Sects. 2.3.2 and 4.3.1. In the same way, statistical parameters such as moment, skewness, kurtosis, and entropy are computed as per Sect. 2.3.3. Now we combine all the features such as moment, skewness, range, kurtosis, and entropy to form a DST trio feature set. Each of the DST trio signatures has a 27-dimensional vector feature. A 27-dimensional vector feature is used as input to NARX, MLP, and RBF networks for categorization of expressions.

8.6 Classification of Distance-Shape-Texture Signature Trio Features

Three artificial networks (RBF, MLP, and NARX) are used to classify the expressions on four benchmark datasets such as Cohn-Kanade, JAFFE, MMI, and MUG.

8.6.1 Multilayer Perceptron

The D-S-T signature trio is formed by a vector of 27 elements of each facial image. These features are also normalized and fed as an input variable to the network of MLP. It produces the output depending on the minimum error. The training process is completed by minimizing the mean square error [10] as $e_k = 1/2 \sum (t_k - y_k)^2$ for six classes. Here t_k and y_k represent the target and desired response. The different class labels set as $k = 6$ in the training procedure.

The four steps of the training process are mentioned as weights initialization, Feed-forward, minimizing the errors through backpropagation, and modification of biases and weights. In the first step, small values are assigned to initial weights. The input unit represents as x_i $(i = 1, \ldots, n)$, where n indicates the inputs received information. After that it transmits input signal to every hidden neuron z_j $(j = 1, 2, \ldots, 8)$. The biases are denoted as v_o and w_o. Every hidden neuron computes the output using a tan$h$ activation function. These outputs are transmitted to each output unit z_j. A linear activation function is used to get the output response. At the time of backpropagation errors, each output unit computes its measured y_k with respect to target t_k to compute the desired error of that unit. Depending on these errors, the factor δ_k ($k = 1, ..., m$) is measured as output y_k and went into the back of all the previous layers. In this experiment, m indicates the output (The value of m is 6). In a similar way, δ_j ($j = 1, .., p$) factor is determined for every hidden neuron z_j. In this experiment, we set the hidden units as $p = 8$. In the last phase biases and weights are modified using the factor of δ. The threshold and learning rate are denoted as ζ and η. The stopping training criteria is $e_k \leq \zeta$. In the testing phase, six basic emotions are identified depending on the maximum output values.

8.6.2   Training Using Nonlinear Auto Regressive with eXogenous Input

The NARX [11] network is an architecture of the dynamical neural network. The network receives as input a window of past input and output values and computes the current output. The NARX model is defined as

$$y(t) = f(u(t - Du), \ldots, u(t - 1), u(t), y(t - Dy), \ldots, y(t - 1)) \qquad (8.1)$$

Here, $u(t)$ and $y(t)$ represent the inputs and outputs of the network at time t, respectively. The time lags of input and output are denoted by Du and Dy, and f represents a nonlinear type function used backpropagation through time [11] for approximation. The backpropagation through time network has three layers as input, hidden, and output layers. The output neurons have recurrent connections from the hidden neurons. The hidden neurons compute through a linear or nonlinear transformation function of the input unit based on the function. The hidden states $h(t)$ and outputs $y(t)$ at time t are derived as

$$h(t) = \phi(w_{hx}x(t)) + b_h \text{ and } y(t) = \gamma(w_{yh}h(t)) + b_y \qquad (8.2)$$

where the weight of the input unit to hidden unit and hidden unit to output unit matrices are represented as w_{hx} and w_{yh}. The biases are denoted as b_h and b_y. The hyperbolic tangent functions (ϕ) use in the hidden unit. In the same way, the linear transfer function (γ) is used for the output unit. In the training phase, the NARX network optimizes to get optimal weights by minimizing the errors between the predictions y and the target outputs.

8.6.3 Radial Basis Function Network

The radial basis network [12] has three layers such as input, hidden, and output. Here n represents the neurons of input and m indicates neurons of output. The hidden neurons reside in the mid position of input and output layers. The hypothetical connections are formed from input layers to hidden layers. In the same way, the weighted connections are formed from the hidden layers to output layers. The Gaussian function computes the output of RBF. In the training phase, the training images are labeled into six classes. The Distance-Shape-Texture trio is extracted from the same training set and fed as an input of that network. During the testing, extracted features are considered to measure the system performance of expression recognition. The output response of the RBF is classified into six classes beyond the expressions.

Here, we propose the training mechanism of the RBF. In the first step, small random values are assigned as weighted to input units. Each input unit x_i ($i = 1, \ldots, n$), where n represents the input receiving feature. This input feature is transferred to each hidden unit and calculates the radial basis function. A radial function is chosen as the center among the input features. In the hidden layer, A radial basis function is used as activation function to transform the input vector: $v_i(x_i) = \exp(-\frac{1}{2\sigma_i^2}||x_{ji} - X_{ji}||^2)$. Here $||.||$ represents a norm of the input feature, X_{ji} represents the centers of the input features, σ_i indicates the ith width of input and x_{ji} indicates the variable of jth input. Now we assign small random values for the weights of the output layers. Now it calculates as

$$y_{ne} = \sum_{i=1}^{h} w_{im} v_i (x_i + w_o) \qquad (8.3)$$

where hidden nodes are represented by h, y_{ne} represents the mth output value in the output layer for the nth coming pattern, w_{im} indicates the weight between ith unit and mth output node and w_o indicates the bias at nth output. The network computes the minimum error using mean square error to stop the training.

8.7 Experiment and Result

The four benchmark datasets are considered to test the system performances. We assess the D-S-T signature trio based facial expression recognition by applying on Cohn-Kanade (CK+) [13], JAFFE [14], MMI [15], and MUG [16] databases. The Distance-Shape-Texture signature trio is represented by a vector of 27 variables. The MLP, RBF, and NARX networks are applied to recognize the emotions. We also study the evaluated results for comparison with the different state-of-the-art approaches. The six basic emotions are indicated as disgust, anger, fear, sadness, happiness, and surprise.

8.7.1 Experiment on CK+ Database

The Cohn-Kanade (CK+) database consists of 100 university students aged between 18 and 30 years. To evaluate the system performance, a total of 393 images are selected to measure the performances of three different networks. In this dataset we use as 70% images for training, 15% images for testing, and remaining 15% for the validation. The total images are divided as 72 for anger, 43 for fear, 54 for disgust, 69 for surprise, 84 for happiness, and 71 for sadness. We use three artificial networks such as MLP, RBF, and NARX to categorize the expressions into different categories.

Table 8.1 represents the performance of the trio signature through MLP. The anger, sadness, and surprise are classified correctly. The disgust recognizes 52 images positively and 2 images are in a mismatch with anger. The happiness identifies 80 images properly and 4 images are misclassified with disgust. The fear detects 41 images positively and 1 image is confused as anger.

The NARX network is evaluated to measure the performances of different expressions of trio signature which is available in Table 8.3. The anger classifies properly 70 images and 2 images are misidentified with disgust. The disgust recognizes 52 images rightly and 2 images are confused with anger. The fear recognizes 41 images perfectly and 2 images are confused with sadness and surprise. The happiness recognizes 83 images and 1 image is confused with sadness. The sadness identifies 69 images properly and 2 images are wrongly classified with surprise. In the same way, the 67 images are classified correctly as surprise.

Table 8.1 The recognition matrix of D-S-T signature trio on CK+ dataset through MLP

	Anger	Disgust	Fear	Happiness	Sadness	Surprise
Anger	72	0	0	0	0	0
Disgust	2	52	0	0	0	0
Fear	1	0	41	0	0	0
Happiness	0	4	0	80	0	0
Sadness	0	0	0	0	71	0
Surprise	0	0	0	0	0	69

Table 8.2 The performance of D-S-T signature on CK+ dataset through MLP

	FAR	FRR	ERR
Anger	0.009	0	0.007
Disgust	0.011	0.037	0.015
Fear	0	0.046	0.005
Happiness	0	0.047	0.010
Sadness	0.003	0	0.002
Surprise	0	0	0

Table 8.3 The recognition matrix of D-S-T signature trio on CK+ dataset through NARX

	Anger	Disgust	Fear	Happiness	Sadness	Surprise
Anger	70	2	0	0	0	0
Disgust	0	52	2	0	0	0
Fear	0	0	41	1	1	0
Happiness	0	0	0	83	1	0
Sadness	0	0	0	0	69	2
Surprise	0	0	0	0	0	67

Table 8.4 The performance of D-S-T signature on CK+ dataset through NARX

	FAR	FRR	ERR
Anger	0	0.027	0.005
Disgust	0.005	0.037	0.010
Fear	0.005	0.046	0.010
Happiness	0.003	0.011	0.005
Sadness	0.006	0.028	0.010
Surprise	0.006	0	0.005

The performance of the proposed approach is measured in terms of the false rejection rate (FAR), false acceptance rate (FAR), and error rate (ERR). The values of FRR, FAR, and ERR show the system performance of the D-S-T signature through MLP on the CK+ dataset indicated in Table 8.2. The FAR value of anger is 0.009 that means it produces a 9/1000 false accept rate. The disgust yields FRR as 0.037. The disgust produces 0.015 as ERR. It also indicates that the system has the highest recognition rate of expressions.

The parameter of FAR, FRR, and ERR are considered to measure the system performances of the D-S-T signature using NARX. Table 8.4 shows the evaluated results of FAR, FRR, and ERR. The FAR value of disgust is 0.005 that means it produces a 5/1000 false accept rate. The disgust yields FRR as 0.037. The disgust produces 0.010 as ERR. It also indicates that the system has the highest recognition rate of expressions.

The RBF network is also evaluated in Table 8.5 to show the performance of expressions of trio signature. From this Table, we see that anger and sadness are classified properly. But the fear identifies correctly 41 images and 2 images are in a mismatch with surprise. The happiness recognizes properly 82 images and 2 images are in misclassification with anger and surprise. The surprise detects 67 images properly and 2 images are wrongly identified with sadness and disgust.

The values of FAR, FRR, and ERR are used to compute the system performances of the D-S-T signature using RBF. Table 8.6 mentions the computed results of FAR, FRR, and ERR to measure the performance. The FAR value of disgust is 0.003 that means it produces a 3/1000 false accept rate. The anger yields FRR as 0.027. The

Table 8.5 The confusion matrix of Distance-Shape-Texture signature trio on CK+ database using RBF

	Anger	Disgust	Fear	Happiness	Sadness	Surprise
Anger	70	0	0	0	0	0
Disgust	0	54	0	0	0	0
Fear	0	0	41	0	1	1
Happiness	1	0	0	82	0	1
Sadness	0	0	0	0	71	0
Surprise	0	1	0	0	1	67

Table 8.6 The performance of D-S-T signature on CK+ dataset through RBF

	FAR	FRR	ERR
Anger	0.003	0.027	0.007
Disgust	0.029	0	0.002
Fear	0	0.046	0.005
Happiness	0	0.023	0.005
Sadness	0.009	0	0.007
Surprise	0.009	0.029	0.012

Fig. 8.2 FAR of CK+ through MLP, NARX, and RBF

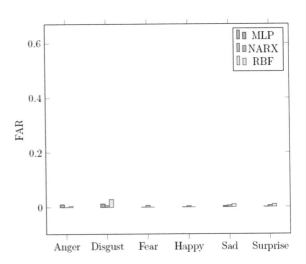

system has the highest recognition rate in expressions if it has the lowest FRR. The disgust produces 0.007 as ERR.

The comparison of the FAR for D-S-T signature through MLP, NARX, and RBF on CK+ is shown in Fig. 8.2. The FAR graph analysis of the D-S-T signature using MLP yields a poor recognition rate in anger. The MLP based FAR graph analysis of the D-S-T signature shows a less promising performance than the NARX based

Fig. 8.3 FRR of CK+
through MLP, NARX, and
RBF

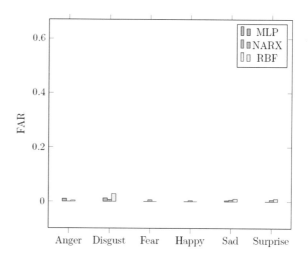

Fig. 8.4 ERR of CK+
through MLP, NARX, and
RBF

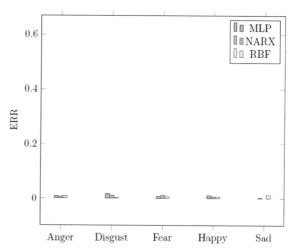

network. From this graph analysis, we also conclude that the D-S-T signature yields a promising recognition rate of individual expressions through RBF.

The comparison of the FRR for D-S-T signature through MLP, NARX, and RBF on CK+ is shown in Fig. 8.3. The FRR graph analysis of MLP based D-S-T signature yields a poor recognition rate in fear. The FRR graph analysis of the D-S-T signature using NARX performs the promising recognition rate of expressions. It is also showed that the D-S-T signature using RBF indicates a promising classification rate of individual expressions.

The comparison of the ERR for D-S-T signature through MLP, NARX, and RBF on the CK+ is shown in Fig. 8.4. The ERR graph analysis of the D-S-T signature yields a poor recognition rate in sadness for MLP. The ERR graph analysis of the

Table 8.7 The recognition matrix of Distance-Shape-Texture signature trio on JAFFE dataset through MLP

	Anger	Disgust	Fear	Happiness	Sadness	Surprise
Anger	21	0	0	0	0	0
Disgust	0	20	0	0	0	0
Fear	1	0	11	0	1	1
Happiness	0	0	0	14	0	0
Sadness	0	0	1	0	13	0
Surprise	0	0	0	0	0	14

Table 8.8 The performance of D-S-T signature on JAFFE dataset through MLP

	FAR	FRR	ERR
Anger	0	0	0
Disgust	0.013	0	0.010
Fear	0.012	0.213	0.041
Happiness	0	0	0
Sadness	0.012	0.071	0.020
Surprise	0.012	0	0.010

D-S-T signature shows promising performance. From this graph analysis, it is also showed that the RBF based D-S-T signature yields a promising classification rate of individual expressions.

8.7.2 Experimental Result on JAFFE Database

The JAFFE [14] dataset has a total of 213 gray level images for the identification of emotions. These expressions are considered as six basic and one neutral of Japanese females. In this experiment, we use a total of 97 images to measure the performances. The dataset is divided as 70% for training, 15% for testing, and 15% for validation.

Table 8.7 indicates the performance of recognized expressions of trio signature using MLP. The anger, disgust, happiness, and surprise are identified correctly. The fear recognizes correctly 11 images and 3 images are in misclassification with anger, sadness, and surprise. The sadness classifies 13 images positively and 1 image is confused as fear.

The results of FRR, FAR, and ERR are evaluated to show the performance of D-S-T signature through MLP on the JAFFE dataset indicated in Table 8.8. The FAR value of fear is 0.013 that means it produces a 13/1000 false accept rate. The fear yields FRR as 0.213. It represents the lowest recognition rate of expression. The fear produces 0.041 as ERR. It also indicates that the system has the highest recognition rate of expressions.

Table 8.9 The recognition matrix of D-S-T signature trio on JAFFE database using NARX

	Anger	Disgust	Fear	Happiness	Sadness	Surprise
Anger	20	1	0	0	0	0
Disgust	0	18	2	0	0	0
Fear	1	0	13	0	0	0
Happiness	0	0	0	12	2	0
Sadness	0	0	0	0	12	2
Surprise	0	0	1	0	0	11

Table 8.10 The performance of D-S-T signature on JAFFE dataset through NARX

	FAR	FRR	ERR
Anger	0.013	0.047	0.021
Disgust	0.013	0.010	0.031
Fear	0.037	0.071	0.042
Happiness	0	0.142	0.021
Sadness	0.024	0.142	0.042
Surprise	0.024	0.083	0.031

The NARX network is evaluated to measure the performances of different expressions of trio signature which is available in Table 8.9. The anger identifies correctly 20 images and 1 image is misclassified with disgust. The disgust recognizes 18 images positively and 2 images are misclassified with happiness. The fear classifies correctly 13 images and 1 image is confused with anger. The happiness recognizes 12 images perfectly and 2 images are confused with sadness. The sadness identifies correctly 12 images and 2 images are in a mismatch with surprise. In the same way, the 11 images are classified correctly as surprise and 1 image is confused with fear.

The parameter of FAR, FRR, and ERR are considered to measure the system performances of the D-S-T signature using NARX. Table 8.10 shows the evaluated results of FAR, FRR, and ERR. The FAR value of disgust is 0.013 that means it produces a 13/1000 false accept rate. The disgust yields FRR as 0.010. The disgust produces 0.031 as ERR. It also indicates that the system has the highest recognition rate of expressions.

The RBF network is also experimented in Table 8.11 to measure the system performance of the trio signature. From this Table, we indicate that the anger, disgust, happiness, and surprise are classified correctly. But the fear identifies 13 images positively and 1 image is in a mismatch with disgust. The sadness detects 13 images properly and 1 image is wrongly identified as fear.

The FAR, FRR, and ERR are used to compute the system performances of the D-S-T signature using RBF. Table 8.12 produces the computed results of FAR, FRR, and ERR. The FAR value of disgust is 0.013 that means it produces a 13/1000 false accept rate. The disgust yields FRR as 0. The system has the correct recognition rate in disgust. The disgust produces 0.010 as ERR.

Table 8.11 The recognition matrix of D-S-T signature trio on JAFFE dataset through RBF

	Anger	Disgust	Fear	Happiness	Sadness	Surprise
Anger	21	0	0	0	0	0
Disgust	0	20	0	0	0	0
Fear	0	1	13	0	0	0
Happiness	0	0	0	14	0	0
Sadness	0	0	1	0	13	0
Surprise	0	0	0	0	0	14

Table 8.12 The performance of D-S-T signature on JAFFE Dataset through RBF

	FAR	FRR	ERR
Anger	0	0	0
Disgust	0.013	0	0.010
Fear	0.012	0.071	0.020
Happiness	0	0	0
Sadness	0	0.071	0.010
Surprise	0	0	0

Fig. 8.5 FAR of JAFFE through MLP, NARX, and RBF

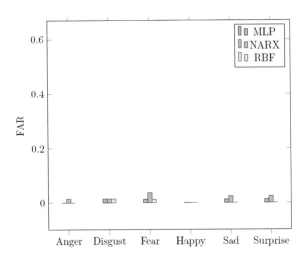

The performance of the FAR for the D-S-T signature through MLP, RBF, and NARX on the JAFFE dataset is shown in Fig. 8.5. The FAR graph analysis of the D-S-T signature yields a poor recognition rate in disgust. The FAR graph analysis of the NARX based D-S-T signature shows the promising recognition rate in expressions. From this graph analysis, we also conclude that the RBF based D-S-T signature yields a promising recognition rate in expressions.

Fig. 8.6 FRR of JAFFE
through MLP, NARX, and
RBF

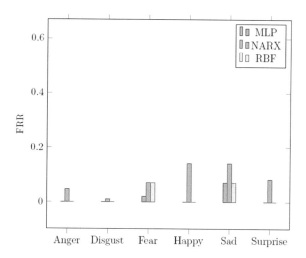

Fig. 8.7 ERR of JAFFE
through MLP, NARX, and
RBF

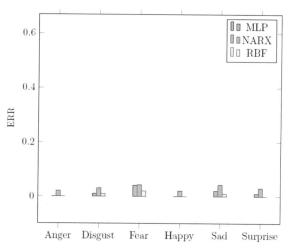

The comparison of the FRR for D-S-T signature through MLP, RBF, and NARX on JAFFE dataset is shown in Fig. 8.6. The FRR graph analysis of D-S-T signature using MLP yields a poor recognition rate in fear. The FRR graph analysis of the D-S-T signature using NARX performs the poor recognition rate of expressions in happiness. It is also showed that the RBF based D-S-T signature indicates a promising classification rate in happiness expression.

The comparison of the ERR for D-S-T signature through MLP, RBF, and NARX on JAFFE dataset is shown in Fig. 8.7. The ERR graph analysis of D-S-T signature yields a poor recognition rate in happiness for MLP. The ERR graph analysis of the NARX based D-S-T signature shows a less promising performance than the MLP based D-S-T signature. From this graph analysis, it is also showed that the RBF based D-S-T signature yields a higher detection rate in anger.

Table 8.13 The recognition matrix of D-S-T signature trio on MMI dataset through MLP

	Anger	Disgust	Fear	Happiness	Sadness	Surprise
Anger	28	2	4	0	5	1
Disgust	3	30	3	1	1	1
Fear	1	1	16	1	5	1
Happiness	1	3	4	12	1	3
Sadness	1	0	0	1	27	1
Surprise	0	1	1	3	1	15

Table 8.14 The performance of D-S-T signature on MMI dataset through MLP

	FAR	FRR	ERR
Anger	0.043	0.300	0.106
Disgust	0.050	0.230	0.089
Fear	0.077	0.360	0.117
Happiness	0.038	0.500	0.100
Sadness	0.087	0.100	0.089
Surprise	0.044	0.285	0.072

8.7.3   Experiment on MMI Database

MMI dataset is a more indispensable dataset due to their spontaneous expressions. In this experiment, we use a total of 113 images to measure the system performance of emotions. They were evaluated as 70% for training, 15% for testing, and remaining 15% for validation.

Table 8.13 indicates the performance of identified expressions of trio signature using MLP. The anger identifies correctly 28 images and 12 images are misclassified with all expressions except anger. The disgust recognizes properly 30 images and 9 images are in misclassification with fear, anger, happiness, sadness, and surprise. The fear recognizes 16 images properly and 9 images are in a mismatch with remaining expressions. The happiness identifies 12 images positively and 12 images are in misclassification with remaining expressions. The sadness detects 27 images properly and 3 images are wrongly identified as anger, happiness, and surprise. The surprise recognizes 15 images positively and 6 images are in misclassification as happiness, sadness, disgust, and fear.

The results of FRR, FAR, and ERR are indicated in Table 8.14 to show the performance of the D-S-T signature through MLP for MMI dataset. The FAR value of fear is 0.050 that means it produces a 5/1000 false accept rate. The fear yields FRR as 0.23 It represents the lowest recognition rate of expression. The fear produces 0.089 as ERR. It also indicates that the system has the highest recognition rate of expressions.

Table 8.15 The recognition matrix of D-S-T signature trio on MMI dataset through NARX

	Anger	Disgust	Fear	Happiness	Sadness	Surprise
Anger	37	3	0	0	0	0
Disgust	4	33	2	0	0	0
Fear	0	0	23	1	1	0
Happiness	0	0	0	23	1	0
Sadness	0	0	0	3	26	1
Surprise	0	1	0	0	0	18

Table 8.16 The performance of D-S-T signature on MMI dataset through NARX

	FAR	FRR	ERR
Anger	0.029	0.075	0.039
Disgust	0.029	0.153	0.056
Fear	0.013	0.080	0.022
Happiness	0.026	0.041	0.028
Sadness	0.013	0.133	0.033
Surprise	0.006	0.052	0.011

The NARX network is also evaluated to measure the performances of different expressions of trio signature which is available in Table 8.15. The anger classifies correctly 37 images and 3 images are in a mismatch with disgust. The disgust recognizes properly 33 images and 6 images are wrongly classified with anger and fear. The fear detects 23 images positively and 2 images are in misclassification with happiness and sadness. The happiness recognizes 23 images properly and 1 image is in misclassification with sadness. The sadness identifies 26 images correctly and 4 images are wrongly classified with happiness and surprise. In the same way, the 18 images are classified correctly as surprise and 1 image is confused with disgust.

The parameter of FAR, FRR, and ERR are considered to measure the system performances of D-S-T signature using NARX. Table 8.16 shows the evaluated results of FAR, FRR, and ERR. The FAR value of disgust is 0.029 that means it produces a 29/1000 false accept rate. The disgust yields FRR as 0.153. The disgust produces 0.056 as ERR. It also indicates that the system has a poor recognition rate in disgust.

The RBF network is also evaluated in Table 8.17 to show the performance of different expressions of trio signature. The anger recognizes properly 34 images and 6 images are in misclassification with disgust and happiness. The disgust identifies 37 images positively and 2 images are confused with fear and surprise. The fear classifies properly 19 images and 6 images are in a mismatch with anger, disgust, sadness, and surprise. The happiness recognizes 14 images correctly and 10 images are confused with remaining expressions. The sadness recognizes 18 images positively and 12 images are in a mismatch with remaining expressions. The surprise detects 17 images perfectly and 5 images are in a mismatch as fear, happiness, and surprise.

Table 8.17 The recognition matrix of D-S-T signature trio on MMI dataset through RBF

	Anger	Disgust	Fear	Happiness	Sadness	Surprise
Anger	34	3	1	2	0	0
Disgust	0	37	1	0	0	1
Fear	1	2	19	0	2	1
Happiness	2	1	1	14	3	3
Sadness	1	4	2	3	18	2
Surprise	2	0	1	1	0	17

Table 8.18 The performance of D-S-T signature on MMI database using RBF

	FAR	FRR	ERR
Anger	0.043	0.150	0.067
Disgust	0.071	0.051	0.067
Fear	0.039	0.240	0.067
Happiness	0.038	0.416	0.089
Sadness	0.033	0.400	0.095
Surprise	0.044	0.190	0.061

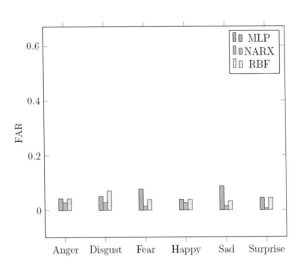

Fig. 8.8 FAR of MMI through MLP, NARX, and RBF

The FAR, FRR, and ERR are used to compute the system performances of the D-S-T signature using RBF. Table 8.18 shows the computed results of FAR, FRR, and ERR. The FAR value of happiness is 0.038 that means it produces a 38/1000 false accept rate. The happiness yields FRR as 0.416. It indicates a poor recognition rate for happiness. The happiness produces 0.089 as ERR.

The performance of the FAR D-S-T signature through MLP, RBF, and NARX on the MMI dataset is shown in Fig. 8.8. The FAR graph analysis of the D-S-T signature

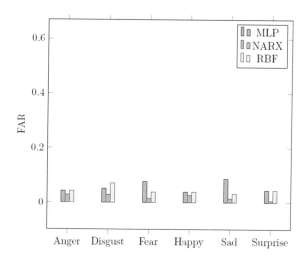

Fig. 8.9 FRR of MMI through MLP, NARX, and RBF

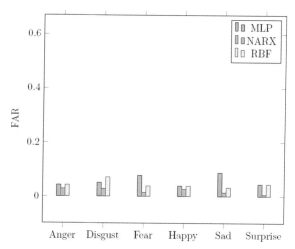

Fig. 8.10 ERR of MMI through MLP, NARX, and RBF

using MLP yields a poor recognition rate in sadness. The FAR graph analysis of the D-S-T signature using NRAX shows a less promising recognition rate in surprise. From this graph analysis, we also observe that the RBF based D-S-T signature yields a promising classification rate in fear.

The comparison of the FRR for the D-S-T signature through MLP, RBF, and NARX on the MMI dataset is shown in Fig. 8.9. The FRR graph analysis of the D-S-T signature using MLP yields a poor recognition rate in sadness. The FRR graph analysis of the D-S-T signature using NARX performs a poor recognition rate of expressions in anger, disgust, and happiness. It is also shown that the RBF based D-S-T signature indicates a promising identification rate in fear and sadness.

The comparison of the ERR D-S-T signature through MLP, RBF, and NARX on MMI dataset is shown in Fig. 8.10. The ERR graph analysis of MLP based D-S-T

Table 8.19 The recognition matrix of D-S-T signature trio on MUG Dataset through MLP

	Anger	Disgust	Fear	Happiness	Sadness	Surprise
Anger	17	0	0	0	1	1
Disgust	1	29	1	0	0	0
Fear	1	1	12	0	0	0
Happiness	0	3	1	26	0	0
Sadness	1	0	0	0	19	1
Surprise	0	0	1	0	0	25

signature yields a poor recognition rate in sadness. The ERR graph analysis of D-S-T signature using NARX shows a less promising recognition rate in anger. From this graph analysis, it is also shown that the RBF based D-S-T signature yields a higher detection rate than the MLP and NARX networks.

8.7.4 Experiment on MUG Database

MUG [16] dataset is evaluated to measure the performances of emotions. In this experiment, we select a total of 197 images to classify the expressions. The dataset is divided as 70% for training, 15% for testing, and 15% for validation.

Table 8.19 represents the effectiveness of facial expressions of trio signature using MLP. The anger classifies correctly 17 images and 2 images are in a mismatch with sadness. The disgust recognizes properly 29 images and 2 images are misclassified with anger and fear. The fear detects 12 images properly and 2 images are in misclassification with anger and fear. The happiness detects 26 images properly and 4 images are in a mismatch with disgust and fear. The sadness identifies 19 images positively and 2 images are confused anger and surprise. The surprise correctly classifies 25 images and 1 image is in mismatch as fear.

The results of FRR, FAR, and ERR are indicated in Table 8.20 to show the performance of the D-S-T signature through MLP for JAFFE dataset. The FAR value of fear is 0.023 that means it produces a 23/1000 false accept rate. The fear yields FRR as 0.142. It represents the lowest recognition rate of expression for fear. The fear produces 0.035 as ERR.

The NARX network is considered to measure the performances of expressions of trio signature which is available in Table 8.21. The anger classifies 18 images positively and 1 image is in misclassification with disgust. The disgust recognizes 29 images perfectly and 2 images are misclassified with fear. The fear detects 13 images properly and 1 image is confused with happiness. The happiness recognizes 29 images and 1 image is confused with sadness. The sadness identifies 19 images correctly and 2 images are wrongly classified with surprise. In the same way, the 23 images are classified correctly as surprise and 1 image is misclassified with disgust.

Table 8.20   The performance of D-S-T signature on MUG dataset through MLP

	FAR	FRR	ERR
Anger	0.024	0.205	0.035
Disgust	0.036	0.064	0.042
Fear	0.023	0.142	0.035
Happiness	0	0.133	0.028
Sadness	0.008	0.095	0.021
Surprise	0.017	0.038	0.021

Table 8.21   The recognition matrix of D-S-T signature trio on MUG dataset through NARX

	Anger	Disgust	Fear	Happiness	Sadness	Surprise
Anger	18	1	0	0	0	0
Disgust	0	29	2	0	0	0
Fear	0	0	13	1	0	0
Happiness	0	0	0	29	1	0
Sadness	0	0	0	0	19	2
Surprise	0	1	0	0	0	23

Table 8.22   The performance of D-S-T signature on MUG dataset through NARX

	FAR	FRR	ERR
Anger	0	0.052	0.007
Disgust	0.018	0.064	0.028
Fear	0.016	0.071	0.021
Happiness	0.009	0.033	0.014
Sadness	0.008	0.095	0.021
Surprise	0.017	0.041	0.021

The parameter of FAR, FRR, and ERR are considered to measure the system performances of the D-S-T signature using NARX. Table 8.22 shows the evaluated results of FAR, FRR, and ERR. The FAR value of disgust is 0.018 that means it produces an 18/1000 false accept rate. The disgust yields FRR as 0.064. The disgust produces 0.028 as ERR. It also indicates that the system has the highest recognition rate of expressions.

The RBF network is also evaluated in Table 8.23 to show the effectiveness of facial expressions of the trio signature. We notice that anger and fear are classified perfectly. The disgust identifies 31 images positively and 1 image is in misclassification with surprise. The happiness identifies correctly 26 images and 4 images are in a mismatch with anger, disgust, and fear. The sadness recognizes properly 20 images and 1 image

Table 8.23 The recognition matrix of D-S-T signature trio on MUG dataset through RBF

	Anger	Disgust	Fear	Happiness	Sadness	Surprise
Anger	19	0	0	0	0	0
Disgust	0	31	0	0	3	1
Fear	0	0	14	0	0	0
Happiness	2	1	1	26	0	0
Sadness	0	0	1	0	20	0
Surprise	0	1	0	0	0	25

Table 8.24 The performance of D-S-T signature on MUG dataset through RBF

	FAR	FRR	ERR
Anger	0.016	0	0.014
Disgust	0.018	0	0.014
Fear	0.015	0	0.014
Happiness	0	0.133	0.028
Sadness	0	0.047	0.007
Surprise	0	0.038	0.007

Fig. 8.11 FAR of MUG through MLP, NARX, and RBF

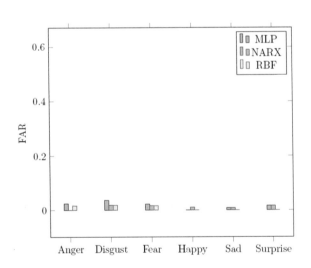

is in misclassification with fear. The surprise classifies 25 images properly and 1 image is wrongly identified as disgust.

The FAR, FRR, and ERR are used to compute the system performances of the D-S-T signature using RBF. Table 8.24 shows the computed results of FAR, FRR, and ERR. The FAR value of disgust is 0.015 that means it produces a 15/1000 false accept rate. The disgust yields FRR as 0. The system has the correct recognition rate in disgust. The disgust produces 0.014 as ERR.

Fig. 8.12 FRR of MUG
through MLP, NARX, and
RBF

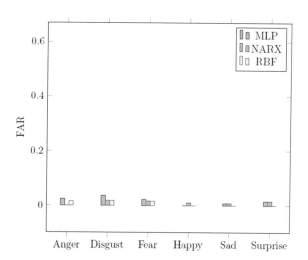

The performance of the FAR for the D-S-T signature through MLP, RBF, and
NARX on the MUG dataset is shown in Fig. 8.11. The FAR graph analysis of the
D-S-T signature using MLP yields a poor recognition rate in disgust. The FAR graph
analysis of the D-S-T signature using NARX shows a less promising recognition
rate in disgust. From this graph analysis, we also observe that the RBF based D-S-T
signature yields a promising identification rate in surprise.

The comparison of the FRR for the D-S-T signature using MLP, RBF, and NARX
on the MUG dataset is shown in Fig. 8.12. The FRR graph analysis of the D-S-
T signature using MLP yields a poor recognition rate in disgust. The FRR graph
analysis of the D-S-T signature using NARX performs a poor recognition rate of
expressions in disgust and surprise. It is also shown that the RBF based D-S-T
signature indicates a promising classification rate in sadness and surprise.

The comparison of ERR for the D-S-T signature through MLP, RBF, and NARX
on the MUG dataset is shown in Fig. 8.13. The ERR graph analysis of the D-S-T
signature using MLP yields a poor recognition rate in disgust and surprise. The ERR
graph analysis of D-S-T signature shows a less promising performance in disgust.
From this graph analysis, it is also shown that the RBF based D-S-T signature yields
a higher detection rate than the shape and texture signatures.

8.7.5 Compare Analysis with Three Artificial Networks and State of the Arts

The comparison task of the recognition rate of CK+ dataset with various neural
networks is presented in Table 8.25. We also show the comparison of expression
recognition rate with the different state of the art. The MLP based DST trio signature

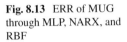

Fig. 8.13 ERR of MUG through MLP, NARX, and RBF

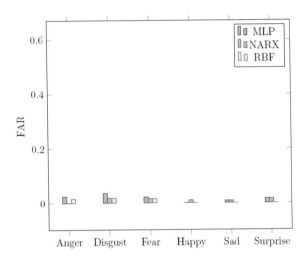

achieves 97.8% of average recognition rate with 100% of recognition rate for anger, disgust, and surprise and 95.2% as the lowest recognition rate for happiness. The NARX based DST trio signature acquires 97.4% of average recognition rate with correct recognition for surprise and 95.3% as lowest recognition for fear. In the same way, the RBF based DST trio signature achieves 97.8% as average recognition with correct recognition for disgust and sadness and 95.3% as the lowest recognition rate for fear. The proposed MLP, NARX, and RBF based DST trio signature methods are considered to measure the comparison with the existing literatures [5–9, 17–20]. It is also established that proposed MLP and NARX based procedures give promising recognition rates for expressions.

The JAFFE dataset is also considered for the comparison of the recognition rate of different neural networks which is shown in Table 8.25. The MLP based DST trio signature achieves 95.2% of average recognition rate with 100% of recognition rate for anger, disgust, happiness, and surprise and 78.6% as the lowest recognition rate for fear. The NARX based DST trio signature acquires 90.2% of average recognition rate with the highest recognition for anger and 85.7% as the lowest recognition for happiness. In the same way, the RBF based DST trio signature achieves 97.6% as average recognition with correct recognition for anger, disgust, surprise, and happiness and 92.9% as the lowest recognition rate for fear. The proposed MLP, NARX, and RBF based DST trio signature methods are considered to measure the comparison with the existing literature [5–9, 17, 19, 20]. It is also established that the proposed RBF based procedure yields a fantastic classification rate for emotions.

The MMI dataset is also evaluated for comparison task of identification rate of expressions of various networks. Table 8.25 shows the comparison of facial expression recognition with a different state of the art. The MLP based DST trio signature achieves 70.3% of average recognition rate with 90% of recognition rate for sadness and 50% as the lowest recognition rate for happiness. The NARX based DST trio signature acquires 91.1% of average recognition rate with correct recognition for

Table 8.25 Performance measure on publicly available datasets of six basic emotions with various state-of-the-art procedures

	Network	Anger	Disgust	Fear	Happiness	Sadness	Surprise	Avg.
DST trio using MLP	CK	100	96.3	95.3	95.2	100	100	97.8
DST trio using NARX	CK	97.2	96.3	95.3	98.8	97.2	100	97.4
DST trio using RBF	CK	97.2	100	95.3	97.6	100	97.1	97.8
[5]	CK+	96.1	95.7	95.8	98.4	95.9	95.8	96.3
[6]	CK+	98.1	100	95.8	100	93.8	100	97.9
[7]	CK+	98.6	98.1	97.7	98.8	98.6	100	98.6
[8]	CK+	100	100	100	100	100	100	100
[9]	CK+	98.6	100	97.7	94	98.6	98.6	97.9
[17]	CK+	87.8	93.3	94.3	94.2	96.4	98.4	94.1
[18]	CK+	87	91.5	90.9	96.9	84.5	91.2	90.3
[19]	CK+	76.2	94.1	86.1	96.3	88.2	98.7	91.5
DST trio using MLP	JAFFE	100	100	78.6	100	92.9	100	95.2
DST trio using NARX	JAFFE	95.2	90	92.9	85.7	85.7	91.7	90.2
DST trio using RBF	JAFFE	100	100	92.9	100	92.9	100	97.6
[5]	JAFFE	100	100	78.6	85.7	100	100	94
[6]	JAFFE	100	95.2	71.4	92.8	92.8	100	92.0
[7]	JAFFE	85.7	90.0	85.7	92.9	85.7	100	90.0
[8]	JAFFE	100	100	78.6	100	100	100	96.4
[9]	JAFFE	100	100	100	100	71.4	100	95.2
[17]	JAFFE	100	86.2	93.7	96.7	77.4	96.6	91.7
[18]	JAFFE	89.3	90.7	91.1	92.6	90.2	92.3	91.1
DST trio using MLP	MMI	70.0	76.9	64.0	50.0	90.0	71.4	70.3
DST trio using NARX	MMI	92.5	84.6	92.0	95.8	86.7	94.7	91.1
DST trio using RBF	MMI	85.0	94.9	76.0	58.3	60.0	81.0	75.9
[5]	MMI	82.8	81	71.4	87.5	100	66.7	81.5
[6]	MMI	100	85.7	64.2	100	61.1	80	81.8
[7]	MMI	97.5	94.9	96	91.7	93.3	100	95.5
[8]	MMI	100	85.7	64.3	100	61.1	80	81.9
[9]	MMI	77.5	97.4	92	87.5	90	86.4	88.5
[18]	MMI	80.1	78.2	81.3	83.2	77.1	81	80.1
[19]	MMI	65.6	72.5	72.5	88.2	71.1	93.8	77.4
DST trio using MLP	MUG	89.5	93.5	85.7	86.7	90.5	96.2	90.3
DST trio using NARX	MUG	94.7	93.5	92.9	96.7	90.5	95.8	94.1
DST trio using RBF	MUG	100	100	100	86.7	95.2	96.2	96.4
[5]	MUG	93.5	100	100	95.6	96.6	94.4	96.7
[6]	MUG	96.7	100	100	100	93.1	100	98.3
[7]	MUG	94.7	96.8	92.9	93.3	95.2	100	95.7
[8]	MUG	96.8	100	96.2	100	93.1	100	97.7
[9]	MUG	100	96.8	100	96.7	100	100	98.6

happiness and 84.6% as the lowest recognition for disgust. In the same way, the RBF based DST trio signature achieves 75.9% as average recognition with the highest recognition for disgust and 60% as the lowest recognition rate for sadness. The proposed MLP, NARX, and RBF based DST trio signature methods are considered to measure the comparison with the existing literature [5–9, 17–19]. It is also established that the proposed NARX based procedure yields a fantastic classification rate for emotions.

The MUG dataset is also evaluated for the comparison task of identification rate with various networks which is available in Table 8.25. We also show the comparison of expression recognition rate with the different state of the art. The MLP based DST trio signature achieves 90.3% of average recognition rate with 96.2% of recognition rate for surprise and 85.7% as the lowest recognition rate for fear. The NARX based DST trio signature acquires 94.1% of average recognition rate with the highest recognition for happiness and 90.5% as the lowest recognition for sadness. In the same way, the RBF based DST trio signature achieves 96.4% as average recognition with correct recognition for disgust and fear and 86.7% as the lowest recognition rate for happiness. The proposed MLP, NARX, and RBF based DST trio signature methods are considered to measure the comparison with the existing literature [5–9]. It is also established that the proposed RBF based procedures yields a promising recognition rate than the MLP.

8.8 Conclusion

This chapter proposed a Distance-Shape-Texture signature trio based facial expression recognition of three artificial neural networks such as MLP, NARX, and RBF. Three different networks are used to evaluate the recognition rate of expressions. The performance of the proposed procedure is experimented by the recognition rate and comparison with the state of the art. The experimental results also show the promising recognition rate of facial expressions of the Distance-Shape-Texture signature trio.

References

1. T.F Cootes, G.J. Edwards, C.J. Taylor, et al., Active appearance models. IEEE Trans. Pattern Anal. Mach. Intell. **23**(6), 681–685 (2001)
2. T. Ojala, M. Pietikäinen, D. Harwood, A comparative study of texture measures with classification based on featured distributions. Pattern Recogn. **29**(1), 51–59 (1996)
3. G. Tzimiropoulos, M. Pantic, Optimization problems for fast AAM fitting in-the-wild, in *Proceedings of the IEEE International Conference on Computer Vision*, pp. 593–600 (2013)
4. Y. Tie, L. Guan, Automatic landmark point detection and tracking for human facial expressions. EURASIP J. Image Video Process. **2013**(1), 8 (2013)
5. A. Barman, P. Dutta, Facial expression recognition using distance signature feature, in *Advanced Computational and Communication Paradigms* (Springer, 2018), pp. 155–163

6. A. Barman, P. Dutta, Facial expression recognition using shape signature feature, in *2017 Third International Conference on Research in Computational Intelligence and Communication Networks (ICRCICN)* (IEEE, 2017), pp. 174–179

7. A. Barman, P. Dutta, Texture signature based facial expression recognition using NARX, in *2017 IEEE Calcutta Conference (CALCON)* (IEEE, 2017), pp. 6–10

8. A. Barman, P. Dutta, Facial expression recognition using distance and shape signature features. Pattern Recogn. Lett. (2017)

9. A. Barman, P. Dutta, Facial expression recognition using distance and texture signature relevant features. Appl. Soft Comput. **77**, 88–105 (2019)

10. D. Chakrabarti, D. Dutta, Facial expression recognition using eigenspaces. Procedia Technol. **10**, 755–761 (2013)

11. H. Jaeger, Tutorial on training recurrent neural networks, covering BPPT, RTRL, EKF and the "echo state network" approach, vol. 5. GMD-Forschungszentrum Informationstechnik (2002)

12. M. Rosenblum, Y. Yacoob, L.S Davis, Human expression recognition from motion using a radial basis function network architecture. IEEE Trans. Neural Netw. **7**(5), 1121–1138 (1996)

13. P. Lucey, J.F. Cohn, T. Kanade, J. Saragih, Z. Ambadar, I. Matthews, The extended Cohn-Kanade dataset (ck+): a complete dataset for action unit and emotion-specified expression, in *Computer Society Conference on Computer Vision and Pattern Recognition-Workshops* (IEEE, 2010), pp. 94–101

14. M. Lyons, S. Akamatsu, M. Kamachi, J. Gyoba, Coding facial expressions with Gabor wavelets, in *Proceedings of Third IEEE International Conference on Automatic Face and Gesture Recognition, 1998* (IEEE, 1998), pp. 200–205

15. M.F. Valstar, M. Pantic, Induced disgust, happiness and surprise: an addition to the mmi facial expression database, in *Proceedings of International Conference Language Resources and Evaluation, Workshop on EMOTION*, Malta, May 2010, pp. 65–70

16. N. Aifanti, C. Papachristou, A. Delopoulos, The mug facial expression database, in *Proceedings of 11th International Workshop on Image Analysis for Facial Expression Database*, Desenzano, Italy, April 2010, pp. 12–14

17. S.L. Happy, A. Routray, Automatic facial expression recognition using features of salient facial patches. IEEE Trans. Affect. Comput. **6**(1), 1–12 (2015)

18. A. Poursaberi, H. Ahmadi Noubari, M. Gavrilova, S.N. Yanushkevich, Gauss–Laguerre wavelet textural feature fusion with geometrical information for facial expression identification. EURASIP J. Image Video Process. **2012**(1), 1–13 (2012)

19. L. Zhong, Q. Liu, P. Yang, J. Huang, D.N. Metaxas, Learning multiscale active facial patches for expression analysis. IEEE Trans. Cybern. **45**(8), 1499–1510 (2015)

20. L. Zhong, Q. Liu, P. Yang, B. Liu, J. Huang, D.N. Metaxas, Learning active facial patches for expression analysis, in *2012 IEEE Conference on Computer Vision and Pattern Recognition (CVPR)* (IEEE, 2012), pp. 2562–2569

Index

© Springer Nature Singapore Pte Ltd. 2020
P. Dutta and A. Barman, *Human Emotion Recognition from Face Images*,
Cognitive Intelligence and Robotics,
https://doi.org/10.1007/978-981-15-3883-4

Printed in the United States
by Baker & Taylor Publisher Services